P9-EEB-521

TENNESSEE WILLIAMS:
Rebellious Puritan

TENNESSEE WILLIAMS:
Rebellious Puritan

NANCY M. TISCHLER

New York : THE CITADEL PRESS

To
MY MOTHER
AND MY HUSBAND
*for their encouragement
and love*

Contents

7

Preface

Tennessee Williams is a latter-day romantic. Both his writings and his life follow the pattern of the romantic nonconformist. If you happened upon this swarthy little man with his square, stocky build, you would hardly credit the romantic characterization. It would seem absurd to locate, under this unprepossessing exterior, a delicate, poetic nature. While his mussed suit, soiled shirt, and generally unkempt appearance suggest Bohemian tastes, nothing about his appearance would reflect the poetry that is his reality, his essence.

Furthermore, an attempt at cocktail-party social amenities would probably fall with a thud. To a compliment on his latest play, this semi-attentive author would probably respond with a noncommittal grunt while his eyes glazed over, signalling a retreat into further remoteness. But if you mistook his shyness for boorishness, you would be mistaken again. Those who know Tennessee Williams well say that among his few friends he displays a quiet, winning charm.

The sonorities of his ante-bellum Southern speech are occasionally interrupted by a startling, screeching laugh. He seems withdrawn because the superficial chatter of the sophisticated world is unreal to him; his work is his reality. At parties, he will sometimes retreat into his own world for prolonged periods, to return with a remark so irrelevant that it startles his companions into embarrassed silence.

This happens on other occasions as well. When being interviewed by Lincoln Barnett for an article in *Life,* Williams proved so uncommunicative that a close friend lectured him soundly. She then put the interviewer and the interviewee in a room of her house so that they would not be disturbed. Upon her return home, some time later, Paul Moor writes, hearing no voices from the room, "she opened the door to find Williams on the couch gazing at the ceiling, and Barnett in a chair, brooding over the pattern of the rug. It was apparent that there had been no communication for some time." Tennessee Williams simply can't understand that behavior which in a nobody may be excused as shyness becomes, in a celebrity, rudeness.

Though Williams has learned to enjoy some luxuries, this does not include expensive clothes. Once his agent's husband suggested that, considering his income, Williams could afford a dress suit. The playwright responded that he would only lose it. He continues to live his unorthodox life on his own terms.

These terms include, first and foremost, his work. He is an artist who relishes the process of writing. He enjoys his friends, including such diverse personalities as Audrey Wood, Carson Mc-Cullers, Maureen Stapleton, Anna Magnani, Elia Kazan, and dozens of others—mostly people who have worked with him.

With a combination of amorality and off-beat humor, he appears to enjoy the lurid suspicions with which gossip surrounds him— of alcoholism, homosexuality, and other aberrations. In fact, he adds fuel to the fire by frequently confessing to interviewers that he pictures no vice in his characters which he has not found in himself. This is a typical exaggeration designed to shock convention-bound people. The iconoclasm and amorality of both his life and his work are consistent with his ideal of "benevolent anarchy."

Shy personally and shocking professionally, an amoral moralist, voracious for applause but firmly independent, Williams is a paradox as a writer and as a person. Insisting that he writes as he must, not as people desire, he has been immensely lucky that so many audiences in the past fifteen years have been willing to eavesdrop on Mr. Williams' inner debates; and those people have been even more lucky that he has been willing to make these very private debates public. His plays have become such assured successes that the organizers of theatre parties consider them as sure-fire as musical comedies. His audiences may respond with disgust and horror to much of the violence that roars across the Williams stage, but they seldom respond with yawns.

Because of his sustained dramatic power and his success on Broadway and off, in little theatre groups all over the country, in actors' workshops, and in major theatres throughout Europe, Tennessee Williams has become a widely discussed, but narrowly understood celebrity. Since his work has changed in both technique and content over the years, while following a consistent thematic and structural pattern, I feel that a summation and an evaluation can help the reader and the viewer of Williams' plays. But no judgment can, at this time, be comprehensive or definitive. His next play may reverse the old patterns.

I have dealt with his plays, stories, poems, and articles as these have mutually reflected and influenced his life, and with the audience and critical reactions to them as these have mutually reflected or influenced his work and the social acceptance of new themes. I have also included detailed plot summaries of the major plays to refresh the reader's mind and to provide, in the case of the little-known works, a basis for discussion.

Whether Tennessee Williams is a major or a minor writer is a subject of heated debate. Some of his works are obvious potboilers;

others are powerful studies of modern man. I personally feel that two plays alone—*The Glass Menagerie* and *A Streetcar Named Desire*—are enough to establish Tennessee Williams as the most important contemporary American dramatist.

TENNESSEE WILLIAMS:
Rebellious Puritan

CHAPTER I

The Early Years

Biography may contribute valuable shortcuts to understanding an artist and his art. Even if the personality, problems, and adventures of Tennessee Williams were less fascinating than they are, they would constitute an interesting commentary on our times. In addition, the biographical element discloses how intensely personal Williams' art is. Writing, for him, is a means of objectifying and universalizing the subjective, individual experience. Out of his milieu—the contemporary South—he constructs a microcosm, crystallizing all human experience; he projects his life as a pattern for the frustrations and satisfactions of modern man.

Tennessee Williams admits that his writing is a form of psychotherapy, and as such brings to light much of his own tormented personality. Most of his themes (his unsystematic view of the human situation hardly deserves the designation of "philosophy") have grown emotionally, organically, dynamically from his own experience. As Dr. Lawrence Kubie, his psychoanalyst, indicated, and he himself agreed, the most important of these experiences were those of his childhood. This is sufficient justification by itself, for discussing Mr. Williams' early years here.

The South, Williams' favorite and most effective setting, is also the setting of his earliest and most pleasant memories. In later years he referred to Mississippi as "a dark wide spacious land that you can breathe in." He was born Thomas Lanier Williams at the Episcopal rectory in Columbus, Mississippi. Neither the name (which reminded him too much of a Southern writer of sonnets to spring) nor the place (few observers of the usual Williams play even faintly suspect that ecclesiastical background) now seems appropriate. But on March 26, 1911, Cornelius Coffin Williams and Edwina Dakin Williams welcomed Thomas Lanier, their second child, into the world and into the Episcopal rectory.

His father came from an old East Tennessee family who had been frontiersmen and Indian fighters in pioneer days. They had then turned to the brutal "dueling-pistol-and-corn-liquor brand of politics that is traditional in that state," as Robert Rice wrote in his recent interview with Williams for the New York *Post*. "Violent and aggressive" is the description that Tennessee Williams himself applies to his paternal ancestry, one member of which had been a right-hand man to Andrew Jackson.

But gentle and lyrical they were too, if Sidney Lanier is considered as well. This paternal ancestor, whose haunting, musical poetry is among the best Southern writing of the nineteenth century, perhaps accounts for the lyric bent apparent in Tennessee Williams. The tone of romantic ante-bellum aristocracy is just as much a part of his paternal heritage as is the violence—and both suffuse Williams' dramas.

Cornelius Williams had been working for the telephone company in Memphis when he met prim Edwina Dakin, a minister's daughter, then singing in an amateur production of light opera. Edwina was as much a Puritan as her husband was a Cavalier, and Tennessee Williams believes that her influence implanted a strong Puritan strain in him.

"I'm a Puritan, too," he insists, "but I'm a rebellious Puritan." Of his gentle, straitlaced mother, he later said, "There is so much in my life she can't accept. My writing shocks her, of course."

This beautiful, genteel, high-strung Puritan apparently did not completely reciprocate her husband's ardor. The strain in their marriage was evident to their children. Since the Williams children spent most of their time with their mother, it was natural for them to take her side in an intense partisan attachment to her.

At the beginning of their marriage, Cornelius Williams held managerial jobs along the Gulf Coast, and the couple set up housekeeping in Gulfport, a lovely little town on the white beaches of the Gulf of Mexico. But he became a travelling salesman before the children were born. "C.C.," as his friends addressed him, was good at this work. Boisterous, energetic, convivial, eloquent, booming and bawdy, this Delta drummer is the original for the sympathetic picture of the aging salesman in "The Last of My Solid Gold Watches," a one-acter suggested by C.C.'s awards from his company for his sales feats. To the "Mistuh Charlie" of the play, his hotel room "was like a *throne*-room. My samples laid out over there on a green velvet cloth! The ceiling fan going. . . . And over here—the washbowl and pitcher removed and the table-top *loaded* with *liquor!* In and out from the time I arrived till the time I left, the men of the road who knew men, to whom I stood for things commanding respect! Poker—continuous! Shouting, laughing—hilarity!" In further transmutations, the boisterous father, ace salesman for the International Shoe Company, became the Big Daddy of *Cat on a Hot Tin Roof* and a symbol of corruption and bullheadedness in Boss Finley of *Sweet Bird of Youth*.

When C. C. Williams went on the road, his wife moved back to her family. And it was there in the Columbus rectory that her first two children were born.

The town of Columbus, Mississippi, where Tom Williams and his sister Rose were born, is an old one on the Tombigbee River, a town of which he comments wryly that it "was so dignified and reserved that there was a saying, only slightly exaggerated, that you had to live there a whole year before a neighbor would smile at you on the street."

Her father, the Reverend Walter E. Dakin, an aristocratic, well-read, liberal churchman, liked to stay with one congregation only long enough to whip it into shape and then move on. In the Bible Belt, an Episcopalian minister would be remarkable for card-playing and whiskey-drinking, but the Reverend Dakin carried his liberality into deeper realms than this. "He was a deeply religious man," recalls his grandson, "but he thought the Old Testament was simply beautiful mythology." Still more remarkable is the fact that Mr. Williams could say of his grandfather in more recent years, "And he never disapproved of anything I wrote."

Little evidence of what Tom was to become appeared in those early years. One note recorded by Robert Rice, however, does presage some of the mature Williams' creativity: "The family spent some time each summer at a mountain resort near Knoxville, Tennessee, to escape the 'malaria country' during its hottest season. His mother recalls that the resort guests gathered most evenings around a log fire and took turns telling ghost stories. One evening a member of the party turned to Tom, then a three-year-old with long yellow curls, and said jokingly, 'Tom it's your turn.'

"It turned out not to be a joke. Without hesitation, Williams began a story, one of the most frightening any of the company had ever heard. They became increasingly spellbound, then suddenly the boy broke off abruptly. 'It's getting scarier and scarier,' his mother quotes him as having said. 'It's getting so scary I'm afraid to go on.' "

His aptitude for horror thus manifested itself early in life. Years later, Brooks Atkinson, drama critic of *The New York Times* and one of Williams' most faithful defenders, summing up his view of modern drama, said, "I think Tennessee Williams is our finest writer, although he sometimes gives me the horrors."

Tom Williams also displayed an early resistance to education.

Mrs. Williams enrolled him in a kindergarten on the campus of Vanderbilt University in Nashville, where they were then living. She took him to class the first day and watched him for ten or fifteen minutes. "I was enchanted," Williams recalls. "I loved all the ABC blocks and the modelling clay. Then all of a sudden I looked up and my mother wasn't there. I lay on the floor and kicked and screamed." Mrs. Williams heard him halfway down the block and returned to rescue him. There was no more kindergarten for him. In the whole of Williams' long career of schooling, there were few peaceful interludes.

Attachment to the mother is a recurrent theme in Williams' work. The number of protagonists looking for their mothers, or as Hadrian says in *You Touched Me!*, "groping for a mother's breast," exceeds the norm. Williams' own attachment to his mother was one of the warmest, yet most unfortunate parts of his youth. His world became increasingly feminine, and he became negatively sensitized to masculine crudities.

When Tom finally started school, his family had shifted to Clarksdale, the "Blue Mountain" of his plays. It is a city of two rivers, the Mississippi and the Sunflower, a beautiful place that symbolizes fond memories of youth. In "The Resemblance Between a Violin Case and a Coffin" (a title probably suggested by his father's middle name), Williams describes the town in romantic terms. On one side of the Sunflower River, he says, "was a wilderness where giant cypresses seemed to engage in mute rites of reverence at the edge of the river, and the blurred pallor of the Dobyne place that used to be a plantation, now vacant and seemingly ravaged by some impalpable violence fiercer than flames, back of this dusky curtain, the immense cotton-fields that absorbed the whole visible distance in one sweeping gesture." Contrasted with the rural magnificence of that view was the other side of the river with "avenues, commerce, pavements and homes of people." These two ways of life were separated by "a yellowish, languorous stream that you could throw a rock over."

Parts of this reminiscent loveliness are recognizable as the memories of Blanche in *Streetcar* and Amanda in *Glass Menagerie*. This is also the immediate setting for *Cat on a Hot Tin Roof* and *Summer and Smoke*. For Williams, the Mississippi Delta has become a symbol of the artist's longing for the "sweet bird" of his youth in a country touched with the merciful blur of remembrance. After his clash with industry and urban squalor, this town and others of the area were increasingly imbued with purity and beauty for him, qualities that frequently stand in terrible contrast to the ugliness of the human animal that inhabits it. Partially because his grandfather had the gracious serenity of the aristocrat, though without plantations or hounds, he, like the landscape itself, blended into the aristocratic pattern. In violent contrast to this symbol, the author was to become increasingly convinced that the mass of men live, not for truth, beauty, integrity, and honor, but for mendacity, materialism, and expediency—the enemies that have rotted civilization from the inside.

Clarksdale was the scene of a second, but again abortive, attempt at Tom's education. This time the schooling was interrupted by disease. He came down with diphtheria. For nine days it was doubtful that he would live. He recalls the ordeal with the hypochondriac's fascination with clinical detail. His legs were partially paralyzed after the crisis; he contracted Bright's disease, an unpleasant kidney ailment; and his tonsils "had completely disintegrated." The sickness had its compensations, however; it kept him out of school and in the comforting warmth of the family.

School had been painful for Tom largely because he was the minister's grandson. His mother's delicacy and his grandfather's work had made him a little Puritan, ill-prepared for the earthier children he was to meet. As these hardier types noticed his shyness and sensitivity, they found him a delight to tease. The young narrator of "The Resemblance Between a Violin Case and a Coffin" tells of being waylaid by young hoodlums of the neighborhood on his way home from school and of being queried unmercifully on the facts of reproduction. His reactions to these "dirty" questions were a blush, a cry, a hurried withdrawal, and a subsequent attack of nausea.

In another revealing passage (in "Three Players of a Summer Game"), Williams records a similar reaction to the candid questions of a little girl playmate. She took him to the local museum, made a beeline for a statue of a reclining warrior, lifted the attached fig-leaf, and, looking into his wide blue eyes, asked "Is yours like that?" "My answer was idiotic; I said, 'I don't know!' and I think I was blushing long after we left the museum. . . ." Tennessee Williams' later determination that no subject can be taboo for the artist was apparently an effort to compensate for the prudery of his childhood, traces of which linger in the recesses of his mind. Much of the evangelical zeal he directs against conventional moral attitudes and judgments grows from the fight he has had to wage within himself. Although his father's Cavalier blood appears to have won the victory over the maternal Puritanism, their conflict found an agonized battlefield in the mind and emotions of the growing boy.

Williams believes that the attack of diphtheria in childhood permanently injured his heart, and doctors have been unable to dissuade him. It did confine him to bed for a year; during this period he spent much time with his grandfather's books. His reading affected his emotions so deeply that he could put away a book and lie on his bed with closed eyes, picturing the events of the story in vivid scenes on his lids. In later years, these ocular effects were to dim somewhat, but the ability to amuse himself with fantasies continues. Some nights he still can close his eyes and evoke enchanting scenes.

Ill health, actual and imagined, was to plague him much of his life. Despite psychoanalytic treatment, entered into partially to

cure it, hypochondria remains with him to this day. He listens for
his heartbeat and watches for other symptoms with abnormal fear.
One of his poems, in a grotesque and frightening image, describes
man as a "pillar of blood" liable to flow downhill at any moment;
in part the morbid meditation goes like this:

> *I build a tottering pillar of my blood*
> *to walk it upright on the tilting street.*
> *The stuff is liquid, it would flow downhill*
> *so very quickly if the hill were steep.*
>
> *How perilously do these fountains leap*
> *whose reckless voyager alone am I!*
> *In mothering darkness, Lord, I pray Thee keep*
> *these springs a single touch of sun could dry.*
>
> *It is the instant froth that globes the world,*
> *an image gushing in a crimson stream.*
> *But let the crystal break and there would be*
> *the timeless quality but not the dream.*

In its final stanzas, the poem asserts the fear that the blood will
succumb to the siege of the world that "is not I." Other poems, and
images in his plays as well, reflect this obsession with health. The
heartbeat is a recurrent motif, usually represented by ticking clocks
and watches. The other major disease motif is cancer, possibly
because the only woman he ever loved died of that disease, and
possibly also because it is an affliction that destroys from the inside and suggests the decay that he also found in the symbol of
Southern plantations.

His ill health kept the boy out of school and brought him more
and more under the influence of his mother, who had always considered him especially fragile. Forbidden to go outside or to play
with other children, he felt his shyness growing, his life turning
inward. He became, in his own words, "delicate and sissified."

Other than his mother and grandmother, his gentle nurses and
friends during his illness, his constant and favorite companion was

his sister Rose. This relationship was not to be affected by the birth
of his brother Dakin. Rose, who was slightly older than Tom,
resembled him in personality and imagination. A lovely, sensitive,
exciting playmate, Rose became for Tom a symbol of loveliness.
The central tragedy of his life has been Rose's failure to make the
crossing from childhood to adolescence. The petals of her brain
"simply closed through fear, and it's no telling how much they
had closed upon in the way of secret wisdom." But in Clarksdale
they were still children and were immensely happy together.

As Tom gained strength, he accompanied his grandfather on
some of his parish calls. One of the parishioners, a young woman
named Laura Young, was to become the key to one of the writer's
most beautiful symbols. "I remember," he said years later, "a lady
named Laura Young. . . . She was something cool and green in a
sulphurous landscape. But there was a shadow upon her. For that
reason we called upon her more frequently than anyone else. She
loved me. I adored her. She lived in a white house near an orchard
and in an arch between two rooms there were hung some pendants
of glass that were a thousand colors. 'That is a prism,' she said. She
lifted me and told me to shake them. When I did they made a
delicate music."

Laura (whose name was given to the daughter in *The Glass
Menagerie*) was the first to associate the qualities of music, glass,
orchards, and love in an impressionable young mind that later was
to find glass and music further associated with his beautiful sister,
whose name became another symbol—Rose. The rainbow colors
that Miss Young's prisms threw off further merged with D. H.
Lawrence's use of the same symbol, the rainbow, to suggest an
earthly paradise of sexuality. The shadowed personality of Laura
turns into that of the heroine in *Battle of Angels* (Williams' first
major play, later rewritten as *Orpheus Descending*). Her orchard
became a confectionery and a setting for love. The shadow that
clouded her appears to have taught the young boy to understand

sorrow or disgrace and to hold out compassion rather than judgment to the sufferer.

Another lesson on the theme of compassion came from still
another outsider whose life touched on that of the Williams-Dakin
family. A Negro nurse named Ozzie took care of Tom and his sister.
She loved the children dearly and they returned that love. One day
however, in a moment of petulance, the boy called Ozzie a
"nigger," a term he had picked up outside his home and that he
was immediately ashamed to have used. The offended Ozzie left
the house for good. Searches by the family were fruitless; the
woman was nowhere to be found. The incident left Tom with a
sense of guilt that he feels to this day, and a hatred of discrimination that lies deeper than intellectual assent to tolerance. In
Streetcar's preface, he inserted a clause asking that the play not be
acted in any theatre where discrimination is practiced. Williams
is no writer of social protest, but he reacts sincerely and violently
whenever he feels that people have been hurt.

During the First World War, when Tom was eight years old, the
Southern idyll came to an abrupt close. His father was transferred
to St. Louis, Missouri. The transfer was a promotion, elevating
Cornelius Williams to sales manager. Because of the war conditions
and his father's stinginess, their new home was in a tenement in a
lower middle-class neighborhood which seemed revoltingly ugly to
the small boy. Both he and Rose found the mid-western city a
hostile place: "The school children made fun of our southern
speech and manners. I remember gangs of kids following me home
yelling 'Sissy!', and home was not a pleasant refuge." It was a "per-
petually dim little apartment in a wilderness of identical brick
and concrete structures with no grass and no trees nearer than the
park."

Because of their grandfather's position, they had always thought
of themselves as leading citizens. "But in St. Louis we suddenly discovered there were two kinds of people, the rich and the poor, and

that we belonged more to the latter. If we walked far enough west we came into a region of fine residences set in beautiful lawns. But where we lived, to which we must always return, were ugly rows of apartment buildings the color of dried blood and mustard." The change was magnified by this contrast. Had he been born there, Williams admits, he probably would not have resented it so much. "But it was forced upon my consciousness at the most sensitive age of childhood. It produced a shock and a rebellion that has grown into an inherent part of my work." Those reactions are, of course, the seeds of *The Glass Menagerie.*

Most of the ugliness Williams has seen in life he associates with St. Louis. It is a place that, to this day, he avoids. When, as a grown man, on a visit to St. Louis in 1947, he was interviewed by a bright-faced reporter asking how it felt to return to his home town, the disconcerting answer was that he found St. Louisans "cold, smug, complacent, intolerant, stupid, and provincial." Needless to say, the statement elicited angry outcries. Then, trying to be somewhat more conciliatory, he said he was sorry, but he could not remember with kindness a city where he spent a "fairly lonely and miserable boyhood" and which he now found it "rather difficult, for that reason, to return to."

But the change from the quiet agricultural town of Clarksville to dirty, noisy, industrial St. Louis was only part of the problem. Tom and Rose also missed the gentle, sensitive grandparents who had given them security and prestige in the community. From the rectory they had been removed to an apartment; and from the serene grandparents they had been removed to day-to-day association with their stormy father.

For the first time in their lives, Rose and Tom found their father to be a part of the household. "C.C.'s" shrewd business sense, his capacity for liquor, his poker playing, and his boisterous good spirits made him popular with his business colleagues. At home he was unpopular—and for almost exactly the same reasons.

Williams acknowledges that, with steadier and earlier doses of his father's obtrusively masculine personality, he might have become less "delicate and sissified." But the almost exclusive companionship of his sister and his mother had already done its work. He is quoted as having summarized his attitude toward his father in the three words, "I hated him." Refuting this statement, Williams says that if his feeling *was* hatred, it has since been mitigated by understanding. "He wasn't really that bad." After his father's death, Williams softened—"I have changed my feeling toward him. After he quit 'the road' my father was a terribly unhappy man who could only escape his great unhappiness through the bottle, poker, and the great esteem and affection of the salesmen who worked under him. My father was a totally honest man; he was never known to tell a lie in his life or to take an unfair advantage of anybody in business. He had a strong character and a sense of honor. He lived on his own terms, which were hard terms for his family, but he should not be judged as long as he remains the mystery that he is to us who lived in his shadow." And, Williams continues, "Maybe I hated him once, but I certainly don't any more. He gave me some valuable things; he gave me fighting blood, which I needed, and now he has given me, through the revelations of my psychoanalysis, a sense of the necessity to forgive your father in order to forgive the world that he brought you into: in my opinion, an important lesson which I hope I have really learned. Forgiving, of course, does not mean accepting and condoning, it does not even mean an end to the battle." The father was devoted to money, but then "all American businessmen seem to have that devotion, more or less, mostly more, and I think it is a sort of reverse sublimation. Disappointed in their longing for other things, such as tenderness, they turn to the pursuit of wealth because that is more easily obtainable in the world. My father got little of either."

The neighborhood kids who called Tom "sissy" and his father,

who nicknamed him "Miss Nancy," were major sources of anxiety
in a city filled with trials for the youngster. At the Eugene Field
School his Southern accent won him ridicule, and his comparatively small stature and weak frame made him a target for bullies.
He hated the school and he hated living in the small, shabby apart-
ments chosen by the father, who gave Mrs. Williams a hundred
dollars a month for food and clothes for the family and kept the
remainder of his ample salary for himself. "I guess," said Tennessee
Williams of his father, "he drank it and gambled it and had himself a ball."

One of these shabby tenements was an old house that Tom
refused to call home. It had windows on two sides only; as a consequence, the room that his sister Rose lived in was a dark cell
overlooking the alley. In the short story that was to become the
seed idea for *The Glass Menagerie* (called "Portrait of a Girl in
Glass"), the author describes the areaway beneath this window
that he and Rose had dubbed "Death Valley":

> There were a great many alleycats in the neighborhood and one
> particularly vicious dirty white chow who stalked them continually.
> In the open or on the fire escapes they would usually elude him but
> now and again he cleverly contrived to run some youngster among
> them into the cul-de-sac of this narrow areaway at the far end of
> which, directly beneath my sister's bedroom windows, they made
> the blinding discovery that what had appeared to be an avenue of
> escape was really a locked arena, a gloomy vault of concrete and
> brick with walls too high for any cat to spring, in which they must
> suddenly turn to spit at their death until it was hurled upon them.
> Hardly a week went by without a repetition of this violent drama.
> The areaway had grown to be hateful to Laura [Rose] because she
> could not look out on it without recalling the screams and the
> snarls of killing. She kept the shades drawn down, and as Mother
> would not permit the use of electric current except when needed,
> her days were spent almost in perpetual twilight. There were
> three pieces of dingy ivory furniture in the room, a bed, a bureau,
> a chair. Over the bed was a remarkably bad religious painting,
> a very effeminate head of Christ with teardrops visible just below
> the eyes. The charm of the room was produced by my sister's

collection of glass. She loved little glass articles, all of them light and delicate in color. These she washed and polished with endless care. When you entered the room there was always the soft, transparent radiance in it which came from the glass absorbing whatever faint light came through the shades on Death Valley.

Tom and his sister painted her room white, hid the outside world behind white curtains, and tried to forget reality in the midst of her glass menagerie. These little glass animals, Williams recalls, "came to represent in my memory all the softest emotions that belong to recollections of things past. They stood for all the small and tender things that relieve the austere pattern of life and make it endurable to the sensitive. The areaway where the cats were torn to pieces was one thing—my sister's white curtains and tiny menagerie of glass were another. Somewhere between them was the world that we lived in."

The association of love and glass, begun with Laura Young, was completed by Rose and her menagerie. Ignored were the heat and fury of the cats and all the passions and fates of the world outside. This picture from memory summarizes the dominating theme of the Williams world. His sensitive mind was to develop toward the feminine rather than the masculine virtues.

This was not affected by the addition of another masculine element in the household, with the birth of Walter Dakin Williams in 1919. The already frail Mrs. Williams fell victim to the postwar influenza epidemic, and her lungs were affected. To lighten the household cares, Tom was sent back to Clarksdale to stay with his grandparents for a year.

Although the year was no recess from school, Tom was happy to get away from the tensions and the ugliness of St. Louis. Recalling that year, he says, "I preferred to play by myself. I had already stopped making connection with other boys." But he was extremely fond of his grandparents, and he got in some good reading in his grandfather's ample library. "I loved Shakespeare," he comments.

"I didn't appreciate the beauty of the language, but I loved the violence. I was mad about 'Titus Andronicus.' " (A significant preference considering the violence of his own plays.)

At the end of his Clarksdale year, Tom returned to the dreariness of St. Louis—to which a new misery was soon added. His sister ceased to be a child, a change neither he nor she could quite understand. The change removed her into an atmosphere her lonely brother couldn't share and left him without a playmate. For Rose the change began the retreat from a world that frightened her. Living more and more within herself, she soon ended all communication with the world, in the total withdrawal of schizophrenia.

In his solitude, Tom found release in a new and strangely satisfying way—in writing. At the age of twelve, surrounded by reality he couldn't bear and books he used for escape, he read Tennyson's "Lady of Shallot." "She was floating down a river in a state of trance," he remembers, "and did something to me." Possessed by that vision, he wrote his first poem. No inspiration could be more typical for Thomas Lanier Williams' entrance into the world of literary creation than the story of a lonely, lovely, romantic lady who is destroyed by the irruption of reality into her world of romance. From loneliness to love to death is certainly the standard Williams pattern. But Queen Victoria's staid laureate would whirl in his grave to think he had any connection with such a playwright.

"I discovered writing as an escape from the world of reality in which I felt acutely uncomfortable," Williams recently said. "It immediately became my place of retreat, my cave, my refuge." In his writing, he could forget that the neighborhood kids called him a sissy and his father called him "Miss Nancy" because he would rather read books in his grandfather's "large and classical library than play marbles and baseball and other normal kid games." Then, almost as soon as he started writing, he ran into his first block: "It's hard to describe it in a way that will be understandable to anyone who is not a neurotic. All my life I have been haunted by the obsession that to desire a thing or to love a thing intensely is to place yourself in a vulnerable position, to be a possible, if not a probable, loser of what you most want."

But the fear that he might not be able to write was overcome; the "barricades of gold and purple tin foil labeled Fear/and other August titles," that were to raise obstacles all his life, were surmounted by the child. No doubt it is this anxiety and the necessity to disprove it that has kept him so steadily at his typewriter. All his life he has taken only one vacation from his writing. Because of his loneliness, he turned to writing; because of his anxieties, he keeps working; and because of fear, he has turned to stories of violence.

Finding that rhyming came naturally to him, and finding it also a solace, an escape, and a means of winning recognition, he continued writing poetry and short stories after he entered Ben Blewitt High School. His given name, Thomas Lanier, which recalled the Southern sonneteer, proved an augury of his early work. He won his first prize (twenty-four dollars from a women's club) for three sonnets to Spring. Under this same name he wrote many lyrics which he characterized as a "bad imitation of Edna Millay." He enjoys quoting the sestet of a later sonnet at parties, an apostrophe to Death, which goes:

> *Rudely you seized and broke proud Sappho's lyre*
> *Barrett and Wylie went your songless way.*
> *You do not care what hecatomb of fire*
> *Is split when shattering the urn of clay*
> *Yet, Death, I'll pardon all you took away*
> *While still you spare me—glorious Millay!*

It was for such effusions that he became the darling of the Southern women's poetry clubs.

During his high school days, he kept himself in spending money by winning advertising contests. Since his father took a dim view of literary activities without financial recompense, the earnings brought in by the young poet's pen caused Mr. Williams to beam approval. (To this day, C. C. Williams' yardstick of financial success is also Tennessee's. A play must draw big audiences over a long period to satisfy his lust for success.) The father's pleasure reached monumental proportions when one of Tom's endeavors was purchased by *Weird Tales* for $35 and another won a $25 prize from *Smart Set.*

The playwright describes the *Weird Tales* story, published in 1928, as a prelude to the violence that is considered his trademark. He drew upon a paragraph in Herodotus to develop a story of the Egyptian queen Nitocris. She "invited all of her enemies to a lavish banquet in a subterranean hall on the shores of the Nile, and . . . at the height of the banquet, she excused herself from the table and opened sluice gates admitting the water of the Nile into the locked banquet hall, drowning her unloved guests like so many rats." This bizarre story, related with great relish, was the product of a sixteen-year-old mind—"sweet bird of youth" indeed!

The *Smart Set* prize was won by his answer to a contest question, "Can a Good Wife Be a Good Sport?" In his vigorously affirmative answer, he pretended to be a good-wife, good-sport who was writing a confession. The effort won third prize.

He won another prize of ten dollars for the best review of the silent film *Stella Dallas.* Movies were always exciting for him—another avenue of escape into romance. "When I was little," he says, "I used to want to climb into the screen and join the action. My mother had to hold me down."

While sitting at the portable typewriter his mother had given him during his illness, he was able to avoid the unhappiness of school. He did well in English, of course, but almost failed math. Every year he became more isolated because of his "withdrawn manner and unfashionable address" that slighted others. More and more poems, stories, and contest essays poured out—but no plays. "I had not yet ever seen a play or thought of writing for the stage," he explains.

Despite these literary successes, which must have been gratifying to the novice writer, his surroundings continued to oppress him. With the prodding of poor health, his distaste for his St. Louis home blossomed into a cluster of neuroses. One of his friends says that young Tom Williams developed a fear of using his voice in public and sat mute when called on to recite in class. He blushed when anyone addressed him or caught his eye and, becoming ashamed of his blushing, blushed all the more. In the preface to a play written years later, Williams recalls the horror of his inability to communicate with outsiders. This, he says, turned him irresistibly toward written expression where his shyness was no handicap. Later he was to find that he could "level" with an audience in a darkened theatre more easily that he could chat with a friend. This awareness of man's solitary condition became frighteningly acute in the adolescent boy, and has never left the mature man. In addition, the boy developed a fear of death that also reached epic proportions. One night it occurred to him that falling asleep was akin to dying. For months thereafter, he fought off sleep at night, holding his eyes open and staring with frightened intensity at the open window.

One of his teachers, Margaret Cowen, who taught him English at University City High, remembered Tommy Williams as a boy "not socially inclined toward the group." He had "too many thoughts of his own. His grades were average. There was no evidence of brilliance in his work. I fear," she lamented, "that he was not well adjusted. In the period I knew him he never was clear about tomorrow's lesson." Then, almost as an afterthought, she commented, "Tommy belonged to another world." He was never clear about lessons then, or shoe invoices and draft registrations later, or driving regulations even now. He would certainly agree that he is far from being "well-adjusted," and no one doubts that he still belongs to another world.

In spite of shyness and absentmindedness, Tom graduated from high school with a respectable B average in 1929. Then, at last, came another temporary relief from the loneliness and unhappiness of St. Louis existence. His father, wanting to cut him free from his mother's apron strings, sent the boy away to college. In the fall of that year, Tom Williams entered the University of Missouri at Columbia, with the intention of majoring in journalism.

CHAPTER II

Education and Apprenticeship

The change from St. Louis to Columbia proved salubrious for the young man. The Southern accent that previously had evoked taunts delighted his college associates, who promptly nicknamed him "Tennessee." Tom was so pleased with the new name that he eventually assumed it.

At the beginning he made the honor list, but from then on his grades went into a steady decline. This was partly a consequence of his joining a fraternity where he learned to smoke and discovered alcohol as a means of overcoming shyness. But a more basic reason was that Tom was in love. Between himself and the girl, Hazel Kramer, a warm relationship had begun when he was twelve and she eleven, and had continued through high school.

When Tom went to college, Hazel still had another year of high school to finish. As the time came for her to apply for admission to Missouri, Cornelius Coffin Williams entered the scene. Hazel's parents were divorced, and she lived with her grandfather, who worked for the shoe company where Mr. Williams was sales manager. One day, Tom's father took Hazel's grandfather aside and told him that if he enrolled his granddaughter at the University of Missouri, Cornelius Williams would promptly withdraw his son. Tennessee Williams to this day doesn't understand his father's motives; perhaps he considered them too young and too poor to be so serious. But whatever the reason, altruistic or not, he never chose to communicate it to his bewildered son. So Hazel went to the University of Wisconsin—and Tom's college career lost much of its glamor.

Two of Tennessee Williams' early short stories reflect something of this frustrated young love, both picturing the poetic undergraduate in relations with an equally sensitive young girl. In one entitled "The Important Thing," the pair find their common interests drawing them closer and closer together until a disastrous day when they combine a picnic with studying together for an exam. The study-picnic ends in a wild, silent struggle on the grass. As they leave, the boy admits he shouldn't have reached for his "important" experience with this friend of what he terms "anonymous gender."

The other college love story is somewhat more flattering to the girl and somewhat less to the man, though here, too, he is pictured as a virile, as well as sensitive and talented, person. In "A Field of Blue Children," a girl spends a night with a young poet whose tastes she shares and whose talents she admires. Unfortunately she is engaged to an attractive, sensible young man for whom she feels great affection. Leaving her dormitory that night she goes to the poet's shabby room, rouses him from bed, and tells him how much she thinks of one of the poems he read at the poetry club that day. In a pastoral idyll he leads her out to see the subject of his poem, a field of blue flowers, into which they sink in the ecstasy of love. The girl, nevertheless, marries her substantial young fiancé and raises her sensible family, returning only once to cry with nostalgia in the field of "blue children." Both stories have a youthful innocence that sets them apart from most of the Williams short stories.

In spite of his love disappointment, Tom liked the university which he found "a nice country-club kind of place." He soon discovered that his choice of journalism as his major was a mistake. He had literary talent, but only a limited interest in news. The University being noted for its school of journalism, a large number of students majored in that subject, and when Williams applied for work on the college paper he found it overstaffed. He was finally assigned death notices and livestock news, the former being more to his taste. This unpromising initiation helped to convince him that fiction, not reality, should be his field.

In the meantime he was happy at the fraternity, even serving for a short time as a member of the wrestling team. Being the only fraternity member eligible for the 118-pound class, he found himself on the mat with an opponent but without any idea of how to proceed. Of this athletic adventure, he recalls, "I attacked my adversary with great fury. I used activity to conceal my lack of skill. I lost the match." And the fraternity thereafter referred to him as "Tiger" Williams.

The decline in grades, the drinking, and the excesses of fraternity life were eyed coldly by C. C. Williams. When Tom failed R.O.T.C. during his third year at Missouri, it was the last straw. Mr. Williams' main source of pride in his ancestors was their military prowess. He himself had quit the University of Tennessee Law School after one year to accept a commission as second lieutenant in the Spanish-American War. Raised in the Southern tradition of patriotic militarism, he was infuriated at this fresh evidence of spinelessness in his son.

Since the Great Depression was by then well on, the elder Mr. Williams felt that his son was misusing a very precious element of life—money. In Mrs. Williams' words, her husband "wasn't poor but felt poor." He plucked his prodigal son from the University and introduced him into the practical world of business. If St. Louis had been "fairly lonely and miserable" for him before, it now became hell. C. C. Williams couldn't have contrived a more precisely designed torture. He financed a quick course in stenography for Tom and got him a sixty-five-dollar-a-month job at the shoe factory as a clerk typist.

The three years that he spent in the International Shoe Company warehouse were the most desperate that Williams was to know. His morning chores began with dusting every shoe in the sample room. His afternoons were spent typing endless order forms consisting mostly of strings of numerals. "The lives of most people," Williams has said, in recalling these chores, "are insulated against monotony by a corresponding monotony in their own soul. . . . Alas for the poet, the dreamer . . . who has been cast into the world without this indispensable solution." The three years were characterized as an "indescribable torment to me as an individual but of immense value to me as a writer, for they gave me first-hand knowledge of what it means to be a small wage earner in a hopelessly routine job."

This "contact with reality" provided the basis for *The Glass Menagerie* and the ideas for several completely un-Williamsian, simple characters who were to appear as The Gentleman Caller (in *The Glass Menagerie*), Mitch in *Streetcar,* and others. It also created the vision of the little man at the mercy of the machine, appearing as the tubercular protagonist in the stories, "The Malediction" and "The Strangest Kind of Romance." This little man, symbolizing all little men everywhere similarly entrapped, spends his days at the factory and his nights with his cat, which offers him love and security. Because his hands and the machines never can achieve the same rhythm, he is constantly jamming the machine. *The Glass Menagerie,* itself, expresses this hatred of routine work. Tom despises his job at the shoe factory, and Laura cannot learn to operate a typewriter.

Tennessee Williams has never been a writer primarily concerned with social issues except where they have forced themselves upon him in a personal way—as did racialism in the case of Ozzie. His experience of machine-age drudgery left him with a compassion for those workers who must submerge their souls in mechanized labor in order to live, the machine becoming their master. Williams tends to blame amorphous "them"—apparently the capitalist oppressors—for this situation. The scene in "The Malediction" that precedes the little man's loss of his job is a particularly vivid vilification of "them":

> The final week of the month the stockholders came in town for a crucial meeting. Glittering black and rushing close to the earth as beetles on desperate errands, the limousines sped toward the plant: disgorged their corpulent contents at private doorways and waited uneasily, like a nest of roaches, in cinder-covered parkways back of the plant.
>
> What was hatching inside the conference chambers no one who worked at the plant could tell. It took some time for the eggs to incubate: secret and black and laid in coagulate clusters, they ripened slowly.
>
> This was the problem: there was a slump at the plant. The stockholders had to decide what action to take, whether to cheapen the product and make it available thus to a wider market or else cut down on production, preserving the margin of profit, and wait for the need of the people to make more demand. This was promptly arranged. The wheels got their orders and stopped: the workers were stopped by the wheels. One third of the plant shut down and the men were laid off: the black roach-nest dispersed from the cinder parkways: the problem was solved.

From the nastiness of this insect imagery it is obvious that Williams was no defender of big business. A product of the Depression, he moved in the natural direction of the time, toward sympathy with the poor. Most of his work, however, is free of so-called "social content." Tennessee Williams was to become the spokesman for the repressed individual rather than for the oppressed class.

The years at the warehouse drove Tom back into his own world. "It was in those years," he says, "that I first began to write seriously." The "serious" writing, as a matter of fact, occasionally intruded into the workaday world as he wrote sonnets on lids of

shoe boxes and forgot orders while working out rhymes. He once
carried a $50,000 order from J. C. Penney in his pocket for weeks,
and fished it out, finally, only because Penney had complained. If
his unconscious or conscious motivation was to precipitate his
dismissal from the job, he was out of luck. "I couldn't be fired,"
he commented, "because of my father."

Tom Williams would return from his work to wage his private
rebellion at night. After dinner, he would close himself in his
room with a pot of black coffee and a supply of cigarettes, and
write until four in the morning. Two hours after he had fallen into
bed, exhausted, his mother would open his door to let out the
billow of stale cigarette smoke and wake him as gently as possible.
Amanda's traditional rousing call in *The Glass Menagerie,* "Rise
and shine," was recorded from bitter memory.

Such a regimen was bound to take its toll on the body and nerves
of Tom, whose physique had never been robust. One night, as he
was writing in his stuffy little room, he became aware of his heartbeat, noticing that it was skipping. Panic-stricken, he rushed out
of the house and walked the streets until morning. His mother's
exaggerated fretting about his health had, by this time, turned
him into a confirmed hypochondriac. The doctor told him the
next morning that he had a heart condition, but failed to mention
that the disorder was functional, not organic. Tom was certain of
impending death. On top of this death fear and the daily torment
at the factory, came the sudden end of an old dream—news from
Wisconsin that Hazel Kramer was to be married. Years later, after
she had married and had died while still young, Williams said of
Hazel, "I never loved anyone as I loved her."

Then, one Sunday in March, 1935, he and Rose went to see
The Scarlet Pimpernel. Both were too nervous in crowds to attempt a bus; so they took a "service car" home. (This is a taxi that
follows a regular bus route and charges a higher fare.) On the
way home, the heart malfunction recurred. Terrified by the pal-

pitations, he could barely breathe and his fingers went numb. He gasped instructions to Rose, who told the driver to take them to the nearest hospital. The symptoms did not abate for two weeks, at which time he was told he need not return to the hated job.

The breakdown was probably psychosomatic, but very real to a twenty-four-year-old man who had a head full of ideas that had never reached paper, and who was already in the grip of a fixated fear of death. Convinced he was going to die, he devoted more attention than ever to analyzing his symptoms. "For years after that I had a terrible cardiac neurosis. Every time I read about someone dropping dead, I thought I'd be next."

His grandfather had retired from the ministry, and his grandparents were now living in Memphis. There Tom went to live and recover his strength. These two gentle people never appear in his major writing, probably because they were the most constantly understanding and sympathetic humans he knew and he considers their personalities too sacred for literary exploitation. His sister, his father, and his mother have served often as reluctant models for Tennessee Williams' altered portraits, but never the grandparents. Ministers whom Tennessee Williams portrays in *Summer and Smoke,* "The Yellow Bird," "One Arm," *You Touched Me!,* and *Cat on a Hot Tin Roof* have no relevance to his grandfather, other than that of being Episcopal clergymen. Instead, they are caricatures, representing the orthodox cant that the old gentleman himself disavowed in religion.

The sojourn in Memphis was lucky for reasons other than physical and mental. It introduced Tom Williams to drama. Near his grandparents lived a girl named Dorothy Shapiro. She was active in a little theatre called The Rose Arbor, which was owned and operated by a Mrs. Roseboro, a woman interested in new talent and prepared to produce anything actable.

Dorothy suggested that they collaborate on a play for The Rose Arbor. It was about two sailors on shore leave who picked up a couple of girls. It was called *Cairo! Shanghai! Bombay!* "I'd never met a sailor then," Williams admits. But this did not distress him, although he did most of the writing. It was a long time before the playwright recognized the value of life experience as the basis for his plays.

Cairo! Shanghai! Bombay! was a modest success. To this day Mrs. Roseboro is of the unique opinion that it is Williams' best. The success provided a powerful stimulant to the young writer. "That was when I first realized that this was a medium that was most attractive. I discovered the thrill of people reacting to my work in front of my eyes."

Audience response has been, from the beginning, immensely important to Tennessee Williams. Although unwilling to allow public opinion to determine his materials, he is nonetheless hypersensitive to every critical reaction and invariably comments about rude or dissatisfied audiences.

When Tom Williams returned to St. Louis, life there, for the first time, became comparatively pleasant for him. His father had given up trying to make a solid citizen of him; so, with his grandmother paying the tuition out of her meagre pension funds and her earnings from piano lessons, he returned to school for his senior year, this time at Washington University in St. Louis. There he could major in drama and in his spare time continue to write fiction and poetry, some of which gained him prizes.

The early poems in the style of Edna St. Vincent Millay that had started appearing "about the time of puberty" had already won him notice among some St. Louis intellectuals. Williams summarized his early poetic career this way: "I took the field with great audacity from the very beginning. I was quite successful, my poetry was much admired in high-school, and I won not only plaudits but many little prizes from women's clubs and poetry groups in Mississippi. I remember when an officer in my mother's chapter of D.A.R. passed away, I composed an elegy to her which was read aloud at the services and resulted in a very moving katharsis."

But now his poetry was ready to move out of the sphere of ladies' literary societies and D.A.R. funerals. By the time he returned to St. Louis, he was convinced writing must be his living; it was already his life. Luckily for both his mental and physical health, Tom discovered sympathetic spirits around St. Louis.

One group that stimulated and inspired him included a number of poets in and around Washington University. It was headed by Clark Mills McBurney, whose verse was published under the name of Clark Mills. Inasmuch as both McBurney and the Williamses lived in Clayton, Missouri, a suburb of St. Louis, the two writers became quite close in the two years that Tom stayed there.

Years later, Tennessee Williams, in the preface to his first volume of published verse, described his relationship with McBurney: "Clark's admiration for my verse was tempered by a more technical approach than my other admirers'." The other poet's reactions were frequently noncommittal—"He was usually given to owlish nods and bronchial noises when I showed him my verse. However, he did admire my plays and stories, and we subsequently formed what we called a 'literary factory' in the basement of his suburban home." They found their exchange of ideas mutually beneficial. "Ideas from my plays went into Clark's verse, and ideas from Clark's verse went into my plays." It was, comments Williams, "a very creative and delightful arrangement, especially since Clark's mother visited us more regularly than the muse with trays of lemonade and sandwiches, and Clark usually had a bottle of wine stashed behind the shelves of poetry."

"It was Clark," Williams added, "who warned me of the existence of people like Hart Crane and Rimbaud and Rilke, and my deep and sustained admiration for Clark's writing gently but firmly removed my attention from the more obvious to the purer voices in poetry." From this time on, his leaning has been consistently toward the *avant garde.* At about this time he "acquired" his copy of Hart Crane's poetry, which he has carried with him ever since—frequently as his whole "library." The acquisition was by the dubious means of borrowing it from the Washington University library without the usual formalities. His justification was, "It had been take out almost no times at all and I felt it wasn't being properly valued."

McBurney's memories of the young Williams are colorful. Robert Rice quotes him as saying, "Tom had fanatical and inexhaustible energy in his writing. His persistence was almost grotesque. It was Dionysian, demoniac. He wasn't aiming basically at material success. He wrote because it was a fatal need. Here was this lost member of his family trying to learn playwriting entirely in the dark. He may have written 100 unsuccessful plays."

Among these early demonic efforts was one done in the summertime, when the McBurney attic was "incredibly like an inferno." Tom suddenly laughed at an idea he had: a fat blond mistress sitting in a rocking chair on the verandah of a Southern plantation house while a wiry little man with a riding whip keeps flicking the whip playfully at her and suggesting that they would find it "cool and quiet" inside. Giggling, squealing, protesting, "I know what you'll do to me inside," she finally acquiesces. As they open the door, she towering above her little seducer, she whimpers, "Well, all right, but you must promise not to hurt me." The plot, with a few alterations, was to become "27 Wagons Full of Cotton" and finally the controversial *Baby Doll.*

At the same time that Clark Mills and his group were dissipating the nightmare quality of the city for Tom, another important step in his dramatic career was taking place. His second theatrical production, called *The Magic Tower,* appeared at a little theatre in Webster Groves, Missouri, just outside of St. Louis. This story about a young married couple living in a garret won Tom another prize—a sterling-silver cake dish!

But vastly more important than such isolated productions was Tom Williams' membership in The Mummers, a small theatrical group under the leadership of Willard Holland. The playwright was to remember this group with abiding affection long after he achieved his Broadway triumphs. He describes them, glowingly, as a "long-haired outfit," but, admits that "there is no virtue, *per se,* in not going to the barber. And I don't suppose there is any particular virtue in girls having runs in their stockings. Yet one feels a kind of nostalgia for this sort of disorderliness now and then." The author was later to associate sartorial non-conformity with his good times and intense feelings and convictions among The Mummers. Williams calls them his "professional youth." They were, he says, "a disorderly theater group of St. Louis, standing socially, if not artistically, opposite to the usual Little Theater group." The latter, says the unsympathetic author, "were eminently respectable, predominantly middle-aged, and devoted mainly to the presentation of Broadway hits a season or two after Broadway. Their stage was narrow and notices usually mentioned how well they had overcome their spatial limitations, but it never seemed to me that they produced anything in a manner that needed to overcome limitations of space. The dynamism which is theater was as foreign to their philosophy as the tongue of Chinese."

Tom Williams had reached his rebellious stage, moving away from the lady sonneteers, the ladies' literary societies—away from his mother's influence and from conservative Southern life. Iconoclasm was becoming his theme and Bohemia his life. By the time he wrote *Summer and Smoke,* ministers and Puritanism had become subjects of satire, and literary societies symbols of human pettiness and intellectual sterility. Among The Mummers, Tom Williams found answers to his troubled questioning about himself and his future, the dynamism, the spark of anarchy that he was seeking. "For about five years—roughly from about 1935 to 1940—

they burned like one of Miss Millay's improvident little candles—
and then expired," Williams says of The Mummers. "Yes, there
was about them that kind of excessive romanticism which is
youth and which is the best and purest part of life."

Their leading figure was Willard Holland, organizer and
director of the group. "Holland always wore a blue suit which was
not only baggy but shiny," says the nostalgic author. "He needed
a haircut and he sometimes wore a scarf instead of a shirt. This
was not what made him a great director, but a great director he
was. Everything that he touched he charged with electricity. Was
it my youth that made it seem that way? Possibly, but not probably.
In fact not even possibly. . . ." The way to judge theatre, says
Williams, is by its effect on audiences, "and Holland's work never
failed to deliver, and when I say deliver I mean a sock!"

Williams' first connection with The Mummers was in their
production of Irwin Shaw's *Bury the Dead*. Since the play ran
short of full length, they needed a curtain raiser. "At the time,"
recalls Mr. Holland, "a lot of college kids were being vocal
against compulsory military training and someone said there was
a boy up at Washington U. 'writes pretty well.'" The call from
Holland was an opportunity that the young writer leapt at.

As Williams remembers it, Mr. Holland called him: "He did
not have a prepossessing voice. It was high-pitched and nervous.
He said, 'I hear you go to college and I hear you can write.' I
admitted some justice in both of these charges. Then he asked me:
'How do you feel about compulsory military training?'" When
Tom assured him that he had left the University of Missouri
because he couldn't get a passing grade in R.O.T.C., Mr. Holland
said, "Swell! you are just the guy I am looking for. How would
you like to write something against militarism? . . . Could you
take some of the headlines and statements being made by people
against war and give us about 12 minutes of stuff to get the
audience in the mood for *Bury the Dead?*" Williams said he could.

"The two things," says Mr. Holland, "Tom's piece, which was called *Headlines* and which he didn't even get program credit for, and *Bury the Dead* were put on on Armistice Day, 1936." Part of the pleasure of writing *Headlines* for Willard Holland must have been the bitter taste he knew it would leave in his militaristic father's mouth.

The evening of theatre was a success. "[Irwin] Shaw's play," Williams says emphatically of *Bury the Dead,* is "one of the greatest lyric plays America has produced." It is "a solid piece of flame." Of the direction, he recalls, "Actors and script, under Holland's dynamic hand, were one piece of vibrant living-tissue." And best of all, for an artist who is always conscious of the audience, the reaction was what it should have been.

Williams adds: "Now St. Louis is not a town that is easily impressed. They love music, they are ardent devotees of the symphony concerts, but they preserve a fairly rigid decorum when they are confronted with anything off-beat which they are not used to. They certainly were not used to the sort of hot lead which the Mummers pumped into their bellies that night of Shaw's play. They were not used to it, but it paralyzed them. There wasn't a cough or creak in the house, and nobody left the Wednesday Club Auditorium (which the Mummers rented for their performances) without a disturbing kink in their nerves or guts, and I doubt if any of them have forgotten it to this day." He mentions nothing at all about the audience's reaction to his own contribution to the evening of theatre, apparently because it seemed inferior by far to the better-known work.

This beginning was to lead Williams deep into off-beat dramatic and intellectual trends. Recalling The Mummers, on whose lives he was, for a time, to pattern his own, he writes: "Most of them worked at other jobs besides theater. They had to, because The Mummers were not a paying proposition. There were laborers. There were clerks. There were waitresses. There were students.

There were whores and tramps and there was even a post-debutante who was a member of the Junior League of St. Louis." Many, although not professional, were fine actors. And "many of them were not. Some of them could not act at all, but what they lacked in ability, Holland inspired them with in the way of enthusiasm." It is hard to define what constituted their intense attraction for Tom Williams. Looking back, he suspects that The Mummers ran "by a kind of beautiful witchcraft! It was like the definition of what I think theater is. Something wild, something exciting, something that you are not used to. Off-beat is the word."

The following year saw the first of his serious efforts put on by The Mummers—a piece called *Candles to the Sun*. Although Williams considers it bad, it was nonetheless a smash hit. He recalls that it got rave notices in all three St. Louis papers. On opening night there was a real demonstration, with "shouts and cheers and stamping, and the pink-faced author took his first bow among the grey-faced coalminers that he had created out of an imagination never stimulated by the sight of an actual coalmine." The St. Louis *Post-Dispatch* carried this colorful review of the play:

> Williams, 25-year-old Washington University senior, is revealed not only as a writer of unusual promise but one of considerable technical skill right now. This theme is spread in realistic, swift strokes, with sound knowledge of locale and a mature appreciation of human affairs. If, impatient with time-honored dramatic technique, he employs two acts and ten scenes, he still has devised effective curtains for all divisions.
>
> "Candles to the Sun," set in the Red Hills mining section of Alabama, dramatizes the yearning of the laboring population, especially of the mothers in that class, for something better. It has poverty, degeneracy, and brutal murder, ending with beans for everybody, hope and the singing of "Solidarity Forever." Our author, in a phrase, shoots the works.

Apparently the standard Williams trademarks were already established: emphasis on mothers, distaste for poverty and humdrum work, violence aplenty, and lack of precision in plotting. The review continues:

> Yet although he has been beguiled by his many colorful opportunities, his writing is rarely unsteady and his play has emotional unity and robustness. It stands on its own feet. Its characters are genuine, its dialogue of a type that must have been uttered in the author's presence, its appeal in the theater widespread.
>
> In the hands of a professional cast, it would doubtless come up more forcefully than on this occasion. Yet the Mummers, all considered, give it more effective treatment than they have to better recognized works.

The critic summarizes the theme as the eventual triumph of beauty over grim poverty and despair and concludes that this social-protest drama was "one of the strongest the Wednesday Club group has ever attempted."

The Great Depression and the general drabness of life in industrial St. Louis had diverted the young writer from his natural inclinations into problems of people he did not know and into social criticism. This direction was wrong for Tom Williams, but it was right for The Mummers, and it was right for the mid-thirties.

His next play had a title which was to become familiar later, when appended to another play—*Fugitive Kind*. It was a story of flop-house characters on skid row in St. Louis, where Tom did some first-hand research. Willard Holland said of it, "To me, *Fugitive Kind* was one of the best things ever written by Tom, let's say because I acted in it and it was such a wonderful Humphrey Bogart part. It was a flop in the sense that the plot structure was too phony and along too melodramatic lines. In other words, if we had let his flophouse guys talk and cough themselves to death to their own amusement it would have been a more satisfactory play." Although The Mummers and many of the spectators felt that *Fugitive Kind,* in spite of its structural flaws, was a good deal better than *Candles to the Sun,* the press, William re-

calls, except for a rave notice in the *Star-Times,* "gave it hell." His
friends remember that he was seized with such a fit of melancholia
at the final curtain that he ripped the script in two and lunged,
with the fortunate interception of well-wishers, for the nearest
open window.

Willard Holland, now a newspaperman in California, gave
Robert Rice an interesting verbal sketch of the young playwright.
"Writing always came easier to Tom than it does to most people.
I call it literary diarrhea—it just poured out of him. His original
manuscripts were the length of three full plays and you could
throw out heaps of typewritten pages and still have more than
enough left over for a full-length play."

Holland was impressed by the very first plays by Tom Williams
that he saw. As soon as he read them, he thought, "Here is
something; nothing like this has hit the American theater since
the early O'Neill stuff. For me it was like being dragged to a
church bazaar and finding Marian Anderson singing there."

As for the boy himself, the older man considered him "an
interesting kid. . . . He was enthusiastic about his work and easy
to work with and an easy person to talk to. You could talk out any
point with him about his plays. He had no temperament about
his work. Right from the beginning I thought of him as a professional." Mr. Holland also admired the "staggering" immersion
that Tom had in his work. "I suppose," he admits, "I had the
same thing and that's why we worked so well together."

Tom's shyness, however, was a barrier even with these people.
The director says that he couldn't get "warmed up to Tom as a
friend. . . . There was something of an iron curtain—perhaps it
had to do with the difficulties he was having with his family—he
drew between himself and other people and it was hard to get
through to him."

The most curious quality that Mr. Holland recalls about the boy
was his laugh: "He had the most inane laugh I ever heard. It

was a high squeaky cackle, a shriek and a cackle. We would be desperately working on something. The blood could be flowing all over the floor; we could be butchering his brain child on the stage, and he would come out with his cackle because something struck him funny. It would drive me mad."

The plays that Tom Williams wrote for The Mummers were largely about sad people with problems. The director comments that he went overboard for characters and dialogue, which remain Williams' two areas of real power. He could sit down at a type-writer and compose a characterization and dialogue for that character that in no way related to any play. This astonishing ability he was to carry into his later work.

On the other hand, he has always been plagued with the inability to construct good plots. But, when the characters are good enough, the audience forgets weak plotting.

Mr. Holland recalls that "his people were really fantastic. You could take a page or pages of dialogue he wrote, give them to an actor, and just put the spotlight on him, and anyone who just happened to walk into the theater couldn't turn away from the strength of it."

A directorial difficulty arising from this talent was the fact that his minor characters would take over. "And another problem we had was keeping actors away from these roles. You couldn't let an actor get hold of a part like that because no one would stand still and let you take a part like that away from him." It remained typical of Tennessee Williams that his minor characters are usually as lively as his main ones, that they frequently usurp the spot-light, that the plays are too long, and it is almost impossible for him to cut them down to a reasonable size.

All through his career, directors and actors have found Mr. Williams easy to work with. He is one of the most docile of play-wrights, and despite his success, he continues to be modest about his talents. In the early days he assumed, wisely, that the people in

the theatre knew more than he about producing a play. Therefore, Holland discovered, as did most other directors over the
years, that this author was "amenable and easy to work with once
you explained what the problem was. He was sensitive to criticism
only when a play was in its produced form, after it had opened.
One of Tom's most likeable traits when he started writing was
that he would listen to people who knew more than he did. If
you tell the average playwright that his play is unproduceable you
crush him, because it may be the effort of five or six months, but
to Tom it just represented some typewritten pages."

Even though he produced reams of his torrential output for The
Mummers, while keeping up his college work and worrying about
home troubles, he never gave his companions the impression of
being tired or run-down. Apparently his health could stand the
strenuous life when he was happy in his work. Writing all night
did not keep him from looking healthy and neat the next day. At
this time, he wore good, quiet tweeds with a shirt and tie. "As a
matter of fact," comments the wry Mr. Holland, "he always
looked like a young bank teller to me."

The plays that Tom Williams wrote for The Mummers, although good enough for an amateur, were not yet of professional
calibre. John Gassner summarized the early Williams' sense of
theatre in an essay that records some of his personal knowledge of
the playwright in his early years. Williams had written poetry
and short stories, but his real métier was the theatre. He found
himself continually thinking "in terms of sound, color, and movement and had grasped the fact that the theatre was something
more than written language."

The playwright himself said of this transition from narrative
and lyric writing to dramatic writing, "The turbulent business
of my nerves demanded something more animate than written
language could be." Poetry, of course, never lost its hold on him,
causing him to fuse the stringent realism, demanded by the stage,

with symbolism and poetic diction. His taste had formed itself before he thoroughly understood his talents; as a result, even the best work of Tennessee Williams is often marred by a misplaced lyricism.

His ability to write good drama, although inborn, required years of self-criticism and control to bring to full maturity. The association with The Mummers was long enough to provide a good portion of the necessary apprenticeship, an apprenticeship that was to continue for years after the extinction of this "brief candle" that was The Mummers.

At the same time he was working with The Mummers, he was taking the university drama course given by Professor William G. B. Carson, a number of whose students have become successful dramatists. A classmate of Williams' was Aaron Hotchner, who has dramatized some of the late Ernest Hemingway's stories.

Professor Carson found Tom a quiet, courteous, pleasant young man. The class operated after this fashion: At the end of the year each student submitted a one-act play. These were then turned over to a committee of three judges (who were unfamiliar with them and with the identities of the authors), and they selected three for production in competition for an annual $50 prize. "I myself," says Professor Carson, "took no part in the deliberations of the judges, though I sometimes stood by to answer questions." He adds wryly that he was seldom able to guess the winner.

The one-act play Tom Williams submitted was called "Me, Vashya," a story of a World War I munitions maker who sold his products to both sides. Although the play had a certain power, the author was again working in alien, and for him barren, territory— ignoring the Southern locale and the Southern characters he was familiar with and later dramatised so effectively.

Professor Carson says that he had expected "Me, Vashya" to be a winner and "was rather dismayed when it was not." One judge excused the decision by insisting that the play could not be cast adequately. (Part of the prize was production of the play at the University theatre.) Among the winners was Aaron Hotchner. Tom was awarded honorable mention.

Williams reaction was violent. "It was a terrible shock and humiliation to me," he has said. "It was a crushing blow to me. I had always thought I was shy, but I discarded all humility. I stormed into Carson's office. (He was a good professor.) I screamed at him. I forgot what my parting shot was, but I remember it was quite a shot. I surprised myself."

The failure of "Me, Vashya," compounded with a series of devastating family crises that year, caused Tom to fall off in his studies, fail Greek, and once again leave college without a degree. The disaster that severed him from St. Louis permanently was not Greek or "Me, Vashya" or his father's materialism. In the years between 1935 and 1939, Rose was losing her mind. Sharing her brother's gentleness, sensitivity, and imagination, she too had felt trapped in St. Louis, but unlike him had not found a creative way out of the trap.

Her relationship with her somewhat aggressive mother was as tense, as full of pent-up emotion, and as mixed as that between the two women in Williams' short play "Something Unspoken." With none of her brother's outlets for rage, she watched the crude stranger, her father, barge into her life. She withdrew into the only place she could—into herself. Frail by nature, the shock of maturing and the coincidental tragedy of a calamitous romance at the beginning of her adolescence had left her unstrung, and unfit to cope with the conflicts in the family. She was finally committed to an institution, an incurable schizophrenic.

Watching Rose's growing insanity was the most horrible experience of Tom Williams' life. In her he saw something of himself and of the romantic beauty that, for him, was and is the best and purest part of life. Here was a moth figure crushed by the brute world—the recurrent theme of Tennessee Williams' greatest dramatic successes. Her delicate beauty finds some expression in almost every Tennessee Williams play, the rose itself standing for the world's beauty and love. Because of his own love for her, her insanity became a personal hell for him. His tributes to her, his loveliest works, unite the pain with the love in a poignant, personal, emotionally charged symbol—the rose, a flower as delicate and evanescent as his sister. As Rose declined, his violence grew.

His sister's removal to an institution severed Williams' last real tie with St. Louis. Again with his grandmother's help, he left the city of his nightmares and finished college at the University of Iowa.

This university is celebrated for riches in its drama department, equipped with facilities for play production superior to those of many professional theatres. The late Professor Mabie's classes were a Mecca to aspiring young playwrights. The enlarged apprenticeship that Tom served in the theatre at Iowa—doing backstage work and occasional bit parts and selling tickets, as well as writing for it—helped him to learn more of the mechanics of the theatre.

Although he had to work hard to stretch his grandmother's small contributions toward living expenses and tuition, he found life at Iowa exciting and congenial. To meet his expenses, he wiped tables in the cafeteria of the University hospital, coached freshman in English, and sold tickets for plays at the University theatre, on commission. "But I have gone to bed numerous nights without supper," he told a friend in a letter. "Such a stringent existence is probably good for the soul—but if some New York producer offers me a fat check for one of my plays. I will certainly be in a receptive state of mind." Still, poverty is not quite so hard to bear when you share it with other adventurous young people, many of whom were as Bohemian as Tom's Mummer friends had been. His iconoclasm and anti-Puritanism gained in intensity during the two years he spent at Iowa.

By the time he earned his degree in 1938, (nine years after entering the University of Missouri), he had written two more plays. One, composed for a seminar at Iowa, was originally entitled (in a rare allusion to Eliot) *April is the Cruelest Month,* but was later changed to *Spring Storm.* Williams read it aloud during a session of the seminar, appropriately in the spring. Professor Mabie and the students listened patiently during the long reading.

On finishing his reading, the young man looked around for reactions. Now he can discuss with amusement what at the time must have cut deep. He noticed "the good professor's eyes had a glassy look as though he had drifted into a state of trance. There was a long and all but unendurable silence. Everyone seemed more or less embarrassed. At last the professor pushed back his chair, thus dismissing the seminar, and remarked casually and kindly, 'Well, we all have to paint our nudes!' "

Williams adds, "And this is the only reference that I can remember anyone making to the play." Actually, the late Lemuel Ayers, who was a graduate student at Iowa that year, read it and gave Williams sufficient praise for its dialogue and atmosphere to cause him to reverse his decision to give up the theatre in favor of his other occupation of waiting on tables. His other play of Iowa vintage, *Not About Nightingales,* was finished after graduation.

His immediate object upon graduating was not so much to write plays as to earn a living. With this in mind, he went to Chicago where, in those depression years, he was not surprised that he couldn't find a job. He tried desperately to get on the W.P.A. Writers' Project, but was turned down because his work lacked "social content," he couldn't prove that his family was destitute, and he retained a touch of refinement in his behavior which made him seem "frivolous and decadent to the conscientiously rough-hewn pillars of the Chicago project."

This idea having failed, he drifted back to St. Louis and finished his fourth long play, the one he had started at Iowa. "It was called *Not About Nightingales* and it concerned prison life, and I have never written anything since that could compete with it in violence and horror," says Williams, "for it was based on something that actually occurred along about that time, the literal roasting-alive of a group of intransigent convicts sent for correction to a hot room called 'The Klondike.'" When it was completed, he submitted it to The Mummers, who, he says, "were eager to perform it but they had come to the end of their economic tether and had to disband at this point." In actual fact, The Mummers appear to have put up some fuss about whether *Not About Nightingales* was really playable.

It is amazing, incidentally, how many of the violent scenes that appear in Tennessee Williams' plays are based on fact; it would seem that he selects rather than invents his cases of the atrocious in man's nature. He considers this play by far the best of his early efforts—perhaps because he hasn't been able to find it in years and thus can't edit his opinion. As far as he knows, there is no manuscript of it extant, unless it is in one of the boxes long ago stored in the St. Louis cellar. He refers to it as his "lost play."

CHAPTER III

Bohemia

Upon his return to St. Louis, Tom found his father as much opposed as ever to his literary aspirations, and determined to reinstate him in the shoe factory. Consequently, his home having become intolerable without Rose or The Mummers, he cut the umbilical cord for good and turned to the life of the itinerant poet. From that day to this, he has been what he terms "that common American phenomenon, the rootless wandering writer." The life would appear on the surface not to be satisfying. Yet, in a short story called "The Poet," Williams describes a Christ-figure, a wandering poet, who finds dignity on earth and salvation in heaven through his vagrant freedom, an existence closely akin to that of the ruminant beast. In such a life resides the anarchy, the dissociation from the intolerable bonds of human affection, the detachment that Tennessee Williams has found essential to his needs as a human being and to his integrity as a poet. Though sympathy is seldom the public response to this choice by the artist, the phenomenon of the isolated artist is becoming so common in modern America that it is now the poet who is a family man, with an insurance business or a medical practice, who evokes comment.

Moreover, Bohemia has, in its own way, become as convention-

bound as the society it is escaping. In Williams' case, the family
had been at constant war with his art; he therefore assumed that
he must reject the one to realize the other. From this point on,
his biography assumes the symbolic aspect of the modern, dis-
sociated, "Puritanical" (*i.e.*, specialized) artist—alienated from his
society both by its impossible demands and by his own needs.

Williams describes this change as leaving the "comparative
cocoon of schools and colleges" and taking to the road "because the
alternative was something too dull to endure." So he turned to the
nearest large centre of Bohemia, New Orleans' Vieux Carré. Still
seeking work, he applied to the New Orleans Writers' Project and
was again rejected because of the lack of social content and protest
in his writing. Williams was obliged to work for little more than
room and board in a twenty-five-cent-a-meal restaurant run by his
landlady. Robert Rice thus describes his days: "Mornings he
handed out flyers containing a slogan of his own composition:
'Meals for a Quarter in the Quarter.' Afternoons and evenings he
waited on tables. Nights he wrote or walked the streets and
marveled."

The figures on the city-scape that charmed him included: "prostitutes and gamblers, sailors who wrote verse, poets who traveled
in boxcars, and unreconstructed Basin Street musicians, sweet old
ladies who quietly drank pain-killer all day, and nasty old men
who quietly molested little boys, alcoholics and hoboes and junkies
and pimps and homosexuals, all in a comprehensive sampling of
those too brave, frightened, pure, corrupt, angry, gentle, clear,
confused, creative, numb to accept the peace, comfort, stagnation
and rot of respectability." The mood and people of Bourbon
Street were later fused into a poem that appeared in his slender
volume of verse, *In the Winter of Cities*. Part of it goes like this:

> He thought of the innocent mornings on Bourbon Street,
> of the sunny courtyard and the iron
> lion's head on the door.

He thought of the quality light could not be expected
to have again after rain,

the pigeons and drunkards coming together from under
the same stone arches, to move again in the sun's
faint mumble of benediction with faint surprise.

He thought of the tall iron horseman before the Cabildo,
tipping his hat so gallantly toward old wharves,
the mist of the river beginning to climb about him.

He thought of the rotten-sweet odor the old Quarter had,
so much like a warning of what he would like to learn.

He thought of belief and the gradual loss of belief and the piecing
together of something like it again.

. . . .

He thought of Irene whose body was offered at night
behind the cathedral, whose outspoken pictures were hung
outdoors, in the public square,
as brutal as knuckles smashed into grinning faces.

He thought of the merchant sailor who wrote of the sea,
haltingly, with a huge power locked in a halting tongue—

lost in a tanker off the Florida coast,
the locked and virginal power burned in oil.

He thought of the opulent antique dealers on Royal
whose tables of rosewood gleamed as blood under lamps.

He thought of his friends.

. . . .

For these rootless people with their eccentric beauty, Williams
felt a kinship he had experienced briefly in St. Louis with the
poetry group and with The Mummers, and at Iowa with other
needy students. With these people, the "rebellious Puritan"
found "a kind of freedom I had always needed. And the shock of
it against the Puritanism of my nature has given me a subject, a
theme, which I have never ceased exploiting."

In New Orleans he came upon a symbol he was to put to memorable use. "If I can be said to have a home," he said some years after, "it is in New Orleans where I've lived off and on since 1938 and which has provided me with more material than any other part of the country. I live near the main street of the Quarter which is named Royal. Down this street, running on the same tracks, are two street-cars, one named DESIRE and the other named CEMETERY. Their indiscourageable progress up and down Royal struck me as having some symbolic bearing of a broad nature on the life in the *Vieux Carré*—and everywhere else for that matter. . . ."

When Williams arrived in New Orleans, he was a proper young man in a neat, conservative suit, polished shoes, dress shirt, and tie. When he left, he was headed for California with an ex-teacher-turned-clarinet-player in a decrepit Chevy; and he was wearing a sports shirt and sandals. His name was now *Tennessee*.

The formal change to the college nickname he justified partially by the fact that some ancestors on his father's side had been Indian fighters in Tennessee. Therefore, that state was a part of his heritage, and sometimes (during those peaceful interludes with his grandparents) of his own life. And later, when he discovered his theme in New Orleans and began to publish a few items in *Story* and *Poetry* magazines, which he classified as his first "serious" artistic efforts, he reasoned that his previous work had degraded his given name. Anyway, Thomas Lanier Williams did sound a bit too much like William Lyon Phelps—an academic mediocrity of that period. After all, he said, the life of an artist is somewhat similar to the defense of a stockade against a band of savages. By the time *The Glass Menagerie* appeared, the old name, Tom (used for the protagonist), served as a cloak for semi-autobiographical confidences.

In more recent years, even the nickname has been nicknamed, and Williams signs himself by the numeral *10*. His friends have made fun of his name. Dorothy Parker said it was as silly as if she signed herself *Palestine Parker*. Nevertheless, the author has now established it as his trademark and has found it, as he anticipated, a handy advertisement. It sounded, he believes, more exotic and commercial than his own name. "I think it helped me. I think it caught people's eyes."

These wandering years left Williams with an abiding sympathy for the hardships of the dedicated artist and an understanding of his problems. A statement in the preface to a collection of his poems published in 1944, could serve as his summary of the situation of the artist in modern America. "If there is ever a world congress of poets, I mean outside the one obliquely described in the section called "Walpurgisnacht" in Joyce's *Ulysses,* I think the problem mainly to be considered is not competitive philosophies of art nor even political ideas. Despite the fuss which many of us make over the latter and its indisputable importance, I think it always remains a little outside our introverted orbit. . . . As for the first, it is altogether a matter of personal feeling and most of the arguments have worn themselves out. I think the problem that we should apply ourselves to is simply one of survival. I mean actual physical survival!" He says that, whenever he meets a young poet, he involuntarily asks, *"How do you live? How do you get along?"* The questions, he admits, are as tasteless as a callously inquisitive visitor at a side show asking "the armless man how he buttoned his trousers." Yet he can't help wondering: "I think it is almost impossible for a young poet to live in contemporary America, let alone contemporary Europe and Asia, and the fact that some of them *do* is far more surprising than the fact that so many *don't*."

To the romantic Mr. Williams, the fragile poet is a pitiful pariah. "The most destructible element in our society," he says, "the immature and rootless artists or poets, is the one that is subjected to the worst lambasting." This he knows from his own personal experience, "and how I have survived is a question I ask myself with the same incredulous wonder that I have asked others."

New Orleans was not his only experience with these outcasts; he has known them in New York and Los Angeles and St. Louis and Chicago, "all the big cities where groups of them huddle together for some dim, communal comfort. I have been a part of their groups because of the desperate necessity for the companionship of one's own kind." He speaks again of the people in the poem—of Irene, "who painted the most powerful primitive canvases I've ever seen and whispered through shutters to men who passed on the street because she had a body that had to live"; of Joe Turner, "who wrote sea-stories more vivid and beautiful than Conrad's. He was a merchant sailor because there was nothing else for him to do when the W.P.A. Writers' Project ceased to exist, and now not only Joe but his manuscripts have disappeared altogether. . . . Hart Crane wasn't the only one," he concludes.

During this nomadic period, Tennessee Williams developed an even greater love for that other nomad, Hart Crane. "Symbolically," he explains, "I have found a lot of books inconvenient to carry with me and gradually they dropped along the way—till finally there was only one volume with me, the book of Hart Crane." Many years later, he still carried the book as his only permanent library. "This does not mean a snobbish or hysterical exclusion of interest in other poets. On the contrary, I think my taste is unusually catholic, for I still enjoy all of the lady poets" that he listed in that first sonnet written many years earlier. His only criterion for a poem is "truthful intensity of feeling." He likes a poem containing this "whether it's in Keats or Auden or even the horrible Mr. Pound, whom I heard over the short-wave from an Axis capital lately." Even so, he values Crane above Eliot "or anyone else because of his organic purity and sheer breathtaking power." For these qualities, Williams classifies him with

Keats and Shakespeare and Whitman. More than anything else, Hart Crane must have appealed to Williams on a purely personal level. He must have felt a kinship with this lonely, Dionysian poet—a homeless wanderer like himself.

With Hart Crane's poetry for a library and his life for a pattern, Tennessee Williams started his travels, or attempted "to find in motion what was lost in space." Like the Tom of *The Glass Menagerie,* he found that the cities swept by him "like dead leaves, leaves that were brightly colored but torn away from their branches." They became reflections of his own non-attachment. He would have stopped, he said, but he felt pursued by something. Perhaps it was the creative need to experience, to move, to write at the peak of excitement that drove him all over the country searching for new sensations in emulation of Hart Crane.

The trip from New Orleans to California that initiated this nomadic anarchy was marked by escapades precipitated by insolvency. "We ran out of gas in El Paso, also out of cash, and it seemed for days that we would never go farther, but my grandmother was an 'easy touch' and I got a letter with a $10 bill stitched neatly to one of the pages, and we continued westward." Another time, when the mendicants ran out of gas, they kept going by siphoning fuel from other cars. His mother refutes this on the bases of both morality and capability: "I don't think Tom would *ever* do a thing like that. . . . Anyway, he couldn't operate a siphon if his life depended on it." From Texas, he wrote his family that he was on his way, and his mother knew that this was the permanent break. The trip to New Orleans she had looked upon as a vacation; this trip to the Coast suggested permanent separation.

During this period, he began to write new poems, most of which he couldn't submit anywhere because he had no reliable mailing address. One submission to a magazine of verse in Chicago was returned to him "with a sharply worded complaint about the omission of return postage and it was signed 'G.D.,' which I assume were the initials of the editor [George Dillon] and not anything more profane!"

As the two travellers neared California and their cash dwindled to nothing, they stopped, one night, at the home of a splendid, large Indian woman, who after one look at their disreputable clothing, announced that she kept a shotgun for dealing with dead-beats. About four the next morning, regardless of this thinly-veiled threat, the two tried to steal away, but the old car back-fired, waking the well-armed landlady. They started to roll and managed to get a few hundred feet away, crouched low and murmuring supplications, when a double-barreled charge of buck-shot sang through the air a few inches above their heads.

Finally they reached their destination, Los Angeles. There, in the summer of 1939, Tennessee Williams worked within sight of the M.G.M. studio, lived on a pigeon ranch owned by the clari-netist's aunt, and went back to his old professional relationship with shoes. He worked at Clark's Bootery for a while, riding the ten miles from the ranch to the store on a second-hand bicycle he had bought for five dollars.

About this time *Story* magazine published "The Field of Blue Children," a short story based on the love adventure of the youth-ful poet and the college beauty. It was the first piece to appear under the name of *Tennessee Williams*. "Then a most wonderful thing happened," says the author. While in New Orleans, he had heard about a play contest being conducted by the Group Theatre of New York. He submitted all four of the long plays he had written up to that time, in addition to a group of one-actors called *Americans Blues*. "One fine day I received, when I returned to the ranch on my bike, a telegram saying that I had won a special award of $100 for the one-acts, and it was signed by Harold Clurman, Molly Day Thatcher, who is the present Mrs. Elia Kazan, and that fine writer, Irwin Shaw, the judges of the contest."

There was a certain amount of confusion regarding the award. The contest was for full-length plays written by playwrights under twenty-five. The plays in *American Blues* were not full-length, and Tennessee Williams was twenty-eight. But he reasoned sophistically that for three years, while he had worked in the shoe factory, he wasn't really alive. "I felt entitled to those three years." Consequently, all of his records have been three years off until a recent spasm of honesty led him to correct a few of the dates and proclaim that he would never lie again.

The Group Theatre, like The Mummers, was a short-lived, long-haired, left-wing, exciting, dynamic group. Irwin Shaw had been a leading member, along with Cheryl Crawford, Maxwell Anderson, Clifford Odets, Lee Strasberg, William Saroyan, Elia Kazan, and Mollie Thatcher. Tennessee Williams' bluesy, off-beat tone and Depression scene appealed to the group, which, at this time, was beginning to break up. Consequently, although the contest was for a full-length play, the judges decided that *American Blues* merited special attention. Miss Thatcher induced the thrifty treasurer of the group, Kermit Bloomgarden, to appropriate an extra $100 as an award for Mr. Tennessee Williams. Miss Thatcher was one of the few people anywhere who knew where Williams was because for weeks she had been getting postcards from him as he traveled across-country with the clarinetist, telling her what General Delivery address he expected to call at next, or on some occasions, simply instructing her to get in touch with him through his mother, who would pass the message on to him with his laundry. Here, as Robert Rice comments, was a "knight of the road who sent his laundry home regularly to his mother!"

In the meantime, Miss Thatcher went far beyond the usual Group Theatre policy of encouraging talented young artists. She told her friend Audrey Wood that Tennessee Williams was "her kind of a writer." Miss Wood was a successful literary agent who had no need to solicit a client, but she became interested. She wrote to Williams in California telling him of her interest. His reply came on an airmail postcard, which she thought amusing, telling her that he had received similar offers from several agents, and then a few weeks later another airmail postcard telling her she was elected. Few associations in literary history have been happier or more fruitful than this oddly-initiated agent-author relation-ship. Miss Wood, it turned out, had all of the practicality and business sense so notably absent in her client. And he, in turn, in his gratitude for her maternal concern for his needs, has brought her other promising clients. His judgments have been good.

The plays in *American Blues,* which precipitated this happy period of the author's life, are quite diverse. Two have the som-brely naturalistic quality of *Streetcar.* Of these, one is a heavily Freudian story of a pregnant girl who spends her days naked in a dark room, admitting only her married seducer; the other, the bewildered cry of a young woodsman trapped in the dual entangle-ment of family life and factory work. A third piece, "The Case of the Crushed Petunias," sounds like the more lyrical appeal for sexuality to appear in his later adaptation of the D. H. Lawrence short story, "You Touched Me!" A fourth was to be expanded into a full-length play, *Camino Real.* And the fifth was the only one to exploit Williams' most effective talent—the depiction of the decadent South. "The Unsatisfactory Supper" was to be combined with another one-acter for *Baby Doll.*

The one-act form is a natural for Tennessee Williams because it conceals his plot weakness and, on the other hand, highlights his genius for creating character through realistic dialogue. These early plays are full of message—perhaps an influence of the W.P.A. rejections—and are excessively poetic. All through his career, Williams has had to keep a tight rein on his tendency to poetize in the wrong spots; and he has never been at his best when preachy. But these flaws would hardly have bothered the Group Theatre.

After winning the prize, Williams retired from his job at the bootery and from picking squabs at the pigeon ranch. He and the clarinet player hopped on their bicycles and rode down to Tiajuana and back as far as Laguna Beach. There they obtained a small cabin on a small ranch, rent free in return for taking care of the poultry. They lived there all that summer on the $100 prize money, and, says Williams, "I think it was the happiest summer of my life. All the days were pure gold, the nights were starry, and I looked so young, or carefree, that they would sometimes refuse to sell me a drink because I did not appear to have reached 21." Toward the end of the summer "as well as the end of the $100, the clarinet player became very moody and disappeared without warning into the San Bernardino Mountains to commune with his soul in solitude, and there was nothing left in the cabin in the canyon but a bag of dried peas."

For a week Williams lived on stolen eggs and avocados and dried peas, and also "on a faint hope stirred by a letter from a lady in New York whose name was Audrey Wood, who had taken hold of all those plays that I had submitted to the Group Theatre contest, and told me that it might be possible to get me one of the Rockefeller Fellowships, or grants, of $1,000 which were being passed out to gifted young writers at that time." Between expeditions to secure nourishment, the author went to work on another long play which he called *Battle of Angels*—"a lyrical play about memories and the loneliness of them." In the midst of his destitution, his devoted grandmother once again saved him. Out of her $86-a-month pension and her small fees from piano lessons, she took several dollars, stitched them neatly to the page of a letter, and sent them off to her prodigal grandson. With the money, he took a bus back to St. Louis, where he finished his first draft of *Battle of Angels* late that fall and sent it to Miss Wood.

"One day the phone rang and, in a terrified tone, my mother told me that it was long distance, for me. The voice," said Williams, "was Audrey Wood's. Mother waited, shakily, in the doorway. When I hung up I said, quietly, 'Rockefeller has given me a $1,000 grant and they want me to come to New York.' For the first time since I had known her, my mother burst into tears. 'I am so happy,' she said. It was all she could say."

The first item of business in New York was to meet his agent, his guardian angel as he was beginning to see her. Audrey Wood remembers this first meeting vividly. She had expected to find Tennessee Williams a man of "high altitude" like Thomas Wolfe. When she walked into her office at 30 Rockefeller Plaza one day after lunch, she glanced at the waiting room which she shared with her husband, William Liebling, and called out briskly to the group of jobless actors, "Anyone want to see me?"

A pale young man stood up and asked, "You Miss Wood?"

She admitted she was.

He picked up his hat to follow her and said, "Then Ah do."

She was surprised at his slight stature but delighted with his inarticulate gallantry, his sweetness, and his humility. "He was wonderful; he'd do anything. This man understood we must get through a certain period. I never in my life had such a hunch on anybody."

One of the prizes that Miss Wood helped Tennessee Williams to win was a scholarship at the New School for Social Research. There he worked with John Gassner and Theresa Helburn on revisions of *Battle of Angels*. In the meantime, he was living on the Rockefeller grant, doled out to him by Miss Wood in twenty-five dollar-a-month installments. It was supplemented by fifty-dollar option payments from Hume Cronyn, who thought of producing some of his one-act plays, but didn't—at least didn't for some years.

Because of this work with John Gassner and Theresa Helburn, both associates to the Theatre Guild, more luck was to come Tennessee Williams' way. Amazingly enough, the Theatre Guild, from which the Group Theatre members had seceded years before, also recognized the talent displayed by this dynamic young writer. In 1940, *Battle of Angels* became the Theatre Guild's first play from the pen of the promising young playwright, Tennessee Williams.

CHAPTER IV

Battle of Angels

John Gassner, who with Miss Helburn, had given Tennessee Williams his scholarship to the New School Seminar, was excited about *Battle of Angels;* in fact, to this day, he considers it one of Williams' most outstanding works. He pronounced it the best script he had seen in five years. Still, he found flaws in it that might interfere with staging it. Williams himself said he then knew frighteningly little about professional theatre. He was therefore eager to learn from more experienced people, but Mr. Gassner laments that the eagerness was wasted: "He did not yet know his way through the maze of plot sustained for an entire evening. He was so poorly guided in the revisions he made for the Theatre Guild that the play as produced was inferior to the script that had been accepted, and he also appeared to have been fixed on D. H. Lawrence somewhat too strongly at this stage to be able to master the play's problems." With all of its flaws, Mr. Gassner considered *Battle of Angels* a work of considerable merit, worth taking an option on for possible production.

In the meantime, disappointed with the coolness of his New York reception, outside of these immensely friendly people, the lonely young writer took his payments from the Rockefeller Foun-

dation and the option money and headed for Mexico. Hopping
from city to city as the spirit moved him, he neglected to leave forwarding addresses with Mr. Gassner. When the option payments
stopped coming, Williams assumed that the Guild had dropped
the play, forgetting that they couldn't know his address. Dis-
couraged, he went on to Los Angeles, where he picked up a New
York paper, to discover that the Theatre Guild was opening its
season with *Battle of Angels.*

Rushing back to New York, he found that Lawrence Langner
had taken charge of his play, that Margaret Webster had agreed to
direct it, and that Miriam Hopkins had chosen to star in it for
her comeback.

Since those days, *Battle of Angels* has undergone many revisions.
But the basic plot and characters have not changed significantly.
(See the chapter entitled "Williams Warmed Over" for changes in
the play when it became *Orpheus Descending.*) In all of its forms,
it is an allegory whose characters are simultaneously abstractions
and humans. Its most unsatisfactory feature is its blatant preaching
of Lawrencian, anti-Puritan credos.

Williams chose the South for his scene, but his chief character,
Myra Torrence, was of Sicilian descent, and he endows her with
stereotyped Latin emotionalism. Her father, sneeringly referred to
as the "Wop" by his racialist neighbors, had owned an orchard on
Moon Lake, which, in the springtime, he converted into a casino
where nooks with lanterns and tables provided the local youth with
privacy for their drinking and love-making. Myra herself, in the
company of a young man from the established Anderson family,
had been a frequent participant. But because the "Wop" had served
"niggers," the "leading citizens" had set fire to the orchard, and
Myra's father had died in the conflagration. This disaster had been
followed closely by another one for Myra. Her lover had married
into a wealthy family, considering money a more rational basis
for marriage than love. Horrified by his betrayal, pregnant with

his child, grieved at her father's violent death, Myra saw no way
out of her trouble. So, in a sort of self-destroying, legal prostitution, she married Jabe Torrence, a crochety, materialistic, selfish,
and malicious old man. Myra's child, luckily, did not live to be
subjected, as she was, to his tyranny.

All this has happened before the curtain rises. As the play opens,
Jabe is slowly dying, too cantankerous to relieve humanity by a
quiet demise. Although he and Myra have made a good living
from his drygoods store, neither makes any pretense of liking the
life they have shared or each other. Myra makes no show of grief
over her husband's approaching death.

As the curtain rises, Myra is waiting in the store for Jabe's return
from the clinic where he has just received the death verdict—
incurable cancer. The local busybodies are there to hear the gory
details while they prepare a sham-festive welcome. When Jabe
appears, looking like death, they gush over his improved "health."
He mutters maledictions and retires to the upstairs bedroom.
There, through the rest of the play, he lies dying, interrupting the
action periodically by thumping his cane on the floor.

Later the same day, a tramp of virile appearance and poetic
talents wanders into the store. He and Myra are immediately
drawn to each other, vacillating between antagonism and childlike
confidences. Val Xavier, the snake-jacketed hobo-writer, is looking
for a job. Myra finally agrees to make him her handyman.

The appearance of a handsome young man in the store sets the
townswomen on a shopping spree. Among them are the sheriff's
frustrated wife, Vee, who has been sublimating in church work and
primitive art à la Grandma Moses, and an anarchistic dypsomaniac
named Sandra. In the course of her conscious—and unconscious—
efforts to thwart their attempts to seduce her handyman, Myra falls
in love with him herself. Her resulting happiness brings her to a
second blooming, the illicit cause of which is obvious to the entire

community. The cane-thumping husband above does not long remain unaware of his wife's affair below his bedroom.

Then one day, the police come after Val on a trumped-up rape charge. The men of the community are only too ready to see "justice" done because Val's advent has caused considerable marital friction. Frantic to escape, Val seeks to leave without the now-pregnant Myra. She insists on accompanying him. A forwarding address would hardly keep her warm of an evening. In the meantime, the equally enamored Sandra enters to propose that Val go with her. Into this melée hobbles the dying husband to announce that he knows what has been going on, that he is the man responsible for the murder of Myra's father, and that he now plans to kill Myra. Whereupon he carries out his threat. As the shot reverberates, Val dashes out the back door. Jabe totters to his prolonged death on stage, hissing that Val has murdered Myra, and a posse hastily assembles to hunt him down. Tracked by bloodhounds, Val is caught and lynched from the "hanging tree" while the store flames up in a final holocaust.

One trouble with the story is that there is too much of it; it is actually much more detailed and involved than this summary suggests. The subplots are not only confusing; some of their involvements are also unnecessary. Tedious dialogue by Greek-chorus-type busybodies, that serves chiefly as exposition, makes the first act too talky and delays the development of the main characters, who are allowed only a few moments on the stage. Besides, the story has too many irrelevant characters. Admittedly, as with most of Williams' minor characters, they are entertaining enough; still, they have no vital role and clog the action of the play. The lack of organic unity is in contradiction to Tennessee Williams' own rules for effective writing. Finally, most of the characters are too often morality-play symbols rather than believable humans.

For instance, Myra as the darkly robust representative of life and procreation is, at times, a virtual Ceres, at other times a Venus.

Disregarding consequences, she goes through violent fluctuations of hatred, love, happiness, and despair. Paired with death, in the person of Jabe, she is like earth in winter; joined with Val, she is springtime and fertility. In the later rewrite of the play, *Orpheus Descending*, Myra becomes a still stranger combination of the Virgin Mary, Proserpine, and Eurydice.

The sources for Myra are obvious: the outcast Laura Young, the passionate Mexican women Williams had seen on his travels, and the D. H. Lawrence fertility goddess. Yet Williams' Mediterranean types, presented as the embodiment of passion, are never so real or so sympathetically presented as his fragile, frustrated Southern ladies. Unlike the latter, Myra and her descendants in Williams' drama are not drawn from his own experience. They are intellectual concepts. (See the chapter on *The Rose Tattoo* for the character of Serafina, his best Mediterranean portrait.)

Against Myra, as protagonist of the fleshy camp in the battle of angels, is Jabe as the epic antagonist, the defender of the spiritual camp. If Myra and Val represent Satan and his fallen angels, Jabe would be God and His triumphant hosts. Certain elements in the drama do, as a matter of fact, imply such an identification. The authoritarian warning thump of his cane (symbol both of his sexual impotence and his moral power) interrupts the fleeting moments of happiness on stage; and his unmerciful judgments of human sin (righteous according to the Old Testament concept of a jealous God) bring punishment, death, and purification by fire. This idea of God is rendered still more repellent by making Jabe the personification, also, of putrefaction and death. And, since conventional morality is on his side, the author seems to be saying that convention-bound morality is a form of death. Encased in Christian terminology, such a sermon could hardly win assent, and it was wise of Williams to change Jehovah-Jabe into Pluto-Jabe, the Greek god of the underworld, for the later version of the play.

In *Battle of Angels,* while Jehovah-Jabe irritates both Jews and

Christians in the audience, another minor character enters to infuriate them even further. Vee, the sheriff's wife, a dedicated churchwoman, is a painter whose primitive canvases exhibit obvious Freudian symbols. In one of the least artistic moments in the play, she totes in her latest opus, a red church steeple. Lest the phallic symbol elude anybody in his audience, Williams further emphasizes the sublimated sexuality of this religious fanatic by discussing her painting of the Last Supper: It seems that she had had a vision of one disciple's face after another, each suggesting a virile young man in town. She climaxes these sublimations of sexuality by ensconcing Christ in the image of Val, who touches her breast in the vision—hardly a spiritual gesture.

Val accents his role as the Christ of the repressed by saying to Myra, "Christ—I, Lady—you," thereby intimating that she is Mary. Furthermore, his name is Xavier—Savior. The name itself, Valentine Xavier, is that of the brother of the saint, who figures in Williams' own ancestry. His dream of escape to Sangre de Cristo, Blood of Christ country, ends in his sacrifice on a tree, a parallel too obvious to miss.

But Val's identification with Christ means, for one thing, that Christ and God are separate and antagonistic in Williamsian theology. This dichotomy is carried further in later plays in which the Christ-figure appears as the compassionate human sufferer while God appears as the merciless judge and executioner imposing an outmoded code of law. In addition, this Christ-figure, through his springtime resurrection, symbolizes fertility and sexuality. The snakeskin jacket even hints that Christ belongs to Satan's team in the contest. As would be expected of an author who had found what he considered his own salvation through rootless wandering, Christ is a poet and a wanderer who would feel at home among the bohemians of the Vieux Carré.

Another allegorical figure is Sandra—Cassandra, the Trojan princess-prophetess who received the gift of foreknowledge and the curse of having none of her prophecies believed. Like her classical namesake, Sandra sounds insane to the local inhabitants as she pronounces her message of doom. In her way, she is as fanatic as Vee, in her flouting of the forces to which Vee has submitted. She is educated—holding a Master's degree in literature. (Blanche in *Streetcar* has the same educational background, perhaps suggesting an affinity in nymphomaniacs for English studies.) She is a Southern aristocrat whose heritage of inbreeding has made her fragile. Since sex gives the illusion of being the farthest distance man can travel from death and since alcohol is a relief from the sense of mortality, a compound of alcohol and promiscuity becomes Sandra's balm for the pain of existence. However, Cypress Hill cemetery, her favorite trysting place, marks her obsession with death. The lesson she believes that the dead teach is *Live!* Her account of the Cassandra of antiquity outlines the pattern of her unorthodoxy. "Her ears were snake-bitten, like mine, so that she could understand the secret language of the birds. . . . You know what they told her, Snakeskin? They contradicted everything she'd been told before. They said it was all stuff an' nonsense, a pack of lies. They advised her to drive her car as fast as she wanted to drive it, to dance like she wanted to dance. Get drunk, they said, raise hell at Moon Lake Casina, do bumps an' wiggle your fanny." Cassandra is perhaps the most exciting character in the story. Unfortunately, though, she has no function in the plot except as another superfluous commentary.

The characters, major and minor, go through their predetermined motions in an equally symbolic setting. The sexual aridity is symbolized by the drygoods in the store; the mock-fertility of the confectionery department, which Myra has decorated like an orchard in springtime, is in keeping with her love affair. Williams describes it as "copiously hung with imitation dogwood blossoms to achieve a striking effect of an orchard in full bloom. The room is almost subjective, a mood of a haunting memory beyond the drab

actuality of the drygoods department." The lights are Japanese
lanterns that give off a rosy glow, a stock Williamsian symbol for
the softening of truth. The memory evoked by this room is, of
course, that of the spring before Myra married Jabe; the irony lies
in the artificiality of the second springtime and the cruelty of this
April.

The other room, a small, dark, locked room, is another standard
Williamsian symbol. Myra has thrown away the key for fear that
Val will want to take her there one day. But Val breaks the lock, as
he breaks all barriers of convention, and the room becomes their
sanctuary of illicit love. Williams uses the locked door frequently
for the locked heart, or for chastity; and the door as womb symbol
is immediately obvious (but not so grotesquely as in the short play
of the *American Blues* collection called "The Dark Room"). Other
parts of the setting reinforce the symbolism—such as dressmaker's
dummies reflecting the lifelessness of Myra's storekeeper existence,
the white phallic columns, and the faintly Gothic architecture of
the whole store, which is intended to suggest a "pillaged temple,"
defiantly profaned by the pagan Val and Myra. The vengeful reaction of this Bible-belt community becomes all the more terrible
with the advent of "something wild" in the country. It is typical
of Tennessee Williams that every detail of the setting—even the
sound effects and the lighting—be as evocative of the mood of the
story as the words themselves. The architecture, the furnishings,
the divisions of the set, the dress and appearance of the characters,
their movements, and their words all carry the meaning of the
story.

But this leaves *Battle of Angels* overcharged with cloying symbolism, and reeling on the edge of melodrama. The poetry was
troublesome in this play, as it was to be in most Williams dramas.
Several speeches, apparently favorites of the author, were overlong
and overpoetic—pushing too hard the barren fig-tree symbol for
Myra, the happiness of the moth in the rain, etc. Williams himself

was aware of the clumsiness of his first scene, the long, talky exposition. What he did not realize was that the clumsiness of the last scene would destroy any chance the play might have had for success.

John Gassner, who watched each step in the painful failure, later analyzed the play's problems—problems, incidentally, that persisted in its revised form. The major difficulty was Williams' effort to "throw together too many of the elements he had dramatized separately in his best one-acters." These include multiplying the dramatic elements instead of fusing them, and the piling up of fortuitous situations, such as the arrival of an avenging fury in the shape of the rape complainant, the killing of Myra, and the lynching of the innocent Val. "Williams, moreover," said Mr. Gassner, "made the mistake of offering an ill-defined cross between a provincial vagrant and a D. H. Lawrence primitive as an example of purity of spirit. A somewhat ill-digested romanticism would have vitiated the play even if its dramaturgy had been finer."

In spite of these flaws, *Battle of Angels* is, in many ways, a powerful play. Mr. Gassner, who fell in love with it at first sight, believes that it "contained some of his most imaginative dialogue and memorable character-drawing. Myra is a rounded portrait, and Williams has yet to improve upon his secondary character, Vee Talbot." They may not compare with Blanche in *Streetcar* or Amanda in *Glass Menagerie,* but they compare favorably with other drama characterizations of this same period. Williams' chief difficulty, as Gassner saw it, was lack of control. "If Williams had been able to exercise restraint," he commented, "he could have made his mark in 1940 instead of having to wait five years." The characters certainly are colorful, the ideas are interesting, the dialogue is frequently both authentic and powerful. The Theatre Guild thought enough of it to invest some $20,000 in its production.

The young author was understandably excited that Margaret

Webster was to direct his first professional effort and that Miriam Hopkins was flying from Hollywood to star in it. Rehearsals went well in Boston, where the play was to open prior to its Broadway run. The only part of the script that really bothered the director was the final scene. She felt that the store's incineration and the heroine's simultaneous violent death toppled the tragedy into melodrama. She asked the young writer to revise this portion. He was willing enough, but could devise no other conclusion. His lack of professional experience showed in his inability to work under pressure. So the director and the cast resigned themselves to doing their best with the final holocaust. On the night of dress rehearsal the ending was flubbed. The stagehand who was to provide the smoke made insufficient use of the smudgepots. Only a few dreary wisps of smoke drifted lazily over the store.

December 30, 1940, was opening night. As the performance got under way, it was apparent that something was wrong. As first the audience was shocked into bridling silence. Then hisses and boos began and soon reached such volume that the actors' words were drowned out. Williams later recalled the tragic night with wonderment. "I never heard of an audience getting so infuriated." The reaction "made Miriam so mad she began to scream her lines above the hissing. Then they stamped their feet, and after a while most of them got up and left, banging their seats behind them." One dignified old Bostonian even paused to shake his fist at the stage before his exit. And for those few who were game enough to linger for the conclusion, injury was added to the insult. For the smoke-pot manipulator made up for his previous dereliction with such billows as nearly to asphyxiate the cast and the remaining auditors. Williams later likened it to "the burning of Rome. . . . Great sulphurous billows rolled chokingly onto the stage and coiled over the footlights. . . . To an already antagonistic audience this was sufficient to excite something in the way of pandemonium. Outraged squawks, gabbling, spluttering spread through all the front rows of the theatre. Nothing that happened on stage from then on was of any importance. Indeed the scene was near eclipsed by the fumes."

The critics groped for words. Only one reviewer was favorable—and he only mildly so—allowing that Williams' talent was "most interesting." The review in the *Globe* started, "One of the most incredible dramas ever presented in Boston. . . ." To another critic Val was a "half-wit living a defensive life against predatory women." What Tennessee Williams had conceived as the tragedy of a wandering poet who brought both salvation and destruction to a love-starved Southern woman, thereby incurring his own crucifixion, became to the Watch and Ward Society indecent exposure of a hillbilly Lothario. Enraged by the combination of religion and sex, they insisted—or at least the Boston City Council did—that the production be closed until bowdlerized to meet Boston standards.

Williams recalls the icy, bright morning after his most catastrophic theatrical disappointment. He and his "brave representative," Audrey Wood, had just read the morning notices of *Battle of Angels*. "As we crossed the Common," Williams remembers, "there was a series of loud reports like gunfire from the street that we were approaching, and one of us said, 'My God, they're shooting at us!' " They were still laughing, a bit hysterically, when they entered the Ritz-Carlton suite, "in which the big brass of the Theatre Guild and director Margaret Webster were waiting for us with that special air of gentle gravity that hangs over the demise of a play so much like the atmosphere that hangs over a home from which a living soul has been snatched by the Reaper." Miriam Hopkins, "understandably shattered and cloistered after the events of the evening before," was absent from the scene. That morning Williams was told that the play must be cut to the bone. Already knowing what to expect, he had come with a rewrite of the final scene in hand. He recalls saying, heroically, "I will crawl on my

belly through brimstone if you will substitute this!" The response
was gently evasive. Then, a few mornings later, he received "the
coup de grâce, the announcement that the play would close at the
completion of its run on Boston." This time he pleaded, with a
note of anguish in his voice, "You don't seem to see that I put my
heart into this play!"

Miss Webster's answer is one that he has never forgotten and yet
never heeded. She said, "You must not wear your heart on your
sleeve for daws to peck at!"

Another reply was less helpful. Someone else, apparently a
financial backer for the play, said, "At least you are not out of
pocket." For this there was no possible response. The playwright
had nothing in his pocket to be out of.

At the end, the Theatre Guild gave him $200 and the advice to
go off somewhere and start revising the play.

Problems came in droves that winter. The Army called the desolate playwright in for a physical and hastily declared him 4F,
thereby reviving his old fears about cardiac trouble. Once again he
started listening with terror for his heartbeat. Then he developed
a cataract in his left eye. He entered the hospital for the first of
four operations and emerged from it both penniless and hopeless.

With another donation of Rockefeller money, he headed for
Key West to start on a rewrite of *Battle of Angels.* He sent it off to
the Theatre Guild, which replied that they had decided to throw
in the sponge. To their members the Guild rationalized: "The
play was more of a disappointment to us than to you. *Battle of
Angels* turned out badly, but who knows whether the next one by
the same author may not prove a success?"

The Theatre Guild may have remained hopeful about the young
author's future, but Tennessee Williams himself was completely
dejected. He ascribed his failure, in part, to his lack of professional
theatrical experience. "Probably no man has ever written for the
theatre with less foreknowledge of it," he reflected. "I had not seen

more than two or three professional productions. . . . My conversion to the theatre arrived as mysteriously as those impulses that enter the flesh at puberty." Furthermore, he knew that, if he wanted to write plays which audiences would sit still long enough to see, he must avoid the mixture of sex and religion; it had proved fatal. He never quite understood, however, why Boston had thought the play obscene. When another version of *Battle of Angels* was published in 1944, he commented that he and the others connected with the production had never for a minute thought that the play might be attacked on such grounds. "If it was in the minds of the others, certainly this suspicion was never communicated to me," he said. "Was I totally amoral? Was I too innocent or too evil—that I remained unprepared for what the audiences, censors and magistracy of Boston were going to find in my play? I knew, of course, that I had written a play that touched upon human longings, about the sometimes conflicting desires of the flesh and the spirit." This struggle, he realized was thematic, implicit in the title of the play. But innocent of any possible complaint that this might engender, he puzzles about his own blindness to alien viewpoints: "Why had I never dreamed that such struggles could strike many people as filthy and seem to them unfit for articulation? Oh, if I had written a play full of licentious wiggling in filmy costumes, replete with allusions to the latrine, a play that was built about some titillating and vulgarly ribald predicament in a bedroom—why then I would feel apprehensive about its moral valuation. However, it seemed to me that if *Battle of Angels* was nothing else, it certainly was clean, it was certainly idealistic." To him, the very experience of writing it "was like taking a bath in snow. It's purity seemed beyond question."

Here, with his typical naiveté, Tennessee Williams discloses both his own concept of morality and his congenital blindness to other views. The desires of Myra and Val are honest. They involve a need for love, a need for freedom, and a need for sexual fulfillment. The fact that Myra is married to someone else appears irrelevant to the author. That marriage, after all, is now and has been, since its inception, a complete farce. The relationship between Myra and Val is more moral, or at least more sincere by far than that which the law had sanctioned. (This idea was to be germane to the later *Baby Doll.*) Bostonians, Roman Catholics, and a good many others cast a jaundiced eye on this theory. But the romantic, refusing to recognize such "unnatural" patterns, insists that sincerity of the emotions rather than the letter of the law should be the moral measure.

Inevitably, the audience reaction left him resentful. "What interests them," he complained, "is themselves, their dignity, their prestige and pretenses. What they want is a flattering mirror, a picture that does the opposite of Dorian Gray's, one that takes off all their blemishes in its reflection." If this was the great American public, then he could never write for them. He remembers, with frightening vividness, his dejection. "I thought for a while I was washed up even before I'd got started." There is an integrity of a perverse sort in this statement, a determination that he and his play were right, that he could not "prostitute" either of them for public acclaim. If anyone changed, it must be the public.

After he had recovered from this series of catastrophes, Williams returned to New Orleans, where he settled for the next couple of years in a slum room in the Vieux Carré. Using his grant and the thin trickle of revenue from royalties on his one-act plays, he began once again the tedious and depressing job of reevaluating himself and rewriting *Battle of Angels,* refusing to desert his rejected brainchild. He was fearful he might never rise above this low-water mark. Williams has always been a slow writer; the dialogue comes quickly, but organizing and developing the play as a whole frequently takes longer than a year. When he ran out of money, he pawned his watch, his clothes, his phonograph—everything but his old portable typewriter.

Out of this and earlier periods in New Orleans grew a number of short stories and one-act plays depicting the people, the mood, and the scene of New Orleans. "The Lady of the Larkspur Lotion" pictures the Southern belle turned prostitute. Like "Portrait of a Madonna," it is an early sketch of a completely degenerated Blanche du Bois. "Lord Byron's Love Letter" is the story of an old woman who, years before, had had an illegitimate child by Lord Byron and still preserves his letters and the idealized memory of the romance that started in Greece. By displaying these letters to tourists, she earns enough money to continue her meager existence in the Quarter. "One Arm" is about a one-armed male prostitute who solicited in this region before his arrest for the murder of a male client. In "The Angel in the Alcove," a male artist "rapes" a young writer who lives in the same rooming house. And "Auto-Da-Fé" records the sick thoughts of a mamma's boy as he turns his pyromaniac fantasies into the mission of cleansing the corrupt Vieux Carré with fire.

His other stories and plays of this time are also of this same cast of the deranged, artistic, lonely, and mutilated—of prostitutes, homosexuals, nymphomaniacs, painters, writers, neurotics—the sick or frightened or confused or alone. New Orleans and his own situation appear to have given Williams an obsession for the pariah theme.

In 1942, Dakin joined the Army, thereby satisfying the demands of the family's military code and also leaving a wardrobe of civilian clothes behind, which Tennessee appropriated. With a new wardrobe and no clear plans for a future that had seemed to have been exceedingly bright only two years previously, he drifted down to Mexico City, where he shared expenses for a while with "a Mexican and the whore he married." From there he wandered over to Acapulco and started on another play, called *Stairs to the Roof*, about a shoe clerk who climbs to the roof of the store to smoke. Here he was working on familiar ground. But then the non-objec-

tive painter he was living with threw him out in the middle of
January, and a composer took him in.

Although his black mood had deepened when the Theatre Guild
rejected his new version of *Battle of Angels,* he continued to work
on revisions, hoping eventually to interest someone in the play.
His previous sponsors were not sufficiently impressed with the
reworking to tempt disaster again, but the head of a New York
drama school showed interest. He wrote Williams that he was
planning to revive *Battle of Angels,* and he forwarded trainfare to
New York. But before the eager writer reached that city, the production was called off.

That winter in New York, his life took on an even more pronounced Bohemian color. Lincoln Barnett has described Williams'
Greenwich Village period in which he was hired as a waiter in a
Village nightclub, "primarily because he had just undergone
another eye operation and the proprietor was enchanted by Williams' black patch on which a friend hàd drawn a fiercely libidi-
nous eye in white chalk." After all his blasted dreams, he was back
to waiting on tables again, his one reliable occupation, it would
seem. "In addition to serving drinks," Mr. Barnett reports, "Williams doubled as an entertainer late at night by reciting bawdy
verse of his own composition." Then he lost this job in a dispute
with his employer over tips. For a time he was kept from starvation
by a group of amiable alcoholics who liked his recitations. "They
wound up each evening at the home of an aging actress, and
Williams found that if he stayed with them long enough someone
would eventually phone for chicken sandwiches." This actress, one
of those who were to merge in the magnificent portrait of the
Princess in *Sweet Bird of Youth,* provided an unsatisfactory diet.
"For days he lived on nothing but highballs and chicken sandwiches and was wolfishly hungry most of the time. There was never
any food in the actress' icebox because she never ate: whenever she
sensed that a collapse was imminent she went to a hospital and had

a blood transfusion; next day she would show up at her favorite bar, her thirst and hemoglobin count back to normal."

Despite this precarious and hectic existence Williams managed to collaborate with a friend, Donald Windham, on a comedy called *You Touched Me!*, a play that was to reach Broadway three years later.

In the meantime, the author turned to other jobs. For a while he ran an elevator in a New York hotel. In 1943, he ushered at the Strand Theatre, and was glad to be wearing any kind of uniform in wartime. When the Rockefeller money finally ran out, he was desperate: "I didn't know where the hell I was headed."

Once again he returned to his perennial haven, his grandparents' home. He had been there only a short time when he got a wire from Audrey Wood telling him to come to New York. His agent had once again accomplished the impossible. After his last seventeen-dollar-a-week ushering job, Tennessee Williams was suddenly whipped off to Hollywood, where M.G.M. paid him $250 a week. When Miss Wood told him the salary for the new job, he was delighted to get that much each month.

"No, no, every week," she corrected him.

"Why, Audrey, that's dishonest," came his reply.

This stroke of luck was to lead to his next play—and to provide an answer to that question echoing from the pages of the Theatre Guild letter of 1941: "but who knows whether the next by the same author may not prove a success?"

CHAPTER V

The Glass Menagerie

The six-months contract Audrey Wood had wangled for her client with M.G.M. on the basis of his one-acters and *Battle of Angels,* proved to be considerably more profitable for Williams than for his boss and the studio. Although the author had expected to work on the best-selling novel *The Sun Is My Undoing,* the studio immediately set him to work on the scenario for *Marriage Is a Private Affair,* a bit of fluff that eventually starred Lana Turner. Williams has since established a mental block about the picture, refusing to remember its title. "I always thought of it as *The Celluloid Brassière,"* he says. The dialogue he wrote was brilliant, he recalls, but not suitable for the story or the star. When his scenario was rejected, he was assigned to another picture starring Margaret O'Brien. His refusal to perform this chore was prefaced by a violently candid evaluation of child actors. He said such prodigies made him vomit.

In the meantime, he had once again entrusted Miss Wood with his money, which he admitted was "peanuts compared to what the names are getting, but it was riches to me," and he had asked her to dole it out to him fifty or seventy-five dollars at a time. He purchased a motor-scooter and a narrow-brim Tyrolean hat adorned with a bright little feather. He must have seemed an eccentric addition to Hollywood society as he roared into the studio lot behind huge, black, shiny Cadillacs and Rolls-Royces. But he was little concerned with the opinion of Hollywood, which he located on the "periphery" of his existence.

After his abortive attempts at writing movie scripts, he offered the film industry an idea of his own which he felt worthy of development. He had worked out the synopsis for a film he referred to as *The Gentleman Caller.* In introducing the outline to his superior at M.G.M., he announced, "This will run three times as long as *Gone With the Wind.* Shortly thereafter, his boss advised him to draw his pay-check quietly each week for the remainder of his contract—three and a half months—and to stay away from the office. Delighted, Williams. sat out the remaining period of his $250-a-week contract on the beach at Santa Monica writing *The Gentleman Caller,* which he renamed *The Glass Menagerie.*

His life was happier now than it had been in some years. He had a good salary, a good idea for a play, and as good health as he ever allows himself to admit. Since he is never happier than when working, the arrangement was ideal. A short story that grew out of this period, "The Mattress in the Tomato Patch," describes his solidly contented landlady, the tanned athletes who roamed the beach and the house, and the richness of the sun-worshipping life— symbolized by the lushness of a bowlful of ripe tomatoes on his desk. Seldom have characters received such benevolent treatment at the hands of Tennessee Williams as in the work of that Santa Monica period—this earthy short story and the gentle play about his frightened sister.

When his contract was up he moved to Provincetown where he finished the play and sent it to his agent. Rather apologetically, he spoke of it to friends as "another of those old uncommercial plays of mine." Paul Moor records that "Miss Wood, much affected by the delicate story, tried to think of a producer who would be sympathetic to it and not botch it. For three weeks it did not leave her office; the fact that Williams never murmured about this apparent inactivity is a sample of his regard for Miss Wood. . . . Finally she remembered Eddie Dowling's touching production of Paul Vincent Carroll's *Shadow and Substance,* and sent it to him. No other producer ever had a chance at it. Dowling bought it, literally overnight."

Never a good critic of his own work, Williams later looked back at both *Battle of Angels* and *The Glass Menagerie* and said of the first, "That play was, of course, a much better play than this one. The thing is, you can't mix up sex and religion, as I did in *Battle of Angels,* but you can always write safely about mothers." He had worked so hard on the complex plot for his first Broadway play that the simple story of the second made it appear inferior. Authors seldom perceive that difficulty in composition bears little relation to the merit of the finished product. The troublesome play is like a maimed or difficult child that one loves all the more for the trouble he causes. To anyone but the writer himself, the fact that *The Glass Menagerie* was so easy to write suggests something of its truth, its naturalness, and its artistry.

The mother Williams had chosen to write about in *The Glass Menagerie* was, naturally, his own. The story is that of his last years in St. Louis—the Depression, "when the huge middle class of America was matriculating in a school for the blind. Their eyes had failed them, or they had failed their eyes, and so they were having their fingers pressed forcibly down on the fiery Braille alphabet of a dissolving economy." Tom, the hero, is working days at the shoe factory and writing nights in his stuffy room or going to the movies. The father of the play, who deserted the family some years earlier, having been a telephone man who fell in love with long distances, haunts the scene pleasantly in the form of an ineluctably smiling photograph. The mother, Amanda Wingfield, is trying to hold the family together and to steer her children into more practical paths than those she has followed herself, for she is a disillusioned romantic turned evangelical realist.

She lectures Tom on the merits of tending to business. By soliciting magazine subscriptions over the phone she finances a secretarial course in business school for Laura, her daughter. When Amanda finds that Laura is too nervous to learn to type, she decides that the girl must marry. This requires exposing her to an eligible bachelor, whom, to his consternation, Tom is to provide. Tom finally approaches Jim O'Connor, a fellow employee at the shoe factory, and invites him to dinner. Overdoing it, as usual, Amanda sets about redecorating the house and revising her daughter's dress and personality. Her frenzy makes the trio increasingly tense as they await the approach of Jim, the gentleman caller.

Jim had known Laura in high school and has been her idol for years. His nice manners appeal to Amanda. The dinner, consequently, proceeds beautifully, with only one slight interruption: the lights go off because Tom has spent the electric-bill money. Candlelight, however, suffices.

After dinner, Amanda hauls her son to the kitchen to provide privacy to the young couple whom this obvious maneuver reduces to painful embarrassment. Very shortly, though, Jim's good nature melts Laura's shyness, and she finds herself sitting on the floor with him chatting cozily by candlelight, sipping dandelion wine. They talk of Jim's ambitions in electro-dynamics and of his night-school courses. Then they turn to a discussion of Laura's collection of tiny glass animals and of her prize, a little unicorn. When, a few minutes later, they start to dance, Jim stumbles and breaks the horn off the little animal. Laura cradles her pet in her palm, musing that he is better off without his horn, for now he can be normal, like the other animals of the menagerie.

In this glimpse, we realize that sweet, simple Laura believes in these little creatures with the same eagerness that Jim believes in electro-dynamics. Finally, in a clumsy effort to apply his half-digested understanding of psychology, Jim decides that Laura has an inferiority complex and that he can cure it with a kiss. Then, horrified at what his action might suggest to this fuzzily romantic girl, he blurts out the secret that he is engaged. Laura, strangely enough, seems to be no more hurt by this clumsiness· than by the breaking of the unicorn. Rather, on learning that her gentleman caller is not an eligible bachelor, she smiles stoically and gives him her now-hornless unicorn as a souvenir.

The tender mood is broken by the gay entrance of Amanda, bearing a pitcher of lemonade and singing a cruelly appropriate song about lemonade and old maids. Jim, finally understanding why he was invited, takes this moment to explain to Amanda that he plans to marry soon. Then he beats a hasty retreat. Amanda turns spittingly upon her son, who in turn stalks off to the movies. She screams after him that he can "go to the moon" since he is nothing but a selfish dreamer anyway. The final scene is a *tableau vivant* of Amanda, looking dignified and beautiful, comforting her daughter while Tom explains that he eventually escaped from the women to follow the pattern of his roving father. This simple story, turning on a dinner party given by a Southern family for an outsider whom they hope to match with their unmarried daughter and the character revelations that occur in its course, constitutes Tennessee Williams' most fragile and lovely play.

In some ways, *The Glass Menagerie* is a variation of the battle-of-angels theme. Tom expresses the same need to escape the nailed-up coffin of his restricted existence that Val expresses in the earlier play; but Tom seems to be more conscious of a corresponding loss that such freedom implies. He rejects the possessive love of his family because he can accept it only by shouldering the responsibility and accepting the imprisonment that go with it. The rejection of this relationship gives him pain, however, as his proposed desertion of Myra apparently did not give Val. This is a more realistic evaluation of human needs and yearnings. The characters also are more realistic. Although Tom and the others in *The Glass Menagerie* may represent attitudes toward life, none are personified abstractions. There is no Jabe to represent death. A subtler type of characterization combined with a simpler, less melodramatic story yields a far more artistic product.

One of the chief characters is sketched only by implication. The father of the Wingfield family hovers over the scene, although he never appears on stage at all. An enlarged photograph of him, which the spotlight occasionally illuminates, reminds us of his part in the formation of the dramatic situation. It is the picture of a handsome young man in a doughboy's cap. Though deeply hurt by his desertion, Amanda considers her erstwhile husband the embodiment of romance, associating him with that time in her life when the house in Blue Mountain was filled with gentleman callers and jonquils. (Blue Mountain is Mr. Williams' poetic name for Clarksdale, the standard symbol in his plays for romantic, happy youth.) Not having seen her husband growing old and ugly enables her to preserve her romantic image of him. That the father does not appear directly in the play suggests that Tennessee Williams could not view him with sufficient objectivity to portray him. The photograph apparently represents the standard view the outside world caught of the gay, soldierly C. C. Williams, whom his son hated so much that the sweetness would have gone out of the play if he had been included.

To Tom Wingfield, on the other hand, his father represents escape. He says of him, in the narrator's preface to the story, "He was a telephone man who fell in love with long distances; he gave up his job with the telephone company and skipped the light fantastic out of town." Then follows a hinted admiration of his romantic disappearance: "The last we heard of him was a picture post-card from Mazatlan, on the Pacific coast of Mexico, containing a message of two words—'Hello—Good-bye!' and no address." Tom's interest in his father's wanderlust, at the beginning of the play, prepares us for Tom's departure at its end. The picture itself, an enlarged photograph of Tom's own face, further emphasizes the similarities of their natures. Thus, while the father still personifies love to the romantic memory of the middle-aged Amanda, he symbolizes another kind of romance to his son—the romance of escape and adventure.

In discarding the real father's part, Tennessee Williams found it necessary to endow the mother with some masculine practicality, thus giving Amanda Wingfield an exceedingly complex personality. Like Myra of *Battle of Angels,* she has her past to recall and her present to endure. One had Moon Lake and love in the vineyard, the other Blue Mountain and gentleman callers. Amanda is, obviously, far more the lady, the Southern aristocrat, than the more voluptuous Myra. The only way Amanda can live with ugly reality is to retreat into her memories; there is no sexual solution for her. Her clothes, her speech, and her ideals for her children declare her belief in the past and her rejection of the present. As the author says of Amanda, "She is not paranoiac, but her life is paranoia."

The feature of this woman, which makes her a more admirable character than the later Blanche of *Streetcar* is the anomalous element of practicality encased in her romantic girlishness. Although she has approached much of her life unrealistically, her plans for her children and her understanding of their shortcomings are grimly realistic. Even when refusing to admit it, she knows Laura will never marry. She then tries to find Laura a protective corner of the business world. When this fails, she rallies for the valiant but hopeless attempt to marry the girl off. This second failure, we feel, is less tragic* for the daughter than for the mother.

* My use of the term *tragic* corresponds with Mr. Williams'. I do not see most of his people as having the stature of the classical or neo-classical tragic heroes, but in their symbolic value they do express heroism. Their status and their values are not so exalted as in the older plays. They are more realistic and pathetic than the traditional hero was allowed to be.

Here we see the quality that Williams suggests from the beginning as the key to her character—her heroism. This, rather than her romantic turn, is her attraction. At the end of the play, when Tom has left, Amanda bends over Laura, huddled upon the sofa, to comfort her. By then, the audience realizes that Amanda herself is in greater need of this sympathy than the quietly resigned Laura. "Now that we cannot hear the mother's speech," says Williams, "her silliness is gone and she has dignity and tragic beauty."

We see this heroism in Amanda in her relations with Tom as well as with the more delicate and more romantic Laura. Although Tom understands the personality of his mother better than any other character in the story, he is more visionary and irresponsible than she is. He cannot see or accept the necessities of their life. Because of this and her previous experience with a romantic husband, she discourages Tom's attempts at a poetic or a nautical career. She returns the D. H. Lawrence novel to the library and nags at him whenever he escapes to a movie. She prods him to take an interest in practical things, like Jim's night classes in electrodynamics. Here, as with her daughter, she is doomed to failure. Consequently, her final line is, "Go, then! Then go to the moon— you selfish dreamer!" Amanda is better able to speak these words with understanding because she shares his yearnings. Her dream has been smashed by reality, but has not been forgotten.

Tom is a poet who is desperately unhappy in his warehouse job, and, as yet, frustrated in his poetry. Since Tennessee Williams knows something of this not-very-tender trap, he speaks with feeling about the afflictions of the machine age. Believing that many, like himself, are poetic rather than mechanistic, he considers surrender to the machine a perversion of man's nature. His escape, heartless though it may seem, is a "necessary and wholesome measure of self-preservation" (as John Gassner expresses it).

Laura, like Rose, obviously can't escape into movies, alcohol, or literature; she simply isn't that violent or decisive. Her retreat is into a world of glass and music. Her father's old phonograph records provide her with escape that the unfamiliar new tunes can't provide. In the short story out of which the play grew, "Portrait of a Girl in Glass," Tom occasionally brings new records to his sister, but she seldom cares for them because they remind her too much of "the noisy tragedies in Death Valley or the speed-drills at the business college." Her collection of glass absorbs her time. She spends hours polishing the tiny animals that are as delicate and fragile as she.

Unable to adapt to the modern scene of electro-dynamics, she lives in a world of candlelight and fantasy. The encounter with the machine age is brief and useless. Laura could no more learn to type than Tom could ever come to like his job. Yet, unlike Tom, Laura seems not to feel the ugliness and entombment of their lives. Incapable of his violence, she never steps into the world for fear it would be impossible to bear. She merely stands at the brink and catches what she can of its beauty without becoming a part of it—a lovely picture of the simple Rose, who all through her brother's life has represented to him everything good and beautiful, soft and gentle.

Laura's early surrender is explained at the opening of the play by an allusion to an illness in childhood which left her crippled, one leg slightly shorter than the other and held in a brace (a physical parallel to Rose's mental affliction). The author explains, "Stemming from this, Laura's separation increases till she is like a piece of her own glass collection, too exquisitely fragile to move from the shelf."

Her mother is both Laura's disease and her brace. It is Amanda's forcefulness that allows Laura to walk at all, but it is also Amanda's example that discourages Laura from walking naturally. At one point, Laura puts on her mother's old coat, which of course is a poor fit for her, an action symbolic of her vague efforts at imitating a personality so alien to her powers and her own nature. She knows that she is like the unicorn or the blue rose, wrong for real life. Laura cannot see that Amanda exaggerates this wrongness by her impossibly romantic dreams. When Laura entered her high-school classes late, the sound of the brace on her leg seemed to her like claps of thunder. She thinks her affliction is dreadful because Amanda thinks it is. This flaw, a symbol of the crippling of a sensitive person thrust into a world unwilling to make allowances for sensitivity, becomes the cause of her separation from reality.

For Tennessee Williams, his sister became a symbol of the sensitive and the outcast, for their sensitivity invariably subjects them to mutilation. It is no accident that Laura's story appears in the collection of early fiction, eventually published under the title *One Arm*. Every important character in the book—the college students, the vagrant poet, the sallow little masochist, the perverted artist, the consumptive factory worker, the one-armed male prostitute, and the girl with her glass menagerie, can be destroyed at a touch. All, like Laura, are crippled in some way. The radiance of such people is like a "piece of translucent glass touched by light, given a momentary radiance, not actual, not lasting."

Laura contrasts with the normal, middle-class, realistic Jim, with whom she falls dreamily in love. Their views show their complete diversity. For example, when they discuss her favorite animal, the unicorn, Laura thinks of him as intrinsically different from his companions, while Jim sees him simply as a horse with a horn. In the same way, Jim sees the defect in Laura's leg as only unfortunately incidental to her normal body, while Laura feels that the flaw transforms her whole being. Jim can sympathize with Laura's world of glass and candlelight for this evening, but his real interests are in the modern mechanical world of self-improvement. He is the only character in the play who goes out of the house into a normal world of "reality." Tom emphasizes this in the opening and closing lines of the play; he is an emissary from another world; he does not belong to the Wingfield world of dreams and fears and unexpressed desires.

Jim is not an especially effective character study because Williams can feel little sympathy with such a substantial and placid citizen. Yet he is a kindly reminder of the reasonable, normal human pattern, like the men Williams had met at the shoe factory—clean-living, honest, sweet-natured, materialistic, eager American businessmen. The gently satirical portrait bears no relationship to the later, bitter portraits of C. C. Williams.

Since it is characteristic of Amanda, more than of the others, to long for everything Jim represents, he is for her an archetype of the "long delayed but always expected something we live for." Unintentionally, Jim breaks up the Wingfield dreams. We suspect that his entrance into the household is part of a recurring pattern. Every contact with the real world has shattered Amanda's unrealistic hopes over the years.

The setting of *The Glass Menagerie* was interesting in its symbolism and technical experimentation. Moving from the deep South to St. Louis for his story, Williams retains the memory of the South, as a haunting presence under the superimposed Midwestern setting. The audience, never seeing the gracious mansion that was the scene of Amanda's girlhood, feels its remembered glory and its contrast to the mean present. Awareness of the past is always an element in Williams' plays. His characters live beyond the fleeting moments of the drama—back into a glowing past and shrinking from a terrifying future. For both Amanda and the later Blanche of *Streetcar,* the South forms an image of youth, love, purity, all of the ideals that have crumbled along with the mansions and the family fortunes.

Since the setting in *Menagerie* is that of a memory play, Tennessee Williams could feel free in its staging. His theory of expression-

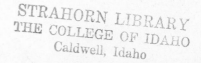

ism is propounded in the introductory production notes, which are, in fact, directly applied in the play. His concept of the "new, plastic theatre" was probably influenced by Erwin Piscator, a German director who had helped him at the New School Seminar. He suggests that in *The Glass Menagerie*'s "considerably delicate or tenuous material, atmospheric touches and subtleties of direction play a particularly important part." Williams justifies such unconventional techniques as expressionism or impressionism on the basis that their subjectivity provides a "closer approach to truth." No playwright should use such devices in an effort to avoid the "responsibility of dealing with reality, or interpreting experience." But he believes that the new drama has followed the other arts in recognizing that realism is not the key to reality.

"The straight realistic play with its genuine frigidaire and authentic ice-cubes, its characters that speak exactly as its audience speaks," he says, "corresponds to the academic landscape and has the same virtue of photographic likeness." Then, with unique optimism regarding current artistic tastes, he continues, "Everyone should know nowadays the unimportance of the photographic in art: that truth, life, or reality is an organic thing which the poetic imagination can represent or suggest, in essence, only through transformation, through changing into other forms than those which were merely present in appearance." The philosophy expressed here is in accord with the nineteenth century romantics and their followers in this century. The expressionistic concepts propounded in this preface have proved so effective in Tennessee Williams' work that set-designers have usually chosen to use expressionistic even when realistic settings are called for in Williams' manuscripts. Williams has a poet's weakness for symbols, and this modern technique frees his hand for scattering them about the stage. Their use to reflect, emphasize, and contrast with the meanings of the actions and the words has become a trademark of the Williams play.

The Glass Menagerie projected symbolic elements in line with Williams' newly enunciated theory. To reinforce the spoken word the author recommends the use of a screen device. A legend or image projected on the screen for the duration of the scene emphasizes the most important phrase. For example, in the scene where Jim remembers that Laura is the girl who was stricken with pleurosis, whom he mistakenly nicknamed "Blue Roses," the legend on the screen accents the peculiarity of the name, and the audience, along with Laura, is made more keenly aware that although blue is beautiful, it is wrong for roses. Eddie Dowling considered this device superfluous and omitted it from the stage production, and wisely so. Mr. Gassner also considered the screen device "redundant and rather precious." Williams is "straining for effect not knowing that his simple tale, so hauntingly self-sufficient, needs no adornments."

Williams' expressionist theory also leads him to another variation from strictly realistic drama. The lighting changes with the mood. The stage is as dim as the participants' lives. Shafts of light flicker onto selected areas or actors, "sometimes in contradiction to what is the apparent center." When Tom and Amanda are quarreling, the light on them is low red, while Laura stands in a pool of light of that "peculiar pristine clarity such as light used in early religious portraits of saints or madonnas." The tone, strength, and occurrence of the lights have the power of emotional emphasis. In a technique reminiscent of Chekhov's, Williams heightens the emotional truths of the scenes and the reality of the internal action through unusual external effects.

The musical accompaniment of *The Glass Menagerie* is another element of Tennessee Williams' expressionism that characterizes his dramas. The theme is a tune called "The Glass Menagerie," composed by Paul Bowles. It is "like circus music, not when you are on the grounds or in the immediate vicinity of the parade, but when you are at some distance and very likely thinking of some-

thing else. . . . It expresses the surface vivacity of life and the underlying strain of immutable and inexpressible sorrow." The music
becames Laura's symbol: of this world which is like a circus for
her—heard from a safe distance; and of her retreat into a world
of music as well as of glass.

The depiction of the Wingfields' apartment also follows the
dicta of expressionism. The ugly uniformity of the tenements
depresses Tom and makes him frantic to escape. The place is
described as "one of those vast hive-like conglomerations of cellu-
lar living-units that flower as warty growths in overcrowded urban
centers of lower middle-class populations." They are, says the
temporarily socially conscious author, "symptomatic of the impulse of this largest and fundamentally enslaved section of American society to avoid fluidity and differentiation and to exist and
function as one interfused mass of automatism." Of the characters
in the play, only Tom seems aware of this grotesque uniformity;
and since the whole story takes place in his memory, he would
naturally exaggerate the dismal reality he sees.

On both sides of the building, dark, narrow alleys run into
"murky canyons of tangled clotheslines, garbage cans and sinister
lattice-work of neighboring fire escapes." The meaning of these
alleys is clear if the reader recalls Tom's picture of "Death Valley,"
where cats were trapped and killed by a vicious dog. The predicament becomes a symbol of his factory work, murderous to his
creative imagination. For Laura, the alley represents the ugly
world from which she retreats to gaze into her tiny glass figures.
For Amanda, too, the alley is the world of her present hopeless
poverty and confusion from which she retreats into her make-
believe world of memory and pretence. Inside the apartment,
where she tries to create an illusion of gentility, her husband's
portrait grins at her futile efforts.

The apartment is entered by a fire escape, "a structure whose
name is a touch of accidental poetic truth, for all those huge

buildings are always burning with the slow and implacable fires of human desperation." On this fire escape, Tom Wingfield seeks liberation from his private hell. It is no mere coincidence that this play's solution (like those of *Battle of Angels* and *Stairs to the Roof*) centers around the stairway. Stairs are the tangible sign of man's change in levels of reality.

It would seem that every item of the setting is symbolic—even the Paradise Dance Hall, across the alley. There sexual gratification provides the cliff-dwellers of the neighborhood a temporary paradise. In their moments of closeness, they achieve the escape that Tom finds in his movies and poetry.

The story, characterization, and setting of this play combine to form a "static" drama, a technique Williams has used in other plays, including the rewrite of *Battle of Angels*. Action is softened by this "patina" of time and distance; framed in memory, it becomes more artistic. The interest of this play depends on neither incident nor situation. Unlike most of Williams' other works that are charged with sensationalism and sex, this story holds the audience by the revelation of quiet and ordinary truths. This play, unique among Williams' dramas, combines poetic and unrealistic techniques with grim naturalism to achieve a gossamer effect of compassion, fragility, and frustration, typical of Tennessee Williams at his most sensitive and natural best. The play is his most effective poetic work.

As soon as Eddie Dowling saw the play, he was interested. He already had a play with "commercial possibilities" ready to put on when he read *The Glass Menagerie*. Delighted with its artistic but probably uncommercial possibilities, he asked his backer, Louis J. Singer, to release him from their arrangement. "I've found a play I love," he told the newcomer to the ranks of Broadway producers. I don't think it will earn a dime but it will make me very happy to do it."

Mr. Singer asked, "Have you arranged for backing?"

"Not yet," replied Dowling.

"You've got a partner."

Dowling then showed the script to George Jean Nathan, who was immediately interested in the part of Laura for Julie Haydon. He also thought the role of Amanda ideal for the woman considered by many to be America's greatest living actress, Laurette Taylor.

As soon as Miss Taylor saw the script, she called her closest friend. "I've found it, Eloise!" she said. "I've found the play I've been waiting for." The aging actress had, in recent years, starred in only a few plays. Her greatest success had been years earlier, when she had one of Broadway's longest runs as *Peg o' My Heart.* Since her husband's death, she had become an alcoholic, and her theatrical opportunities had steadily declined. Producers were afraid to trust her. Recently, however, she had recovered her control and had been looking for a good part. She recognized in the Amanda created by this unknown playwright a flesh-and-blood character who would challenge all the resources of an experienced actress. She accepted the part with enthusiasm.

When Williams heard that Laurette Taylor was to play Amanda, he was astonished. He thought she had died. The only memory of her he could dredge up was of walking by a St. Louis movie theatre and reading the advertisements for the silent film *Peg o' My Heart,* starring Laurette Taylor. He had not gone in.

Before going to Chicago to join the company at rehearsals, Williams went to St. Louis to see his mother. Since *The Glass Menagerie* was on its way to Broadway with big-name stars in its cast, the St. Louis press welcomed the visiting playwright whom it could claim as its own. To the discomfiture of the reporters, he replied to their inquiries with brutally candid recollections of his miserable youth there and his impressions of its ugliness and unfriendliness, thereby alienating many civic-minded St. Louisans.

But one of the interviewers, the man sent by the *Star-Times,* happened to be William Inge, then its amusement-page editor. Inge called Williams to discuss the interview and to suggest some entertainment, since anyone so long away from St. Louis would probably find few of his old friends still there. Williams went to Inge's apartment, located in a housing project. "When he opened the door, I saw over his shoulder a reproduction of my favorite Picasso," wrote Williams of this visit, "I knew that the interview would be as painless as it turned out to be." The two became friends, swimming together at the "Y" every day while Williams was in St. Louis. Since the editor had passes to plays and movies he was to cover for his paper, he took the penniless visitor along with him.

From St. Louis, Williams met the troupe and went on to Chicago for rehearsals. Later, recalling the loneliness of his arrival at Chicago's Union Station, he remembered his delight on seeing a familiar face and figure. "It was a short and nearly square figure in a peculiar costume, like something rooted from the bottom of an old wardrobe trunk." This costume consisted of a grey muskrat coat, the pelts of which were "not enjoying the most pacific relation," and a broad-brimmed hat "of the type that is worn by cinema buccaneers." Staring out from between the turned-up collar and turned-down brim were eyes "much too bright to be described as brown." The face was framed by a "cloudy profusion of hair that is lighter than auburn." This small woman looked as lost and frightened as the young author himself. His heart went out to her.

"Laurette!" he called. She turned and called out his name. "Then and there," he remembers, "we joined forces. The station diminished to a comfortable size; the bitter cold thawed a little, we moved off together with a feeling of union deeper than physical, more than accidental, to find a taxi."

Laurette Taylor was a legend in the theatre long before Tennessee Williams wrote his first play. She brought to the role of

Amanda, which proved to be her last, all her genius for characterization. She worked feverishly to catch the essence of the woman. Her technique was to study the part, learning rather than memorizing, and she drove Eddie Dowling almost out of his mind. From time to time he would murmur, "That woman is crucifying me!" It didn't occur to her that other actors didn't appreciate the changes she made and resented her unreadiness during rehearsals. Everyone else knew his part before she.

However, her interest in the play far outstripped theirs. She actually directed many of the scenes in which she and Julie Haydon appeared, and Williams estimates her directing as "a top-notch job." This continued even after the play was in production. "Almost every night in Chicago," Williams recalls, "there was something new but she never disturbed the central characterization. Everything she did was absolutely in character." She and the author were not always in perfect accord about suggested changes. She tried to talk him into changing one speech, of which he was especially enamoured, the one in which Amanda reminisces about the house full of flowers and suitors. She insisted, "It's just too many jonquils, Tennessee. Can't you cut a few?"

His reply was, "Laurette, it's got rhythm. Ah need all those jonquils!"

One of her major problems was the acquisition of a Southern accent. When they first started rehearsals, the author came up to Miss Taylor and said quietly, as she remembered, "Miss Taylor, Ah hopes yo' don't mahn mah sayin' so but yo' Southe'n accent is a little thick."

"All right," she answered. "How would you like it if I copied you?"

He agreed. At rehearsals after that, she would say, "Talk to me, Tennessee, just talk to me. Don't explain how to pronounce the words, just keep talking."

Their friendship grew, despite the barrier which separates the shy Williams from the rest of the world. Miss Taylor used to say of him, "Tennessee is a *very* sensitive fellow." She couldn't quite understand his kind of sensitivity but she could sympathize with it.

Miss Taylor was never happy with Eddie Dowling in the role of her son, thinking him too old and too mannered in the part. However, they, Julie Haydon, and Anthony Ross formed a highly-skilled team. With such a collection of talent, and with the additional boost of Margo Jones as assistant-director with Eddie Dowling, the outlook seemed good.

Nevertheless, ill luck at first pursued *The Glass Menagerie*. When the company arrived in Chicago, the set-erector was too drunk to work, and without him, it took twenty-four hours of steady work to set up a single scene. Then Jo Mielziner found that Julie Haydon's costume for the second act showed up poorly in the light. Louis Singer, the coproducer, was dubious about the play's chances for success and wanted to back out. He refused to put another dollar into the production. When twenty dollars were needed for another costume, Eddie Dowling, Miss Haydon, and Williams chipped in to buy it. Then Laurette Taylor, who had become almost paralyzed with fear by opening night, was discovered in her dressing room, a few hours before the opening curtain, dyeing a bathrobe which she was to wear in the second act; she was frantic.

But somehow, everything mysteriously fitted together by opening night. The excited audience cried, "Author! Author!" and the red-faced young playwright took a happy bow.

Though tempered with some adverse critical comment on the unevenness of the writing, the intrusion of the narrator, and the poeticizing, the reviews were mostly raves. The critics loved the play and adored Miss Taylor in it. The Chicago journalist and writer, Lloyd Lewis, reported that Miss Taylor had not been the center of so much discussion since *Peg o' My Heart*, exactly thirty years before. Analyzing her remarkable style, he noted,

"When Miss Taylor mumbles in magnificent realism she is still enough of a vocal wizard to be intelligible to her audience, and when she pouts, nags or struts in pathetic bursts of romantic memory she is superb at pantomime. Her descents into hysteria are masterpieces of understatement, dramatic enough that they force the audience to do the acting for her."

Ashton Stevens, the critic for the *Herald-American,* was so entranced he saw *The Glass Menagerie* six more times after opening night. He closed his review by saying, "From neighboring seats I heard William Saroyan mentioned, and Paul Vincent Carroll and Sean O'Casey, and even a playwright named Barrie. But the only author's name I could think of was Tennessee Williams, whose magic was his own." However, the public did not respond at first, and there were many empty seats.

William Inge, who went up to Chicago to see his new friend's play that December, reports that "Williams was in a state of gloom. The reviews had been favorable, but the audiences weren't coming yet. They did, a few weeks later, lashed into it by a steady stream of propaganda from the critics." Inge himself was delighted with the play: "I've been really inspired very few times in the theater. What the play did for me was show me for the first time the dynamic relationship between art and life. After seeing it I seemed to know where to look for material in myself." The two of them spent a dreary New Year's Eve together that year. "We went around to bars and watched others celebrate."

Williams' mother also came to Chicago to see the play that December. Her son had not told her that Amanda was a portrait of herself. He still remembers her reactions with fond humor. As she listened to Laurette Taylor uttering her favorite comments about the family and life in general, "Mother began to sit up stiffer and stiffer. She looked like a horse eating briars. She was touching her throat and clasping her hands and quite unable to look at me. . . . What made it particularly hard for Mother to bear is that she is a tiny, delicate woman with great dignity and always managing to be extremely chic in dress, while Laurette Taylor invested the part with that blowsy, powerful quality of hers—and thank God she did, for it made the play."

When the performance was over, he asked his mother to go backstage and meet Miss Taylor. "She was somewhat constrained," he says in obvious understatement, "but she went." The meeting was one to remember. Laurette Taylor, oblivious of her feelings, promptly said, "And how do you like yourself on the stage?" Mrs. Williams could not quite bring herself to answer that question. She expressed polite surprise that Miss Taylor should consider it her portrait. "Laurette had another tactless idea. 'I have a very intellectual forehead,' she confided in Mother. 'However, the woman in this play is a fool. That's why I wear bangs.'" Williams reports with barely suppressed amusement, "Mother kept her composure but it was a severe test. Later she came to see that to have been portrayed by Laurette Taylor was the greatest tribute she could have and her visit backstage became her favorite story."

Plaudits for the play and the performers continued, and gradually the audiences began to crowd out the returning critics. *The Glass Menagerie* lost its reputation for "preciousness" and became a full-fledged success.

By the time the company had reached New York, its critical reputation had preceded it and stirred up a healthy anticipation. On opening night the audience again called "Author! Author!" and the author, overcome with delight at his newly achieved success and his appreciation of the cast, stepped into the aisle from his fourth-row seat and bowed first to the stage, thereby presenting the first-night audience with an unexpected view of his rear.

Robert Rice calls this opening night a "memorable evening in the theatre." The enthusiasm of the audience was reflected at the box-office. *The Glass Menagerie* ran for nearly two years on Broadway.

When the critics gathered to vote on the coveted Critics' Award, on April 10, 1945, at the Algonquin, it took them only fifteen minutes to choose *The Glass Menagerie* by nine out of fourteen votes. *Harvey* was the runner-up.

Although *The Glass Menagerie* had proved a winner, Williams doubted needlessly that critics would like future plays of his as well. "In this play I said all the nice things I have to say about people," he confessed. "The future things will be harsher." And indeed they were! But harsh or no, Tennessee Williams was to continue to be the "awards man of the younger generation."

His pleasure in his success was marred by something that was to plague the playwright through the rest of his career. Miss Taylor's powerful handling of her part and Eddie Dowling's effective direction evoked comments that the triumph was that of the company rather than of the playwright. Rumor exaggerated Eddie Dowling's suggestions, that the screen device be omitted and that a drunk scene be added, into conclusions that the success was the result of skillful rewriting by talented play doctors. Williams' readiness to listen to those more experienced than he looked like a weakness rather than a virtue to outsiders. For that reason the published version of the play has italicized: "There is *only one important difference between the original and acting version of the play* and that is the *omission* in the latter which I tentatively included in my *original* script." The italics are his; the effect of the statement was to squelch a few of these rumors—but they were to reappear with each of his successes.

Since Tennessee Williams has owed much of his success to the designers, directors, and actors who have caught the fire of his conception and conveyed it vividly and artistically to the audience, these belittling rumors are partially justified. The reader, however, has only to see how fully he conceives the scenery and the people of his dramas to realize that the greatest credit for the final product belongs to the writer. His parts are exciting to play, a fact to which one actor after another has testified; and his dramas are challenging to stage, lending themselves to the impressionistic or expressionistic devices of imaginative designers or directors.

Laurette Taylor was one of many who tried to make the modest Williams see that the talent was his. No actor or actress was indispensable to him. Everyone had worried about Miss Taylor's dependability from the beginning; after her phenomenal success in the part, speculation grew that the play would collapse without her. Her throat began to give her trouble in Chicago, but because she knew the rumors about her alcoholism, she refused to take a rest. She continued in the demanding part—frequently vomiting after a performance, looking white and weak—obviously a sick woman. Williams later recalled how few people sympathized with her in her ordeal. He said that she was keenly aware of the reservation in so many minds about her. She was "determined to beat it. She did. She was neither a well nor a strong person at any time during the run of the play and often continued her performance when a person of ordinary spirit would not have dared to."

No one seemed to realize the sacrifice of personal comfort and health involved in her remaining a year and a half with *The Glass Menagerie*. "She remained in the part that long because of a heroic perseverance I find as magnificent as her art itself." The term which best fits Williams' view of this fine actress as she battled ill health and ugly rumors is *gallantry*. Amanda proved to be her last part. She died in 1946.

Tennessee Williams joined the host of her mourners, insisting that she was "the greatest artist of her profession that I have known. I loved her as a person. I'm afraid it is the only close friendship I have ever had with a player." In her, he experienced a rare glimpse of "something that lies outside the flesh and its mortality. . . . There was a radiance about her art which I can compare only to the greatest lines of poetry, and which gave me the same shock of revelation as if the air about us had been momentarily broken through by light from some clear space beyond us. . . . Having created a part for Laurette Taylor is a reward I find sufficient for all the effort that went before and any that may come after."

Just before she died, Laurette Taylor had retired from her role. When the road company opened in Pittsburgh, with Pauline Lord as Amanda, the notices spoke warmly of Pauline Lord's performance in the part of Amanda. "I have just read the Pittsburgh notices," Miss Taylor wired the adoring author, then adding, "What did I tell you, my boy? You don't need me." These are the last words that Tennessee Williams was ever to hear from Laurette Taylor, but they summarize much of the generous, warm, human understanding of this fine actress.

Shortly after *The Glass Menagerie* had settled into the Playhouse for its long run, Robert van Gelder interviewed Tennessee Williams for *The New York Times*. He found his subject a cleanshaven, individualistic, befuddled young man in his early thirties. He said of him that, when he went to shake hands, he put out both hands as if confused as to which one to use. A man of "quiet candor," Tennessee Williams seemed a "composed, confident dreamer, observant, self-centered, sympathetic, remote." He still disliked New York, as he had on that first visit and as he does to this day, bluntly stating, "I have no interest in the intellectuals or pseudo-intellectuals that I find here. . . . They mean nothing to me creatively." Assuming a pose of disinterest, he disclaimed being impressed by applause, desiring only to write for the "creative theatre."

As his income began to rise, Williams signed 50 per cent of his earnings over to his mother. His friends insisted that his shabbiness was now uncalled-for and was therefore faintly pretentious. So he moved into a suite at a good hotel that had a swimming pool, bought some expensive clothes, and even replaced his old faithful phonograph with a new electric model.

But with increased fame and income came unexpected difficulties. His Bohemian existence left him unprotected from self-seekers. (He even thought it was required by law to put a name card on the door wherever he lived.) So leeches and pack rats appeared in droves. Not so cynical as most who reach this position, he was appalled at the insincerity of the people who came to cadge his time and money. Old friends started complaining that he was high-hatting them because he couldn't spend so much time with them as in the past. Perplexed, he tried to reason out the difficulty he felt: "There is a kind of problem in personal integrity," he decided. "The real fact is that no one means a great deal to me, anyway, but almost anybody will do. I'm rather selfish in picking my friends, anyway; that is, I prefer people who can help me in some way or another, and most of my friendships are accidental. . . . I don't want to be like most people. And I do think there is a problem of personal integrity involved." One of those who especially disgusted him and whom he avoided was his father. After years of trying to discourage his writing, old C. C. Williams suddenly took pride in his hitherto worthless son.

Another touch of ironic satisfaction accompanied the success of *The Glass Menagerie*. The last word Tennessee Williams had had from M.G.M. studios was in answer to a question he had asked while still working for them. He had requested permission to go to the opening of one of his plays in Cleveland, and his boss had answered that he could go one one condition—that he never come back. Now here was the rejected manuscript, née *The Gentleman Caller,* a Broadway success and the subject of heated bargaining by several Hollywood producers, among them, to Williams' immense satisfaction, M.G.M. The play written on M.G.M. time went to Warner Brothers.

For a while the plan was to use Ethel Barrymore for Amanda, but then Feldman of Warner Brothers decided on Gertrude Lawrence. Miss Lawrence wasn't especially interested at first, fearing that she would become typed for mother roles. Finally, though, she agreed, and Feldman was willing to wait two years for her to become available for the part. He managed to satisfy her pride by including some flashbacks of the young Amanda. "Otherwise," said Miss Lawrence, "she [Amanda] would have been only a character study of a middle-aged woman, and I don't want to get mother roles, and unglamorous ones at that. I'd be afraid if I succeeded I'd never do any thing else."

So *The Glass Menagerie* headed for Hollywood, settled in for a long New York run, began road company tours, opened in London (Helen Hayes, the London Amanda, like Miss Taylor gained credit for "making" the show), and finally toured the Continent. Tennessee Williams found that he had finally embraced the "Bitch Goddess" Success.

CHAPTER VI

To the Memory of Lawrence

A constant influence in Tennessee Williams' work and thought has been that of D. H. Lawrence. Tom, in *The Glass Menagerie,* is caught by Amanda reading one of the horrible novels by "that insane Mr. Lawrence," and Tom Williams must have spent a great deal of time the same way.

Once, in the midst of his early vagrancy, Williams stopped off at Taos, New Mexico, to visit Lawrence's widow, Frieda. This encounter inspired the short play recounting the death of Lawrence—*I Rise in Flame, Cried the Phoenix,* which was not produced until 1958, and then off-Broadway. Since it exemplifies the influence Lawrence had upon Williams, it is worth a brief discussion here.

The theme of *I Rise in Flame . . .* is Lawrence's death, immediately after the failure of an exhibition of his paintings in London. Williams says of these Lawrencian paintings: "Primitive in technique and boldly sensual in matter, this exhibition created a little tempest. The pictures were seized by the police and would have been burned if the authorities had not been restrained by an injunction." Here Lawrence was working in an alien medium and one in which, by general agreement, he had little talent.

But since most of his books, especially *Lady Chatterley's Lover,* were under the censor's ban, he appears to have taken an obstreperous pleasure in stirring up even greater indignation among what today would be called the "squares." In Lawrence, as in Williams, a perverse Puritanism leads to making a fetish of sex: Lawrence because he was obsessed with it, Williams because he was frightened of it.

Williams envisioned the old writer in his last stand against an emasculating culture. Lawrence sits before a silk banner which bears his favorite symbol, the Phoenix in its nest of flames. Lawrence looks taut and feverish. "His beard is fiercely red and his face is immobile, the color of baked clay with tints of purple in it. The hands that gripped the terrible stuff of life and made it plastic are folded on the black-and-white-checked surface of an invalid's blanket." Alluding to Lawrence's childhood in a mining town, Williams writes: "The long fingers of the Welch coal-miners, with their fine blond hairs and their knobby knuckles, made for rending the black heart out of the earth, are knotted together with a tightness that betrays the inner lack of repose. His slightly distended nostrils draw the breath in and out as tenderly as if it were an invisible silk thread that any unusual tension might snap in two." The fierce old battler, in his last fight, is raging within. "Born for contention, he is contending with something he can't get his hands on. He has to control his fury. And so he is seated motionless in the sunlight—wrapped in a checkered blanket and lavender wool shawl.—The tiger in him is trapped but not destroyed yet."

Contrasted to the emaciated Lawrence is his handsome, robust German wife, Frieda, who looks "rather like a Valkyrie." She carries a little jar of marmalade left by a timid lady admirer. The card with it reads, "I worship you, Mr. Lawrence, because I know that only a god could know so much about Life!" Lawrence smiles and muses wryly, "In looking for God so unsuccessfully myself, it seems that I have accidentally managed to create one for an anonymous spinster in a blue pea-jacket." He is searching, even in these last hours of his life, for a god to worship (sounding like the hero of *Suddenly Last Summer,* a closely-related play). When he says he would gladly tear his heart out and burn it on an altar before such a deity, Frieda comments on his sentimentality and narcissism: "You can't stand Jesus Christ because he beat you to it. Oh, how you would have loved to suffer the *original* crucifixion."

Lawrence, irritated by the mundane reality to which his wife insists on reducing his dreams, demands that she and the dovelike women who flutter around the Phoenix and suffocate him in their destructive devotion leave him to die alone. "I want to die like a lonely old animal does, I want to die fiercely and cleanly with nothing but anger and fear and other hard things like that to deal with at the finish," he tells her. Struck by the actuality of his approaching death, she softens toward him. A love scene and a quarrel which follow illustrate something of their tempestuous life together.

Just then, Bertha, a soulful friend, comes to describe the public reaction at the London exhibit. It was what Lawrence had anticipated: the figures were called "grotesque. . . . lumpy, obscene, misshapen, monstrous, deformed." The public laughed, and a "group of ladies' club members attempted to slash the picture of Adam and Eve."

This final failure to communicate the driving force of his life saps Lawrence's remaining strength. Feebly, from his invalid's chair, he comments on the setting sun, using his customary sexual imagery: "The young blond god is beginning to be seduced by the harlot of darkness. . . . Now she has got him, they're copulating together! The sun is exhausted. The harlot has taken his strength and now she will start to destroy him. She's eating him up. . . . Oh, but he won't stay down. He'll climb back out of her belly and there will be light. In the end there will always be light.—And I am the prophet of it!"

His relationship with Frieda has become symbolically transformed into the cosmic. He believes himself as fierce as the light, one who has had to take the world by storm. "I wanted to stretch out the long, sweet arms of my art and embrace the whole world!" he laments. But the world is like a woman. It isn't enough to go to it with love. "The world's a woman you've got to take by storm." This, then, is his approach to art. "I doubled my fist and I struck and I struck. Words weren't enough—I had to have color too." But the world's reaction was feminine revulsion. "They banned my books and they wanted to burn my pictures! That's how it is.— When you first look at the sun it strikes you blind.—Life's blinding. . . ." With this summation of his light that has been shining unheeded in the cannibal darkness, Lawrence rages out of the house to die alone with nature.

The play is short and powerful. It conveys the struggle waged by this ferocious, frail fox of a man, and it also discloses the sources of Williams' admiration for the old phoenix: his metaphysical veneration of the physical—a cosmic view of sex—and his powerful emotionalism. But for Tennessee Williams, sex is not the Lawrencian salvation, but a momentary relief, and, as such, it becomes the key to the action of *You Touched Me!, Summer and Smoke, The Rose Tatoo, A Streetcar Named Desire,* and *Cat on a Hot Tin Roof.* The human need for the warmth of another person and the Puritan horror of the physical are the recurrent adversaries in Williams' continued battles of angels. In *I Rise in Flame, Cried the Phoenix,* Bertha, the soul, and Frieda, the body, struggle over the expiring male, Lawrence; it is a favorite Williasmsian figure. Other Williamsian symbols include crucifixion, human sacrifice, and the battle between light and dark in the universe.

While realizing that much of D. H. Lawrence's work is "chaotic and distorted by tangent obsessions, such as his insistence upon the woman's subservience to the male," Williams believes that "all in all his work is probably the greatest modern monument to the dark roots of creation." And he especially appeals to the playwright as the "life-long adversary of those who wanted to keep the subject [of the mystery and power of sex, and the primal life urge] locked away in the cellars of prudery."

Williams' poems, as well as his plays, testify to his veneration of this preacher of sexuality. "Cried the Fox," a poem dedicated to D.H.L., pictures the older author as a fox chased by the hounds over scenery fraught with sexual symbolism.

Williams' empathy with Lawrence inevitably led him to a collaboration, although with Lawrence already dead, it was necessarily indirect. He adapted, with a collaborator, one of Lawrence's short stories, in the play *You Touched Me!* Actually it was an earlier play than *The Glass Menagerie.* After the failure of *Battle of Angels,* Williams had stayed for a while in New York before heading for Key West and the Bohemian culture centers of which he is so fond. During this New York stay he saw a great deal of his friend, Donald Windham, who lived at the West Side Y.M.C.A. His visits were motivated. Williams loves the water to the point of calling himself a "compulsive swimmer." Every afternoon, wherever possible, he dons bathing suit and cap and beats his choppy but determined way the length of the pool and back until he is winded. Since the cheapest swimming facilities in the country are usually at the local "Y," he has an intimate knowledge of Y.M.C.A.'s all over America. At this indigent point in his career, he was delighted to have free access to a pool.

During dry moments and rest periods, the two began to work on a play. Both admired Lawrence and believed that "You Touched Me," a short story in the collection *England, My England,* would make a good play. They decided to expand it into a lyrical comedy, which might be more acceptable to the prudish public than the intense *Battle of Angels* had been—and might therefore produce some sorely needed income.

The short story on which the play is loosely based is about two spinster sisters who live with their dying father in an English pottery house. A charity boy named Hadrian, who had been brought into the house by their lonely father and has been absent for some years, returns. Now a virile young man whose masculinity the sisters resent, he has returned in the hope of getting his hands on some of the old man's money. He sees an opportunity in marriage to one of the daughters, Matilda, and talks their father into insisting on the marriage. The father tells Matilda that unless she accepts the unwelcome proposal, she will be disinherited. Eventually she agrees; so everyone gets his share of the estate, and sex proves the triumphant solution to life's Gordian knot.

The play enlarges and alters the short story in certain respects. The setting preserves the pottery house of the story, but adds detail. "The stage should have atmospheric charm," and although the sets are more realistic than usual with Tennessee Williams' dramas, they still are not to be "heavy like Ibsen. . . . The house has grace and beauty as do many things which nevertheless are not in vital contact with the world". (For a moment it sounds like a background for Laura's glass unicorn.) One level of the stage has a small room containing relics of voyages, the others contain standard Victorian furnishings. Here, Williamsian symbolism is at work again; the voyage room is symbolic of the vital life outside.

You Touched Me! has curious resemblances to *The Glass Menagerie.* Matilda, though a healthier and prettier version of Laura, lives a timid, secluded life. She too is dominated by a hoveringly attentive older woman, (not her sister but her aunt, her father's sister) Emmie. The two represent different types of virginity—congenital and acquired. Emmie is militant in her chastity. That she is nursing hopes of marrying the local rector is no contradiction. The authors make it quite clear that this "ecclesiastical capon" offers no threat to Emmie's superiority over the flesh. The courtship is entirely verbal and "spiritual."

The old potter is transformed into a drunken, profane, chantey-roaring ex-sea captain living out the end of his life trying to forget an unsatisfying marriage and a smashed career. He had wrecked his ship while drunk on duty, and Emmie had destroyed his marriage by spiritualizing his wife. All he can do now is to contrive his daughter's escape from Emmie's blighting grasp. This hope is promised fulfilment in the reappearance of young Hadrian who, during his five-year absence has migrated to Canada and fought the war as an R.C.A.F. bombardier.

Hadrian is described as a "clean-cut, muscular young man in the dress uniform of a lieutenant in the Royal Canadian Air Force. There is something about him which the unsympathetic might call sharp or fox-like"—that is, to the initiated reader, a variant of Lawrence himself. He has, notes the playwright, "a look, certainly, that might be observed in the face of a young animal of the woods who has preserved his life through tense exercise of a physical craft and quickness; an alert, inquisitive look. To avoid a complication in casting the part, we will not say that he has red hair, but hair of that color would suit his kind of vital, quick awareness." Behind that quickness is something else—a need, a sensitivity, a sad, patient waiting for something. Confirming this D. H. Lawrence hero as a nature-sex symbol is the fact that Hadrian enters playing a penny-flute and looking like Pan.

For Matilda, Hadrian represents the same unacknowledged hope of escape that the Gentleman Caller did for Laura; and, like Laura, Matilda reacts with shy stiffness to this foxlike marauder from the world outside. He, like everything vital, frightens her. With amazing gentleness, he tries to draw her out in conversation, tries to coax her out of her fright—she gradually relaxing and responding. In what may be considered the central speech of the play, Hadrian expresses vaguely revolutionary doctrines, among them his sense of guilt over the deaths he inflicted as a bombardier. Though he knows that the guilt is not his, individually, he cannot shake off a feeling of responsibility for the horror.

When Matilda smiles and says, "Everything's slipped back to normal," he responds, "Excuse me, but I can't smile. Y'see 'back to normal' was not quite all we dreamed of." He wants "change." Break through the old frontiers, he says, the "frontiers of thinking." This can be done by putting less faith in fences—"more in the open range. Now the war's over—we've got to explore new countries of the mind, and colonize them." The world doesn't need peace, it needs to embark on the new war—for life rather than against it. "The war to create a world that can live without war . . . " and suggests, "All the dead bodies of Europe, all the corpses of Africa, Asia, America, ought to be raised on flagpoles over the world, and the cities not built up but left as they are— a shambles, a black museum . . . in case you forget—and leave the world to chance, and the rats of advantage." Vague as this bright-eyed idealism may sound, Matilda is impressed and moved.

She also senses in Hadrian's sympathy an understanding of her loneliness and isolation. Hadrian tries to show himself capable of gentleness as well as masculine dynamism. Because of his uncertain origin, he has spent his life looking for the love that most people find in their parents. "I grew up reaching for something that wasn't there any more—maybe the breast of my mother. . . . Something warm and able to give me comfort—I guess that's what I'm still reaching for. To be warmed—touched—loved!"

One night both Hadrian and Matilda realize that what they are groping for is to be found in one another. Hadrian has exchanged sleeping quarters with the Captain; and Matilda, thinking her father is in his usual bed, comes in to say good night. When she touches his forehead with a caress, she realizes that this is Hadrian. Running out the door, she is startled by her excitement at the touch. And Hadrian, lying in bed, thinks the gesture of intimacy and love he has been groping for ever since he was a child is the touch of Matilda.

Meanwhile, there is off-stage activity symbolic of that on-stage. A fox makes periodic forays on the henhouse. Emmie, in an effort to kill the fox, manages to shoot the only rooster, with probably unconscious intention, thereby reducing the net amount of masculinity in the area. Eventually, either fox or madness (the Captain thinks the death of the rooster has made all of the chickens demented) annihilates the ranks of the chicken coop.

In counterpoint with the main love affair, the birdlike courtship between Emmie and her clergyman goes on with duets, tiny jokes, and embroidered chasubles. Just as they are about to reach an "understanding," the drunken Captain throws one of the maid's butterfly garters into the lap of the horrified little rector. This, suggesting the Captain's lecherous interest in the buxom little servant, sends the Reverend Guilford Melton scurrying and brings the full force of Emmie's vitriolic tongue to bear on the blinking, remorseful Captain.

In the meantime, Hadrian tries to show Matilda that he understands her and will not hurt her. "She is so full of tenderness that if you touched her she would probably faint," he comments. "Some women are like that. All of this unspent tenderness grows and grows until it gets to be something enormous. Then finally there is so much of it, it explodes inside them—and they go to pieces." Her gentleness is not threatened, he explains, in the dynamic future he envisions, because without the very virtues that Matilda embodies, his ideal postwar world would be impossible. "The future knows the good things of the past. Just as well as it knows the deceit and confusion. It doesn't want to leave everything behind." There are parts of the past that must be incorporated into the future . . . "Such things as music—poetry—and gentleness." This outlined future "is only fierce for a little while so that after a time it can afford to be gentle. Much more gentle than the wrong, deceitful past of the world could be—could afford to be. . . ."

As in the short story, the Captain encourages the romance, insisting that Hadrian save Matilda from Emmie, and threatening to disinherit her unless she agrees. Emmie runs off to confer with her parson-suitor, and these two enemies of sexuality go over plans to block the Captain, finally deciding to have him declared incompetent and placed in a Christian retreat for alcoholics.

Everything comes to a head when Hadrian receives a telegram ordering him back to duty. He has only one night to convince his delicate recluse to accept the world of the future. She, having locked herself in her room, is tricked into opening the door to Hadrian. When he maneuvers himself into her bedroom, she retreats, and Emmie locks Hadrian in the bedroom and calls the police. Triumphant, she discloses her plans to tell the constable that Hadrian forced his way into the room intending to rape Matilda. But Hadrian, after escaping down the drain pipe, convinces Matilda to tell the policeman that she had merely had a nightmare. When she does, Emmie's hold over her is broken.

The dénouement is completed the following morning when Hadrian is preparing to leave. Matilda comes in, accepts his proposal, changes clothes, and runs off with him. Emmie reacts with unaccustomed grace and the Captain with justified delight. The play ends with the promise of Emmie's marriage and the Captain's regeneration; and as the young couple leave to a cry of "Forward!" Emmie runs off to the church clutching the chasuble she has just finished embroidering for the Reverend Melton.

Certain features are un-Williamsian: the soap-opera ending, the wholesomeness of all the sympathetically presented characters, the political commentaries, the careful plotting, and some really saccharine dialogue—to wit:

> HADRIAN: . . . but it's *you* that I want, Matilda—not books, not poems! [She has just offered him a book of her poetry which she had dedicated to Hart Crane.]
> MATILDA: What's—stopping you, you fool?
> HADRIAN: Little girl with broken doll. Matilda! Matilda, Matilda, Matilda! Ring out little bells in heaven, little Silver Matilda, little bells!

But the genuine Williams' touches are there too: the action's centering around Palm Sunday, the satire of the religious hypocrite, the fragile figure of the frightened woman in a destructively creative world, the symbolism in scenery, dialogue, and action, and the insistent discussion of sex. Being an adaptation and a collaboration, the play obviously is not representative of Tennessee Williams. Its portraits, however, are almost replicas of portraits in *The Glass Menagerie* and *Summer and Smoke,* both of them better plays.

For example, as mentioned earlier, Matilda and Laura are almost identical, although Matilda, not being crippled, can more easily adapt to the world. Laura is, by all counts, the more artistic study; her delicate, vague, sweet, stoic charm makes her believable and heart-rending. Emmie and Amanda also possess similarities— age and dominance. But Amanda is a far superior portrait—a compassionate, powerful, tragic study of the human heart—where Emmie is a satirical caricature. Hadrian and Jim are very much alike too, in their materialism, their enthusiasm for the new frontiers of science, and in being strong and gentle at the same time. But both Jim and Hadrian are symbolizations rather than actual people. They do not quite come to life as do Williams' neurotics and homosexuals. Besides, Williams' men almost never have the reality or depth of his women. The possible exception to this would be the studies of his father, of which the Captain is one of the first. His lusty, loud, drunken masculinity is a prevision of the magnificent Big Daddy of *Cat on a Hot Tin Roof.*

The play was important for a reason other than its settling of an overdue debt to D. H. Lawrence. It was the first Williams work to be directed by Margo Jones. In 1943, she had worked on productions at the Cleveland and Pasadena Playhouses. And because of her enthusiasm for Tennessee Williams, she was eager to help direct *The Glass Menagerie*.

It was only after *The Glass Menagerie's* success that *You Touched Me!* reached Broadway, opening September 26, 1945, at the Booth. The cast again was excellent: the choice parts of the Captain and Emmie went to Edmund Gwenn and Catherine Willard; Marianne Stewart was Matilda, and Montgomery Clift played Hadrian.

Most of the critics were disappointed. Lewis Nicols deemed the play "not an improvement nor an advancement; in fact it represents quite a step down." He labeled it Williams' "fall from grace." *The New Yorker* called it an "elaborate and intensely literary version of 'Snow White,'" and said it sounded like a compression of a year's editorials from *PM* in its political commentary. Joseph Wood Krutch was annoyed with the theme. Rather than a romantic comedy, he felt that the authors had concocted "an intense, half-symbolical drama in which boy-getting-girl seems intended to represent the triumph of good over evil." The Lawrence-type of sexuality here appears funny rather than deep; the now old-fashioned earnestness about sex doesn't achieve its purpose. The tie of sex to politics especially fails: "There may be some connection between phallic worship and a new league of nations," notes Mr. Krutch, "but it is not to me immediately a very clear one." The critic continues to laugh at the symbolism and the message, saying of Hadrian, "Almost at his first appearance we see the hero playing a penny flute, and no reader of Lawrence needs to be told what that means. Very shortly thereafter he is in the midst of a passionate speech about a new world order, and to me it never does become quite clear whether society is to be saved through better international understanding or whether, as Lawrence sometimes seemed to think, all we need is more and better copulation." Several of the critics felt they could hear three distinct voices, those of Mr. Lawrence, Mr. Windham, and Mr. Williams, each speaking out separately rather than in unison. Euphemia Wyatt called it "a music box which plays four different tunes." The Captain is a character study from O'Neill, the scenes between the spinster and her rector-suitor are a debased James, the Matilda-Hadrian love story is a happy Chekhov; and the fox-chicken, flute-playing, bomb-dropping symbolism is from Ibsen and, of course, Lawrence.

Only the ever-faithful John Gassner, though admitting that the play fell short of *The Glass Menagerie,* insisted that it also had its virtues—"it again revealed an aptitude for sensitive characterization and dialogue." But even he felt that the major flaws were the obvious lack of personal observation and the absence of the Williams' signature of anguish.

Tennessee Williams himself refuses to carry a torch for this potboiler. It is one of the few Williams efforts that has not been rewritten and reprinted.

CHAPTER VII

A Streetcar Named Desire

Life took on a strangely distasteful quality for Tennessee Williams after *The Glass Menagerie* proved the smash hit of 1945. He describes the change in one of his most personal and interesting essays, "The Catastrophe of Success," an effort to make his own experience a commentary on the upsetting phenomenon of success. "I was snatched out of virtual oblivion and thrust into sudden prominence, and from the precarious tenancy of furnished rooms about the country I was removed to a suite in a first-class Manhattan hotel. . . . My experience was not unique. Success has often come that abruptly into the lives of Americans. The Cinderella story is our favorite national myth, the cornerstone of the film industry if not of the Democracy itself." This dream that warps so many careers is antithetical to life itself, to the very nature of man. "The sort of life which I had had previous to this popular success was one that required endurance, a life of clawing and scratching along a sheer surface and holding on tight with raw fingers to every inch of rock higher than the one caught hold of before, but it was a good life because it was the sort of life for which the human organism is created. . . . I was not aware of how much vital energy had gone into this struggle until the struggle was removed. I was out on a level plateau with my arms still thrashing and my lungs still grabbing at air that no longer resisted. This was security at last." But the security proved depressing. He thought this was just a period of adjustment. "Tomorrow morning I will wake up in this first-class hotel suite above the discreet hum of an East Side boulevard and I will appreciate its elegance and luxuriate in its comforts and know that I have arrived at our American plan of Olympus. Tomorrow morning when I look at the green satin sofa I will fall in love with it. It is only temporarily that green satin looks like slime on stagnant water."

But the next morning, the inoffensive little sofa still looked revolting, and he was getting too fat for his new $125 suit. "In the suite things began to break accidentally. An arm came off the sofa. Cigarette burns appeared on the polished surface of the furniture. Windows were left open and a rainstorm flooded the suite. But the maid always put it straight and the patience of the management was inexhaustible. Late parties could not offend them seriously. Nothing short of a demolition bomb seemed to bother my neighbors." For a time he lived on room service, which provided its own disenchantment. "Some time between the moment when I ordered dinner over the phone and when it was rolled into my living room like a corpse on a rubber-wheeled table, I lost all interest in it. Once I ordered a sirloin steak and a chocolate sundae, but everything was so cunningly disguised on the table that I mistook the chocolate sauce for gravy and poured it over the sirloin steak."

Generalizing from this distaste, he decided what he was experiencing was a more trivial aspect of a spiritual dislocation, of which he soon experienced a more disturbing manifestation—he found himself becoming indifferent to people. "A well of cynicism rose in me. Conversations all sounded as if they had been recorded years ago and were being played back on a turn-table. Sincerity and kindliness seemed to have gone out of my friends' voices. I suspected them of hypocrisy. I stopped calling them, stopped seeing

them. I was impatient of what I took to be inane flattery." He got
so sick of hearing people say, "I loved your play!" that he found he
could not say "Thank you" any more. "I choked on the words and
turned rudely away from the usually sincere person. I no longer
felt any pride in the play itself but began to dislike it, probably because I felt too lifeless inside ever to create another. I was walking
around dead in my shoes and I knew it but there were no friends
I knew or trusted sufficiently, at that time, to take them aside and
tell them what was the matter."

After three months of this curious condition, he decided to have
another eye operation "mainly because of the excuse it gave me to
withdraw from the world behind the gauze mask." The mask, it
turned out, served a spiritual purpose. "While I was resting in the
hospital the friends whom I had neglected or affronted in one way
or another began to call on me and now that I was in pain and
darkness, their voices seemed to have changed, or rather that unpleasant mutation which I had suspected earlier in the season had
now disappeared and they sounded now as they had used to sound
in the lamented days of my obscurity." Once again he caught the
notes of sincerity and understanding for which he had originally
sought these people out. As for the operation itself it was only
relatively successful; it left him with an apparently clear black
pupil in the right position, or nearly so. But in another figurative
way, it had served a deeper purpose.

From the whole experience, he concluded that it was not impossible to survive the catastrophe of success. "It is never altogether
too late unless you embrace the Bitch Goddess, as William James
called her, with both arms and find in her smothering caresses
exactly what the homesick little boy in you always wanted, absolute protection and utter effortlessness. . . ."

Concerned with what his life would gradually become if he
submitted to these seductive embraces, he retreated from New
York to Texas, to New Mexico, and finally to Mexico. Taking with

him his old, hand-crank phonograph, his old clothes, and a recording of "Under the Bamboo Tree," his theme was "civilization—
take it away!" Williams had previously discovered in Mexico,
where he had lived, a paradisiac *vie horizontale* in Acapulco. He
characterized Mexico as an "elemental country where you can
quickly forget the false dignities and conceits imposed by success,
a country where vagrants innocent as children curl up to sleep on
the pavements and human voices, especially when their language
is not familiar to the ear, are soft as birds'." He wrote in a ham-
mock all morning, swam all afternoon, and spent evenings chatting
over rum-colas on the verandah, as in the short story "The Night
of the Iguana."

An odd thing happened that year. On his way to Taos, New
Mexico, he came down with agonizing abdominal pains that
landed him in the hospital. The trouble was a ruptured appendix,
but he overheard one nun whisper to the other that it might be
cancer. When the operation, to which he referred with his hypochondriacal love of such detail, as the removal of "three inches of
purple small intestine," was over, he left the hospital, convinced
that he was under a death sentence.

When he got to Chapala, in Mexico, he started feverishly on a
play, *The Poker Night*—later renamed *A Streetcar Named Desire*
—which he believed would be his last. He therefore sought to have
it express everything he had to say.

Early in the summer of 1946, having decided to die on Nan-
tucket Island, he took a cottage there for the season. Because he
had long admired Carson McCullers, whose sensitivity to human
relationships and love of the South are so much like his own,
Williams felt he must meet her before he died. He therefore wrote
his fellow Mississippian a letter explaining the imminence of his
death and his desire to see her before he left the land of the living.
So Carson McCullers came from her home in Nyack, looking
surprisingly like her own heroine, Frankie Addams, wearing blue

jeans, a sweatshirt, and a baseball cap. "The moment she came down the gangplank of the ship from the mainland, in her baseball cap, with that enchanting radiant crooked-toothed grin of hers," recalls Williams, "something very light happened in me. I dropped my preoccupation with the thought that I was doomed and from then on there was the process of adjustment to the new situation...."

Before Miss McCullers had been with him more than a few hours, Williams had become so fond of her that he wanted her to stay as his houseguest for the summer. She, responding with the same degree of fondness, accepted. This began a friendship which has steadily deepened. "I want you to know how much I love Tenn," Miss McCullers told Robert Rice, who was interviewing her for the *New York Post,* "how tenderly I feel toward him. And he has a great tender feeling for me as he does for a sister." Obviously he does, for he has given her a ring that belonged to Rose.

Williams had become enthusiastic about her novel, *A Member of the Wedding,* and believed it would make a good play. With this in mind, he borrowed a portable typewriter for her and put her to work on it. All summer they spent their mornings at opposite ends of a long table, she working on *A Member of the Wedding* and he on *A Streetcar Named Desire.* Afternoons they swam, and evenings they read poetry aloud or Miss McCullers played the piano. "It was a lovely summer," she said, summarizing their happiness together. Both plays were successes. Williams had Carson McCullers submit her manuscript to Audrey Wood, who gave her the boost to success that she had given the devoted Williams. Both Miss Wood and Miss McCullers were delighted at his intervention.

By 1947, Tennessee Williams had finished his new play, for once certain that he had a good play and one that should be a hit on Broadway. It is his one drama with what he calls an "epic" quality. He considers it his masterpiece.

A Streetcar Named Desire describes a triangle, the apex of which

is Stella (star). She is the sister of Blanche, an impoverished Southern gentlewoman, and wife of Stanley, a lusty barbarian of Polish
immigrant descent. Stella, forgetting her dismal childhood at Belle
Reve, the decayed family plantation, has been revelling in narcotic
sex with Stanley, content to live for that in a New Orleans slum.

Until Blanche reenters her life, Stella is blissfully oblivious of
her degradation. Blanche, frail and neurotic, had stayed on at
Belle Reve after Stella's escape. She had watched the tubercular
deaths of her other sister and her mother, and stood helplessly by
while the estate was drained by her father's and grandfather's "epic
fornications." She had married a delicate poetic youth, only to
discover that he was a homosexual. The miseries of that marriage
were climaxed by his suicide precipitated, in part, by his sense of
failure to satisfy her sexual needs. Turning to sex as a refuge from
nightmare reality, she had become a nymphomaniac and a town
"character." The end was her expulsion from her teaching job and
eventually from town. In frightened flight from the mounting
horrors of her existence, she seeks a haven with her sister, Stella.

But the tension she brings with her soon destroys the peace she
has expected to find there. Reacting to Stanley's brutality and sub-
humanity, she obliges Stella to acknowledge her husband's crude-
ness, and in the resumed relationship between the sisters, Stanley's
dominance is threatened. In the ensuing struggle between Stanley
and Blanche for Stella, Blanche is the doomed loser.

Blanche also sees a final chance for her own salvation. A mama's
boy, Mitch, finds in Blanche the purity and loveliness he has
associated with his mother. They reach out to each other in mutual
understanding of loneliness and longing. "Sometimes there's God
so quickly," Blanche rhapsodizes.

Aware of the change in Stella as she begins to show revulsion to
the overt display of sexuality which is his sole attraction, Stanley
declares open war on Blanche. When his inquiries into her sale of
Belle Reve yield nothing, he investigates her behavior in her home

town and bares the scandals that forced her into flight. He destroys her relationship with Mitch by disclosing this to him. With Mitch gone and Stella away in the hospital having a baby, Stanley completes Blanche's annihilation by raping her. This reduces her to lunacy, and in the last scene she leaves the house on the arm of a doctor, headed for the asylum.

Although Blanche is the catalyst around whose visit the play revolves, Stella is the key figure. Her previously unconscious choice of Stanley's sexuality is now put on trial. Not only does Stella revert to her former values, but her sympathy goes out to Blanche for her tragic marriage and its aftermath of desperate clutching for love, as she tries to shield Blanche from Stanley. Her inner conflict reaches a climax when she and Blanche come back from a genteelly festive evening to see him and his poker pals in barbarous revelry. In a drunken rage, Stanley throws the radio out the window and lunges with clenched fist at his pregnant wife. Then Stella goes over to Blanche completely and rushes out the door. This moment of truth, however, is followed by another. For all his animalism, Stanley is all that keeps Stella from decaying like Blanche. Without him, she too might sag into a tragi-comic caricature of the outdated aristocrat. So, when Stanley cries out for her, Stella rushes back into his arms. Later, when Blanche tells her about the rape, she must pretend that Blanche is mad to avoid losing Stanley. She may never love Stanley as she did in the past, she may now devote herself to her children, but she has chosen to accept reality and not the lost world of Blanche du Bois.

The power of the play lies largely in its poignant theme, which Elia Kazan expresses as, "a message from the dark interior. This little twisted, pathetic, confused bit of light and culture puts out a cry. It is snuffed out by the crude forces of violence, and this cry is the play." Williams is said to have summed up the theme as, "If we don't watch out, the apes will take over."

Kazan's director's notebook for *Streetcar,* applying the Stanislavaskian principle of searching for the "spine" of each character, is a masterpiece of analysis. He says, "This play is a poetic tragedy. We are shown the final dissolution of a person of worth, who once had great potential, and who, even as she goes down, has worth exceeding that of the 'healthy,' coarse-grained figures who kill her." He sees the play as a conflict between two civilizations—the dying aristocracy and the vital, modern, cynical democracy. Blanche, played brilliantly on Broadway by Jessica Tandy, represents tradition and idealism, seeing herself as she would like to be, denying what she is, trying to appear special and different. She is in the tradition of heroines of medieval romances as revived in the pale images of the English "Pre-Raphaelites." "Because," Mr. Kazan says, "this image of herself cannot be accomplished in reality, certainly not in the South of our day and time, it is her effort and practice to *accomplish it in fantasy.* . . . The audience at the beginning should see her bad effect on Stella, want Stanley to tell her off. He does. He exposes her and then gradually, as they see how genuinely in pain, how actually desperate she is, how warm, tender and loving she can be (the Mitch story), how frightened with need she is—then they begin to go with her. They begin to realize that they are sitting in at the death of something extraordinary . . . colorful, varied, passionate, lost, witty, imaginative, of her own integrity . . . and then they feel the tragedy."

Blanche is universal in being a woman dependent on men, aware of her waning physical appeal, terrified of her looming extinction. She drinks to dim her world, seeks sex to forget her loneliness, and when the real world catches up with her, she retreats into the all-out fantasy of madness.

As for Stella, Kazan sees her hostility toward Blanche—she is "so patronizing, demanding and superior toward her . . . makes her so useless, old-fashioned and helpless . . . everything that Stanley has got her out of." So her "spine" is cling to Stanley at any price, though she realizes, finally, that the price is exorbitant. Mr. Kazan sees her as losing interest in the sex-act where she is taken but not fulfilled or recognized. So she can never feel the same about Stanley again. Her hope lies in her children.

One day, during rehearsals, Williams explained his own idea about the playing of Stella. As Kim Hunter was playing her she had, Williams thought, "too much vivacity, at times she is bouncing around in a way that suggests a co-ed on a benzedrine kick. I know it is impossible to be literal about the description 'narcoticized tranquillity' but I do think there is an important value in suggesting it, in contrast to Blanche's rather feverish excitability." Then, clarifying the difference between the two women, he said, "Blanche is the quick, light one. Stella is relatively slow and almost indolent. Blanche mentions her 'Chinese philosophy'—the way she sits with her little hands folded like a cherub in a choir, etc. I think her natural passivity is one of the things that makes her acceptance of Stanley acceptable."

In all the controversy about how much directors and actors have contributed to the Williams plays, it seems necessary to point out how clearly the author himself sees each of his characters. They have grown in his mind for years. Blanche incorporates both Sandra (Cassandra) of *Battle of Angels* and Amanda of *The Glass Menagerie* into a personality that is softer, sweeter, more subtle, more tragic. The effective contrast with her sister emphasizes her tragic stature.

Williams see the situation as a parable of the fall of Rome to the blue-eyed marauders from the North, of the destruction of all beauty by brutality.

Stanley, the destroyer, is quite right about Blanche, but in an ugly, realistic, harshly unsympathetic way. Again, quoting from the Kazan notebook: "He's got things the way he wants them around there and he does *not* want them upset by a phony, corrupt, sick, destructive woman. *This makes Stanley right!* Are we going into the era of Stanley? He may be practical and right ... but what the hell does it leave us?" This violent character was played to the hilt by Marlon Brando.

The play is not only distinguished for its mood and its characterization—Blanche is Williams' finest creation—it also is outstanding for its successful plotting. As in *The Glass Menagerie,* the plot is simple. It moves from hope and frustration to destruction and despair. The characters themselves provide probability for every action. When we know Stella, we know what her choice must be, and we know also how Blanche and Stanley will react. Less consciously poetic than *Menagerie,* this play undoubtedly stands as Tennessee Williams' finest work. Williams attributed its success largely to Elia Kazan's inspired direction. "Kazan was to this play what Laurette was to 'Menagerie,' " he commented. "I'd be happy to trust him with anything I ever wrote."

It was inevitable that the two would work together. Kazan had been active in the Group Theatre which had awarded Williams his first recognition in 1939. Molly Day Thatcher, Kazan's wife, persuaded the Group to award him a prize and had influenced Audrey Wood to become his agent. The experimental techniques that Mr. Kazan and the Group Theatre had advocated were the very ones Tennessee Williams was using in his plays. Thus the Williams-Kazan collaboration seemed predestined.

At first Williams' respect for Kazan made him diffident. Watching a rehearsal of *Streetcar,* Williams was struck with an idea for the production. Turning to an associate, he asked if it would be proper to tell Kazan about it. On receiving an affirmative answer, he waited until a break in the rehearsal before approaching Mr. Kazan with his suggestion.

The play was also blessed with a remarkable cast. Jessica Tandy came into the part of Blanche by one of those odd coincidences that have marked Williams' career. Hume Cronyn, who had been interested in Tennessee Williams after seeing his one-acters, had occasionally taken options on his plays. One day he called on Audrey

Wood to thank her for giving him permission to use "Portrait of a Madonna," a short play based on a New Orleans woman strongly suggestive of Blanche, if Blanche had lived on for several more years. It had played for several performances at the Actors' Lab on the West Coast. Cronyn had directed it, with his wife, Jessica Tandy, playing the leading role. When Miss Wood told him she had just received Williams' latest script, Cronyn asked for permission to read it. Immediately he saw that the part of Blanche was an expansion of the *Madonna* and therefore an ideal role for his wife.

"Who do you think should play Blanche?" Andrey Wood asked him.

Mr. Cronyn, pleased that she asked the very question he was only too eager to answer, quickly suggested his wife—Jessica Tandy.

Miss Wood considered for a moment and then said reflectively, "You may be right."

Miss Tandy was pleased to hear of this, but not yet assured that she had the part. She recalls that there could be no certainty of her selection since, as yet, the play had neither producer nor director. "Certain that when these two rather vital factors appeared," she says, "there would be the customary flight to the West and a mad search for names with box-office appeal, I put the whole thing out of my mind." Nevertheless, the following June, she received a call from Elia Kazan, who had just come to New York to finish shooting *Gentleman's Agreement* and to do some preliminary casting for *Streetcar*. "Neither he nor Irene M. Selznick, the producer," remembers Miss Tandy, "was familiar with my stage work, he informed me, but they had heard of my performance in *Portrait of a Madonna*. After a couple of reading sessions, he seemed satisfied with me and I had acquired a new theatrical god. A subsequent reading for Miss Selznick resulted in a contract."

John Garfield was first proposed for the part of Stanley, but it finally fell to a lesser-known talent, Marlon Brando. The role of Stanley established him as an important actor, and his playing of the part convinced Williams that he was the perfect actor for the Williams' virile male roles. When *A Battle of Angels* was made into a film (renamed *The Fugitive Kind*), Mr. Brando again was to star.

The critics admired everything about the *Streetcar* production—the lighting, the directing, the acting, even the writing. Jessica Tandy won special notice for her brilliant handling of a demanding part. Brooks Atkinson called her "a trim, agile actress with a lovely voice and quick intelligence. Her performance is almost incredibly true. For it does seem almost incredible that she could understand such an elusive part so thoroughly and that she can convey it with so many shades and impulses that are accurate, revealing and true."

A few critics suggested that the real genius of the production might be Elia Kazan rather than Tennessee Williams, but most recognized Williams' predominant contribution. Miss Tandy insisted that it was the part rather than the acting that was great: "I have a theory that Tennessee's lines could be read as one reads a telephone book and their beauty would still come through." When Uta Hagen eventually replaced her, the play remained a favorite. Even when Tallulah Bankhead took over the part for a New York City Center revival in 1956, her immensely individual style gradually altered to suit the part, and Blanche triumphed over Tallulah. At first, when she stressed the bawdiness in Blanche's lines, Williams told her her performance was the worst he had seen. But by the time she opened in New York after the preliminary run in Miami, he said that he "shed tears almost all the way through, and . . . when the play was finished, I rushed up to her and fell to my knees at her feet. The human drama, the play of a woman's great valor and an artist's truth, her own, far superseded, and even eclipsed, to my eye, the performance of my own play. Such an experience in the life of a playwright demands some tribute from him and this late, awkward confession is my effort to give it." To this tribute, in an open letter published in *The New York Times,* Miss Bankhead replied curtly, also in the pages of the *Times:* "I have read the communique of Tennessee Williams in the *Times* of last Sunday in which he undertook to sober up. Mr. Williams' talents as a playwright are considerable, but in his manifesto he forever scuttles the ancient legend, *in vino veritas.*"

Most critics felt *Streetcar* a superior play to *Menagerie.* The lyricism is more relevant since it is limited to the speeches of the over-refined Blanche. The presentation is more natural, Williams having abandoned the gauze curtains that annoyed some viewers of *The Glass Menagerie.* Reviewers found it more coherent, more lucid, and discerned no loose ends.

Like *The Glass Menagerie,* this play is well-constructed. The action moves steadily and easily to its inevitable conclusion. Each scene is constructed like a one-act play, Williams' forte; yet together the scenes have an impressive accumulative effect. There is a convincing balance of humor and pathos, of illusion and reality. Nowhere has Tennessee Williams made better use of his abilities: his talent for picturing violence, for accurate dialogue, for compassionate revelation, for understanding of basic human problems.

Nevertheless, certain drawbacks exist. A basic one, pointed out by John Gassner among others, is the ambivalence of the author's attitude. This, of course, has persisted in all of Williams' work. The brute Stanley is pictured as the personification of disgusting normality. But this is hardly consistent with the Lawrencian phallic worship. Apparently Williams wants the audience to believe that Stella is wrong in loving Stanley but right in living with him. The conflict between Blanche's sex drives and puritanical traditions ends in a reality that is distorted and ugly. Yet Stella, who finds a socially acceptable form of the same drives, is hardly admirable. Should we consider Blanche the heroine or the villain of the piece? Her flirtation with Stanley suggests that she is attracted to him and actually desires the rape. We see her acting seductively toward the newsboy as she must have done in her affair with the seventeen-year-old pupil that cost her her teaching job, yet we are supposed to see her as the embodiment of the classic virtues. Though her way led to the madhouse, Blanche, according to Williams, "was the most rational of all the characters I've created and, in almost all ways, she was the strongest." We apparently are intended to see Blanche, then, as idealism debauched. On the other hand, we know that Williams has at least intellectual enthusiasm for that which debauched her—the sexual gratification that solved all of the problems in *You Touched Me!*

The difficulty is clear enough—Tennessee Williams can't decide whether he's for sex or against it. The dichotomy of *Streetcar* is actually more natural to him than is the obviously forced solution of *You Touched Me!* It is his perennial Puritan-Cavalier, aesthetic-physical split. His will and his intellect push him one way while his natural inclination and background pull him another.

Joseph Wood Krutch is one of the few critics who sees behind the story a parable that might in part justify the ambiguity. Stella is the representative of a decayed aristocracy. Stanley is the natural man. And "virility, even orgiastic virility, is the proper answer to decadence." So the decaying aristocracy is rejuvenated by its union with a "representative of the people." Whereas one side of the audience is inevitably with Stella, the other will share Blanche's revulsion, thinking "better decadence than this obscene surrender." Mr. Krutch, in evaluating Blanche, insists, "Her instincts are right. She is on the side of civilization and refinement. But the age has placed her in a tragic dilemma. She looks about for a tradition according to which she may live and a civilization to which she can be loyal. She finds none. Ours is a society which has lost its shape." Behind Blanche lies a past which seems to have been civilized. "The culture of the Old South is dead, and she has good reason to know that it is. It is, however, the only culture about which she knows anything. The world of Stella and her husband is a barbarism—perhaps, as its admirers would say, a vigorous barbarism—but a barbarism nonetheless." In this dilemma, "Blanche chooses the dead past and becomes a victim of that impossible choice. But she does choose it rather than the 'adjustment' of her sister. At least she has not succumbed to barbarism."

Thus, ambivalence becomes a virtue rather than a vice, if we see the play in its social context and consider the natural inclinations of its author. The decision seems to lie in the taste of the viewer, whether he prefers the absolute standards and the single view of the tragedy or the relative standards and the complex view. Tennessee Williams makes no claims to objectivity or to classical tragedy in his art.

A corollary to this problem of ambiguity is the question of the tragic proportions of the play. Without the single vision, can the play be a tragedy? Are not the tragic implications reduced by Blanche's failings? She loses some chance of tragic stature from the very first when she is seen as a neurotic and an alcoholic. As the play progresses, she loses even more, especially in her seduction scene with the newsboy which discloses her nymphomania. If these had all been the result of the decline of the family fortunes, she might still have had a claim to tragic stature by virtue of her symbolic significance. But then the revelation of her marriage, the discovery of her husband's homosexuality, the compounded deaths —a series of traumas supposedly impelling Blanche into abnormalities—all make her not a tragic heroine, but a case history. As Mr. Gassner argues: "The aristocratic family's fortunes declined, it is true, and left her economically insecure; but she could have supported herself honorably as a teacher had she not become a victim of neurosis." Nor, in his judgment, can the homosexual young husband's death explain the wife's seduction of a boy and her opening a brothel for the neighboring army camp. Her illness is believable, but hardly inevitable, and not tragic. Blanche, then, although she has the intelligence, idealism, and tragic vision necessary for the classic heroine, falls short because psychopathology substitutes for Fate.

Also detracting from the tragic possibilities is Stanley's extreme brutality in the rape scene. Mr. Gassner believes that, Williams, having missed the insight of tragedy and settled for pathos, had to turn Stanley into the brutal executioner. He performs the act of destruction that Blanche should have performed for herself, having had within her the seeds of her own destruction.

By absolute standards, the argument is quite just. But this assumes that Williams sought to write classical tragedy, which was not the case. Tennessee Williams' concept is that of moth beauty destroyed by brute ugliness. He did not see Blanche as a Medea or an Electra. Her quality is pathetic softness, not tragic strength. Nor is there any catharsis to cleanse the audience of its distress when the action moves like a reversal of Darwin's vision—back to the apes. Our sense of justice and our love of beauty are outraged; we leave the theatre troubled, not tranquil.

Streetcar might shock, disgust, or frighten its audiences, but it interested and stirred them. Brooks Atkinson wrote: "They come away from it profoundly moved and also in some curious way elated. For they have been sitting all evening in the presence of truth, and that is a rare and wonderful experience. Out of nothing more esoteric than interest in human beings, Mr. Williams has looked steadily and wholly into the private agony of one lost person."

The play won for Tennessee Williams both his second Critics' Award and the Pulitzer Prize. Broadway learned that Tennessee Williams was no flash in the pan, but a solid-gold playwright.

In Europe, *Streetcar* stirred up strong reactions. Vivien Leigh played Blanche in the London production (as well as in the film), and her husband, Sir Lawrence Olivier, directed the play. Miss

Leigh won unanimous praise from London critics, who echoed the familiar cant that she was the redeeming element in an otherwise pointless play. The *Daily Express* concluded that *Streetcar,* lauded "across the Atlantic as highflown drama," was merely "highflown melodrama." Nevertheless, the critics admitted that is was "by far the best thing Vivian Leigh has given us." To *The London Evening Standard, Streetcar* was just the stimulant the West End stage needed, "the greatest event in the contemporary London theatre" (despite the fact that *Death of a Salesman* was in London at the same time, starring Paul Muni as Willie Loman), predicting, with relish, that it would provoke controversy.

The forecast proved accurate. The play had been produced under the sponsorship of the Arts Council, organized to help productions of artistic quality by absorbing the losses of the failures by pooling the profits of the successes. Since the British government exempts the organization from entertainment tax, the Council is subjected to some measure of government control.

In December, 1949, by which time audiences were queuing up twenty-four hours in advance for gallery seats and a member of the Royal Family had refused to attend a charity performance, certain Members of Parliament asked the Chancellor of the Exchequer to explain how the British nation had come to sponsor such obscene drama. Janus, of *The Spectator,* supported them. "I have not seen 'A Streetcar Named Desire,' " he proclaimed with self-righteous pride, "but from the notices of it I have read in *The Spectator* and other papers, I have gathered that culture is not its outstanding characteristic. On the face of it, the exemption puts it in very unfair competition with other plays certainly not inferior in merit. And if the exemption is justified on the ground that this is a non-profit-making enterprise, it would be desirable to know precisely what this means and by whom the accounts are audited."

American critics counterattacked. How could the English, asked Brooks Atkinson, be so blind as not to see how Blanche's "genteel-

murky past, muddled present or dark future can matter a stick of gum to anybody but Blanche." If this chiaroscuro form, he mused, seems formless to the English mind—then perhaps the difference in taste is simply too great to bridge.

The French production, an adaptation by Jean Cocteau from a translation by Paule de Beaumont, had an even stormier reception. The inclusion of Negro belly dancers in the background of the production and other bits of pantomime, such as robbery and near-rape, imposed surrealist sensationalism upon the play. The critics again praised the acting but regretted the waste of talent and refinement on "this shabby example of American art." Jean Jacques Gautier, in *Figaro,* stressed the: "undressings, morbid strangeness, fights, enough alcohol to swim in, card games, squalling murders, eroticism, and . . . obscenities." *Theatre Arts* commented that *Un Tramway Nommé Désir* "was greeted by the most intense critical revulsion since the days when critics and playwrights dueled at dawn in the Bois de Boulogne." It was banned in some parts of France. Regardless of the protests (or perhaps because of them), *Streetcar* became the greatest box office smash in European memory. Tennessee Williams was now internationally famous—or notorious.

A small flurry about a Spanish production caused a miniature international incident. Williams was reported to have refused permission for a production because of the low intellectual level of the Spanish people and the possible damage a Spanish production would do his work in other countries. A Roman Catholic newspaper picked this up and preached to Williams at some length on the ancient and noble tradition of the Spanish theatre. Williams was shocked. He called the whole teapot tempest a "total misallegation. I never wrote anybody in Spain about anything, anytime, anyhow! Theatre is a completely non-political, international thing (as I regard it) and I would love for the Spanish people to see all of my plays. Foreign rights are one of the many things I leave in the hands of my agents." Miss Wood told reporters that her letter had made no reference to the intelligence quotient of Spaniards. She had simply withheld permission for an amateur production of *Streetcar* on the practical grounds that it might interfere with a subsequent professional offering.

The New York opening of *A Streetcar Named Desire* at the Barrymore Theatre on December 3, 1947, was a memorable one for Tennessee Williams. This time the audience, when it cried "Author! Author!" got a full-front view of his smiling, mustached, chubby face. After the performance, members of the company were invited along with a number of celebrities, to a party at "21." Until the morning papers arrived there was the usual tension. When the rave notices started coming in the party became jubilant. Williams wandered among his guests with a smile on his face, accepting congratulations with real pleasure. Finally, he discovered he was standing quite alone, and then he felt a hand at his elbow. It was Audrey Wood, who looked at him and asked, "Tenn, are you really happy?"

"Of course I am," he answered, surprised at her question.

"Are you a completely fulfilled young man?" she demanded sternly.

"Completely," he said. "Why do you ask me?"

His agent looked at him and said quietly, "I just wanted to hear you say it."

And indeed he was a completely fulfilled young man. His premature swan song was a success and he had years left to write many more plays searching into the human heart and soul.

CHAPTER VIII

Summer and Smoke

In the meantime, Tennessee Williams had been rewriting an old play originally called *A Chart of Anatomy,* to be retitled *Summer and Smoke.* It had been begun during his retreat from the involvements of *Menagerie*'s success. He stopped in Texas for a visit with Margo Jones, then promoting her Dallas theatre project.

Margo had been "riding herd all over eastern Texas" in the hope of gaining acceptance for her little theatre idea, and in the meantime directing *Joan of Lorraine, On Whitman Avenue,* and *The Glass Menagerie.* Her love was the little theatre. Having worked with Williams at the Pasadena and Cleveland Playhouses on *You Touched Me!,* she knew that he shared her ideas. Later she had directed his short poetic drama "The Purification" and two other one-acters, before becoming co-director of *Menagerie.* In every case, she had found him pleasant to work with and an author whose plays lend themselves beautifully to little-theatre presentation. She had returned to Texas determined to establish such a theatre there. Finally she had found local sponsors in Dallas and had also received a Rockefeller grant. Margo chose Dallas on the assumption that a city with enough cultural interest to maintain a permanent symphony orchestra would also support a repertoire theatre.

There the "Texas Tornado" discovered the perfect location for her "Theatre '47" (to be renamed year by year, to emphasize its contemporaneity). Gulf Oil Company had built a small, air-conditioned theatre for the World's Fair in 1936, which, like other exposition structures, was now unused. The auditorium seated fewer than 200 people; the seats were arranged in tiers on all four sides of a small rectangular stage. This was perfect for her concept of an intimate theatre-in-the-round.

With a company of devoted Broadway actors and a minimum of scenery, she established a repertoire theatre. Her idea of an intimate theatre-in-the-round wasn't original, but it was fresh to Texans. The audience feels related to the action of the play, since everyone sits close enough to the stage to see every expression of the actors; this also means that the acting style can be quieter, more natural.

Among the five plays Margo Jones used for Theatre '47 was one called *Farther off from Heaven,* by an unknown playwright Williams had introduced to her, William Inge. Another was *Summer and Smoke.*

Margo Jones understood this subtle play and endowed it with the atmospheric quality it demands. Mr. Rosenfield of *The New York Times* called the production a unified "orchestration" of dialogue, stage movement, and background.

The play itself falls short of Williams' best. Although it has most of the Williams trademarks and more control than most of his plays, it lacks fire. Like other of his plays, *Summer and Smoke* grew out of a short story ("The Yellow Bird") and the theme is again Puritanism in battle with Lawrencian sex.

The simple plot narrates the unfulfillable love of two neighbors, Alma Winemiller, the daughter of a minister, and John Buchanan, the son of a doctor. Though different in their ways of life, they are sufficiently attracted to one another to try, over a period of years, to communicate. Alma's upbringing had made her excessively sensitive and repressed. Her senile mother has regressed to infantilism, compelling Alma to assume the responsibilities—and deportment—of the lady in a minister's household. Her minister-father is drearily puritanical. She has become hypochondriacal and subject to hysterical attacks and is unable to talk naturally with young men. Her social life, outside her duties as hostess at the rectory, is confined to a petty circle of culture addicts. During their meetings at her house, she gazes longingly out of the window for a sight of the carefree John, who leads an uninhibited life while pursuing his medical studies.

The play begins with a childhood episode in the town's park. Meeting at the foot of the statue of the angel named Eternity, Alma gives John a package of hankerchiefs to use instead of his sleeve. Although irritated by the gift, he uses the opportunity to assure himself that Alma has a crush on him and to steal a kiss.

In the next scene, also before the statue, but years later, John has become a doctor while Alma has become hostess at the rectory. There is a renewal of the old mutual attraction; they plan to go out for a drive provided she meets his condition that she wear a plumed hat and he meets her condition that he observe the speed limits. When John delays the promised date, Alma invites him to her literary circle, to which he hesitantly comes. He cannot stand the cattiness and pettiness of the "intellectuals" and soon leaves.

Alma's hypochondria makes her fear that she has heart trouble, and a hysterical attack takes her to the doctor's house in the middle of the night. There, instead of his father, she finds John with the voluptuous Rosa Gonzales. Overcoming her repulsion, Alma describes her symptoms to John, who diagnoses it as a *doppleganger* (double personality—her secret self is in conflict with her public self). He gives her some sleeping tablets and agrees to take her on the promised excursion.

This he does. A few days later, he appears at her door in a

white suit and drives her out to Moon Lake Casino. After an attempt to hold her hand, he invites her to a more fundamental demonstration of mutual affection in one of the private rooms upstairs. Horrified, Alma takes a taxi home.

As the summer draws to a close, John becomes more involved with Rosa, and Alma takes more sleeping tablets which make her feel like a "lily on a Chinese lagoon." The play reaches its climax at a party at John's house, with Rosa and her racketeer father as the chief guests and the occasion the projected marriage of John and Rosa. John suddenly leaves his house and wanders, in a dreamlike trance, into Alma's living room and kneels with his head on her lap. Just when it seems that they are communicating, a shot rings out from the Buchanan house. John's father has come home (having been notified of the party by Alma), has ordered the guests out, and has been shot by the infuriated racketeer. The wound proves fatal.

After his father's death, the repentant John goes to a neighboring town where an epidemic is raging and where his father had organized the medical services. John's work is a success, and he returns as the town idol. Since marriage would complete the pattern of his new respectability, he proposes to Nellie Ewell, a girl who has been taking voice lessons from Alma and flirting with John all through the play.

Alma is now left to resolve her life without the hope that John might become the completing part of her half-fulfilled life. Trying to find a substitute, she strikes up a friendship with a lonely travelling salesman, with whom, in the last scene, she walks off arm-in-arm—headed for Moon Lake Casino—and a career as the town prostitute.

One critic commented that *Summer and Smoke* is really not a play, but only the outline of a play. It has a kind of dancelike movement, balanced, regular, precise, and obviously contrived. Its structure is elegance itself, but it is not life.

The characters are excellent as allegorical figures, but are not living people. They do not stir the sympathy of the audience like Blanche or Amanda. Alma, to many auditors, is an affected and silly hypochondriac. Her symbolic role as "spirit" is too obvious. Symbolism gives little pleasure when it is so transparent. The symbolic role of John, the young doctor, is equally obvious in its representation of the flesh and the world of science. Nellie has no basis for any claim to dynamic characterization either. She is too sweet and grows up too fast to be plausible. Her pertinence to the drama is vague until the last act, when she serves as the unlikely key to the dénouement. The minor characters are worse. The senile Mrs. Winemiller, in her uninhibited infantilism, furnishes a lively contrast to her prim husband; but none of the minor characters are more than stereotypes or caricatures.

Then there is Williams' own apparent ambivalence toward Alma. As with Blanche, he sometimes treats her with ironic distaste, sometimes with warm sympathy. In mood, the play shifts from satiric wit to lyric romance to violent melodrama. It is therefore an uneven play though, if well directed, this can be masked by a unifying atmospheric charm. Because of the plot contrivance and the symbolism, a realistic production approach would be unwise. The best approach—and this is true for most of Williams' plays—is a consistent dichotomy, a balance of forces and moods.

The action of the play's opposing teams—the senses and the spirit, faith and science—is like that in a fixed game. What could be more banal than the thesis that people are split categorically into the physical and the spiritual? Although Williams extends sympathy to the intense person unfortunately trapped on spirit's side, his intellectual assent goes to the dynamic spokesman for the flesh. The captive heroine escapes the desert of Puritanism only to sink in a morass of sex. *Summer and Smoke*'s preachments turn it into a diluted *Battle of Angels*.

But even with its romanticism and ambiguity, *Summer and Smoke* has beauty and truth. The theme has universality. The struggle between the mind and the flesh, between order and anarchy, although not so clear-cut as the artist pictures it, is a universal human conflict. There is a haunting truth in its portrayal of the vain human search for complete communication. In the delicate suggestiveness of the meetings, when each seeks something intangible, ineffable, and impossible from the other, Tennessee Williams is at his best.

Summer and Smoke was a hit in Dallas, but there was no assurance that it would succeed in New York. Brooks Atkinson was one among several metropolitan critics who went to Dallas to see Margo Jones' productions. He said of *Summer and Smoke* that it would be a "calculated risk" to move it to Broadway. "Its buoyant loveliness might disappear into the fly loft. The magic of informal staging in Theatre '47 has completely unpacked the heart of Mr. Williams' poignant narrative. The Broadway style is seldom that sensitive." He thought it the finest play Williams had written, as did several other critics. (This was before they had had a chance to see *Streetcar*.) But most seemed worried that the change to a large theatre might destroy its charm. Some thought, on the other hand, that the play's symbolism might prove more effective with a more elaborate setting, and Jo Mielziner, "Broadway's regal scene-designer," flew down to "appraise the value of scenery to a theatre that has none."

Mielziner had already provided the background magic for *The Glass Menagerie* and *A Streetcar Named Desire* by the time he started work on *Summer and Smoke,* so he knew the demands of a Williams' play. Tennessee Williams was so specific about the colors and effects he wanted that Mielziner, at one point, had to employ nine different colors in varying combinations to achieve a desired effect. Altogether there were 12 sections of border lights, 105 individually hung spotlights, and 50 star effects; 2000 feet of cable were strung backstage; and 80 lighting cues had to be followed in each performance. It took technicians eight hours to hang and angle the lights for the play when it opened in Buffalo. All the spots had been blueprinted and charted by the designer beforehand. Mr. Mielziner concludes his description of this enormous job with, "We could have used fewer lights, but it wouldn't have filled the bill for Margo and Tennessee."

The Broadway production also added background music, by Paul Bowles, who had composed the "Glass Menagerie" tune. The cast included several of the people from the Dallas production. Tod Andrews again played John; Margaret Phillips was cast as the soulful Alma. The director was, of course, Margo Jones.

Its opening was not quite so satisfying as *Streetcar*'s. Williams was not certain of success because he knew that the play, although an earlier one, would be measured by *Streetcar*. He suspected that it wasn't as good. Also, conversations with friends and strangers made him aware that the play was, for some reason, raising questions for which he had no ready answers. As an example of the questions he had been confronting on the road, he described a supper for the cast given by Lester and Cleo Gruber at a suburb in Detroit. "Everything was wonderful: it was the first good time we had all had together on the road and it was wonderfully relaxing after the tension of two openings and some highly charged atmosphere in suites at the Statler and the Book-Cadillac." During the early part of the evening, the party was conducted through the hosts' winecellar. "With our backs to the rathskeller bar, behind which stood a white-jacketed youth passing out drinks as fast as the elbow can bend, the director, Margo Jones, and myself withstood a barrage of questions like a pair of antlered beasts, and withstood them successfully." Thinking that they had settled all possible perplexities, they later progressed from the rathskeller "if progression you call it, from cocktails and highballs to cole slaw and beeftongue. . . .

"The comfortable stupefaction which belongs to the late hours of Sunday had fallen over me, and I had retreated with a plate of food to an alcove in the parlor. This alcove was something of a cul-de-sac. It had a fine view but no exit, and if you've seen or read Sartre you know how discomfiting no exit can be, especially when there get to be women in it. That was what happened. . . . A fresh contingent of visitors arrived at the Gruber residence and headed straight for this alcove. All at once I found myself hemmed in by three women in basic black who had been to a Saturday matinée and had apparently thought of nothing since except the problems of Alma Winemiller, the heroine of *Summer and Smoke*. . . . When you are eating," Williams says, in explanation of the strategy he used the following moments, "a great deal can be accomplished by having a mouth full of food and by making guttural noises instead of speech when confronted with questions such as, What is the theme of your play? What happens to the characters after the play is over? Why do you write? What is your next play about and how do you happen to know so much about women?" In answer to that last question, he suggests that the food might begin to choke you, in which case he recommends that the questionee spit it out.

It seemed to Williams that, for a writer who is not intentionally obscure, and never, in his opinion, obscure at all, "I do get asked a hell of a lot of questions which I can't answer." The uncritical author comments of his plays, "I have never been able to say what was the theme of my play and I don't think I have ever been conscious of writing with a theme in mind. I am always surprised when, after a play has opened, I read in the papers what the play is about, that it was about a decayed Southern belle trying to get a man for her crippled daughter, or that it was about a boozie floozie on the skids, or a backwoods sheik in a losing battle with three village vamps." For fear that in such a statement he might have trampled on sensitive critical toes, he allows that he's not complaining—"Don't misunderstand me. I am thankful for these highly condensed and stimulating analyses, but it would never have occurred to me that that was the story I was trying to tell. Usually when asked about a theme, I look vague and say, 'It's a play about life.' What could be simpler, and yet more pretentious? You can easily extend that a little and say it is a tragedy of incomprehension. That also means life. Or you can say it is a tragedy of Puritanism." Of this, which is closer to his actual themes, he comments, "That is life in America. Or you can say it is a play that considers the 'problem of evil.' But why not just say 'life'?" Inasmuch as this is his view of his writing, he was thoroughly harassed by the women in the alcove.

"On this particular occasion," he continues, "the question that floored me was, 'Why do you always write about frustrated women?'" Frustrated, he feels, is the one thing the women he writes about are not. "What is frustrated about Amanda Wingfield? Circumstances, yes! But spirit? See Helen Hayes in London's *The Glass Menagerie* if you still think Amanda is a frustrated spirit! No, there is nothing interesting about frustration per se. I could not write a line about it for the simple reason that I can't write a line about anything that bores me." And as for Blanche, was she frustrated? "About as frustrated as a beast of the jungle! And Alma Winemiller? What is frustrated about loving with such white-hot intensity that it alters the whole direction of your life, and removes you from the parlor of an Episcopal rectory to a secret room above Moon Lake Casino?"

As it turned out, he didn't have to say any of this to the bright-eyed lady waiting for an answer. "Into the fiery breach jumped— Margo Jones! Her answer came with the speed of a machine gun: 'Tennessee does not write about frustrated women!' she shouted. 'Tennessee does not write about abnormal characters!'

" 'Oh?' asked one lady, 'Then what does he write about?'

" 'People!' said Margo. 'Life!'

"Then, in a somewhat milder tone, she continued, 'Now, honey, I don't know a thing about you women, but just looking at you, I can see you have problems!' "

Under the cover of Margo's diversionary tactics, Williams began "executing a flanking movement. . . . The alcove, the women, the questions and finally even the residence was behind me and I stood on the suburban sidewalk, still with a plate of food and no fork but ten fingers, and I suddenly felt very happy, not that I had escaped from the questions but that there were people who cared enough to ask them." His own belief is that the very fact that he chooses to write about life confuses people, and this is why some find his stories strange and baffling.

Whether it was because *Summer and Smoke* was about life, or because it had shifted into a large theatre, or because too many ladies in basic black were baffled, the play was a failure. Two critics fought heroically in its defense. Brooks Atkinson said that *Summer and Smoke* again showed the artist's sure insight into character that is "almost unbearably lucid." He felt that its insistence on truth and its immense compassion marked it as a fine play. He praised Williams' freedom from convenient categories—his not being willing to resort to psychoanalysis, not being governed by social or political ideas. This he said, is an author writing "out of the free world of the poet: he looks about him at ordinary people, wonders about their private anguish but knows of no way to relieve it."

Joseph Wood Krutch also praised *Summer and Smoke*. The fact that it had a common origin with *Streetcar* seemed to him a demonstration of Williams' gifts. "Only a powerful imagination could have used so profitably the same thing twice. . . ." He notes that again the author's sympathies lie, not with the triumphant vital characters, but with the ineffectual idealist. The fact that this, unlike "The Yellow Bird" or *You Touched Me!* or *Battle of Angels* is no mere object lesson on the dangers of "suppression," no mere plea for "healthy animality," is to Mr. Krutch a strength. He explains that *Summer and Smoke* and *Streetcar* have a dilemma in common. "In both cases the tragedy lies, not in the fact that the heroine resists, but in the fact that she has so little to resist with. 'Gentility' is the only form of idealism or spirituality accessible to her; perhaps, Mr. Williams seems to be saying, the only form now accessible to anyone, and our culture is ugly just because we have no living equivalent for what is by now a mere quaint anachronism." Rather than ridiculing his Southern "ladies" and "gentlemen," Williams is instead "reproaching the rest of the world for having found no equivalent of what their ladyhood and gentlemanliness once represented."

Unfortunately, these two critical giants stood practically alone. Wolcott Gibbs, under the headline "Smoke Gets in Your Hair," calls Alma a "moderately routine victim of sexual repression" and considers the dialogue a "parody of that in both *The Glass Menagerie* and *A Streetcar Named Desire*." Others called it "early stuff," "melodramatic," "episodic," and "laughable." The symbolism came in for the heaviest critical blasts. John Mason Brown felt that Williams, being unable to make his words do what he wanted, had to resort to the O'Neill technique of outward symbols for inner conflicts. Others said this was "nursery symbolism" or "Ibsenesque." Even John Gassner, one of Williams' staunchest advocates, was negative toward it. The author, he said, seems "to be heralding an indiscernible profundity of poetic vision throughout the evening by keeping before us the statue of a winged figure representing eternity. It is difficult to know what eternity has to do with a girl's conversion from frigidity to mundane passionateness."

The *nays* had it, and Tennessee Williams was crushed. He attributed the failure of *Summer and Smoke* to the critics, who wielded the power to make or break a play. They had, of course, brought him success in *Menagerie*'s early days, transforming a seeming fiasco into a smash hit; but now they had turned against him.

His wrath broke into print. In a letter to Irving Hoffman, columnist for the *Hollywood Reporter,* he protested the "exorbitant demands which are made by critics who don't stop to consider the playwright's need for a gradual ripening or development . . . a degree of tolerance and patience in his mentors during this period of transition. Painters have it better. They are allowed to evolve new methods, new styles, by a reasonable gradual process. They are not abused for turning out creative variations on themes already stated. If a certain theme has importance, it may take a number of individual works to explore it fully. . . . It would help enormously if there were professional theatre centers outside of New York, so that the playwright would not always be at the mercy of a single localized group."

Strangely enough, four years and much furor later, *Summer and Smoke* returned to New York to become the most highly acclaimed off-Broadway production of 1952. Perhaps it was unwise to have brought it to Broadway just after the obviously superior *Streetcar.* Perhaps the fault lay in the large-scale production. When José Quintero followed Margo Jones' lead and used a theatre-in-the-round production, the play was again a smash hit. Critics who had blasted the Broadway production fell in love with the off-Broadway presentation at the Circle-in-the-Square—John Gassner, for one, joined the Williams cheering section. Although not every detail of the new production was perfectly realized, Mr. Gassner now thought "the play existed as an artistic unity and as an autonomous reality on the stage. The scenes were fused in an atmosphere of frustration and anguish. There was a nightmare quality in the action as it moved back and forth across the three playing areas of the rectangular stage surrounded by the audience on three sides. . . . Owing to inadequate lighting problems," he commented wryly, "the production had, in effect, too much atmosphere at times. Nevertheless, *Summer and Smoke* was turned into a frequently effective drama when it was atmospherically dissolved and presented as a state of mind and a series of tensions. . . . Realism of treatment," he noted, "is precisely what Williams' novelistic drama cannot stand, because its reality is subjective." This production, whatever the reason, "created a special world for the play or, to be more accurate, a special world *of* the play—a darkness, fatefulness, and irony emanating from confused and blindly driven lives. The production telescoped the dramatic action by cramping the stage movement not merely physically but psychologically." The characters in the play seemed to move within an inner darkness. With the stage movement compressed by the concentrating darkness, "it was not action but tension that was manifest in the darkness." Shaped by this darkness, they were never able to emerge from it into free and sharply lit space. "They seemed to belong to their inner compulsions rather than to environment beyond and independent of them." The genius of the Quintero production was its avoidance of representation in the manner of fourth-wall illusionism. The semi-expressionist, inner reality is the ideal setting for the subjective Williams drama.

This production also introduced a magnificent new actress, Geraldine Page, who is again to star in it in the movie production scheduled this year; it stirred up new enthusiasm and hope for off-Broadway; and it showed Tennessee Williams that he could work with less emotional strain if he utilized the small-scale, off-Broadway theatre. Most important to him, naturally, was the fact that the Quintero production, like the first Margo Jones production, proved that *Summer and Smoke* is a competent piece of craftsmanship.

CHAPTER IX

Roman Springs and Rose Tattoos

Long before the success of *Streetcar*, Tennessee Williams had learned that New York was no place for him. That he stayed there a month after *Streetcar's* opening was a surprise to his friends. His rooms in midtown Manhattan were in an old brownstone house with drafty windows and a conspicuous absence of luxury. Lincoln Barnett, when calling upon him for an interview, was amazed at the unmade bed, the litter of movie magazines, books of philosophy, and albums of Shostakovich and New Orleans jazz on the floor, a blues record on the phonograph, a disordered kitchenette in the background, and Tennessee Williams himself sitting before the portable typewriter at work on another play. He was now conscientiously avoiding the luxurious hotels and the opulent life, eating at cafeterias, playing poker with Negro musicians backstage at the theatre, and swimming at the "Y." To Barnett's query as to whether he believed he was running dry, he answered, "I have more to write than I have strength or energy to write." He had two new plays in his mind, and another in the typewriter.

Williams had decided to take some of the royalties that were beginning to pile up (on *Streetcar* alone at the rate of $2,000 a week) and travel for a while in Europe. He had been there as a boy, but now he wanted to study the European theatre, oversee the London production of *Streetcar,* and to visit Carson McCullers, who was in Paris.

Irene Selznick gave him a handsome set of luggage as a going-away present; but when Kazan went to check on the packing, he found that Williams had all of his belongings in a single bag. This, his phonograph, and his typewriter were all he planned to take. He had overlooked shirts, so Kazan rushed out to buy him some.

The trip was a long and restful one. Williams saw London's reaction to *A Streetcar Named Desire* and France's critical horror at, but box office stampede to, *Un Tramway Nommé Désir.* Then he wandered on down to Rome, where he settled for the winter. He was working on a play called *Cockcrow,* reportedly set in the Italian Renaissance, but dealing with the Monkey Trial, the trial at which a young science instructor in Tennessee was convicted for teaching evolution in his class. Williams told reporters his theme was the difficulty of resolving logic with faith. Either he abandoned the unlikely subject for want of inspiration or his idea was preempted by the Broadway production of *Inherit the Wind;* anyway, *Cockcrow* passed quietly into the limbo of unrealized plans.

He interrupted his European interlude to return to New York for the disappointing Broadway production of *Summer and Smoke.*

Back in Rome again, he fell deeply in love with the city and the Italian people. Their art, their dignity, their physical beauty, their speech, their zest for life appealed to every anti-Puritanical inch of his being. He found in them something of the excitement, naturalness, color, and anarchy that had stirred him in Mexico. He went back to work on an old one-act play, *Camino Real,* while he was in the mood of its Latin setting, and also started work on two specifically Italian pieces.

One was *The Rose Tattoo*. The characters of the play live on the American Gulf Coast, but their roots are in Sicily. Thus he was able to combine the South that he knew with the Sicily that he was growing to love. "What I am getting at in the play," he said, "is the warmth and sweetness of the Italian people." He felt that Italy had shown him a good way of life. Coming to know the Italians and their philosophy of living seemed to him the most important experience of his adult life. "If this is a warmer and happier play than anything I've written it is because of that experience. I would not have missed putting these feelings into a play for anything in the world." For once, the Williams world became comic and honestly lusty, sweet, robust, healthy. He laughed at his critics and said, "If anyone mentions 'neurotic' in connection with this play, I'll reach for a gun."

The play was not completed in Rome. Two years later, settled in Key West at the cottage that was to become as permanent as any home ever is for him, he was still working on it, having by then rewritten it five times. The neighborhood in which his little white frame house is located, incidentally, was later used for the filming of the movie. Some of his furniture is left over from that motion picture which was made on his own doorstep.

The Sicilians of *The Rose Tattoo* are members of a clannish little community. They cling to the old customs and superstitions in a new and confusing country. Here, in the colorful Italianate English phrasing, as in the Southern speech, is a natural poetry that appeals to the poet in Williams. Here also is a passionate aliveness that needs no Lawrencian cerebration for its promotion. The women mature early, love lustily, and react violently to the human drama. These are a people of whom Mr. Williams has been fond for many years—e.g., Myra in *Battle of Angels* and Rosa Gonzales in *Summer and Smoke*.

The heroine, Serafina, is the local seamstress. She is a woman passionately devoted to her man. When first seen, tightly corseted and elaborately dressed, she "looks like a plump little Italian opera singer in the role of Madame Butterfly." She is all aglow with the pleasure of knowing that new life is stirring inside her. Her happiness in her husband, her daughter, her pregnancy, and her life in general is manifest in every detail of action and setting.

When her truckman husband fails to return that evening, she becomes alarmed. She has idealized her husband, Rosario, because he is the son of a baron—a title that may be meaningless to others, but has a genuine aristocratic sound to the barefoot peasant, Serafina. Clean, handsome, perfumed, and rose-tattooed, he has been her whole life during the years of their marriage. She does not know that he is a smuggler and an adulterer who has been gambling at the local casino and carrying on an affair with the blackjack dealer, Estelle Hohengarten.

While Serafina is anxiously waiting for him, Estelle brings her a piece of rose-colored satin to make into a shirt for her lover. Estelle, of course, knows that the seamstress is the wife of her lover; she comes, we assume, out of curiosity and possibly mischief. Serafina, with grim irony, is lecturing Estelle on the joys of domestic love as opposed to wild love, when a goat gets loose and runs through her yard. The Strega, a local witch, comes screaming after it. The goat makes successive appearances during the play as a symbol of sexuality and cuckolding.

Just before dawn, the priest and several black-shawled women gather before Serafina's house to tell her that Rosario is dead. Serafina senses their message without being told and, in the first unbearable agony of grief, loses her baby. Her illness for the next few days keeps her away from the inquest and its disclosures of Rosario's bootlegging and woman-chasing. No one has the heart to tell her this unendurable truth.

When the community gathers for mourning, Serafina announces she wants Rosario's body cremated. Father de Leo, as the voice of the Roman Catholic Church, warns her this would be sacrilege. He knows she will worship the ashes if she keeps them in the house. The doctors, representing the more sensible scientific view, tries to tell the priest something of Serafina's state of mind: "Father de Leo, you love your people but you don't understand them. They find God in each other. And when they lose each other, they lose God and they're lost."

At this moment, an alien figure, Estelle Hohengarten, joins the mourners. All of the women know by now of her affair with Rosario and of the rose she had tattooed on her own breast to symbolize their love. The chorus of Sicilian harpies attacks her, snatches the bouquet of roses from her hand, and flails her around the neck and shoulders with them.

For the next three years Serafina keeps a flame burning at the marble urn containing Rosario's ashes and she mortifies her own flesh. Moping around, dirty and bedraggled, she has been transformed into an object of ridicule to the neighbors and then of anger for her failure to deliver the dresses she has made for their daughters' school graduation. Ignoring the screaming neighbors at her door, Serafina is lamenting her daughter Rosa's love affair with a young sailor. She forbids Rosa to see her Jack, and refuses to meet him herself. To enforce this separation, she has appropriated Rosa's clothes, thus trapping her in the house. Although this keeps Rosa from taking final exams at her school, her teacher appears with news that because of her good record the school will allow her to graduate anyway. But Serafina greets the teacher in a filthy slip shrieking that Rosa has slashed her wrists. The wound turns out to be superficial; the teacher helps her to dress and takes her off to the graduation. Remorsefully Serafina tries to embrace her pretty daughter, but Rosa, embarrassed to have her teacher see Serafina's hysterics, whirls on her and says, "Mama, you look disgusting!"

These wounding words help to bring Serafina to an abrupt self-awareness. She starts to dress for the graduation, only to find that her clothes don't fit any more. Then, searching for the watch she bought for Rosa's graduation present, she can't find it. In the midst of her frenzied search, two "female clowns," of middle years and juvenile temperament, come to her door.

On their way to the Legion convention in New Orleans, they have stopped to pick up the scanty blouse Serafina has agreed to sew for one of them. They force her to finish it, talking, as they watch her, about the anticipated lewd antics of the Legionnaires. Their giggles and squeals reach a crescendo when some roistering Legionnaires pass the window, and they lean out the window to join them in a chorus of "Mademoiselle from Armentières." Serafina can contain her disgust no longer; she screams at them, ordering them to leave the house that contains the ashes of her sainted Rosario. Retorting on the "Wop," they tell her that Rosario was a thief and an adulterer; then, frightened of her anger, they flee.

Serafina has brought the revelation on herself. She has thought of Rosario's lovemaking as a sacrament: "I am satisfied to remember the love of a man that was mine—only mine." Now her dream is threatened with destruction. To reinforce her faith in Rosario and in their love, she turns first to Father de Leo, who admits reluctantly that much about Estelle came out at the inquest, but refuses to divulge Rosario's confessions. Unable to believe what he hints at, Serafina attacks him with her fists like a wild animal. The horrified women of the neighborhood pull her away.

But Serafina is shaken enough to relent toward her daughter's love. When Rosa brings Jack to meet her, Serafina greets the sailor distractedly, but without antagonism. Before allowing the young couple to go off for their picnic with the graduating class, however, Serafina forces Jack to his knees before the combination shrine of the Virgin and Rosario and makes him swear to respect Rosa's innocence.

Alone again at last, Serafina muses over her life. She becomes

aware of her sinful pride in her glorifying love. Insignificant
people become jealous of such love and try to belittle and destroy
it. Her agonized reveries are interrupted by a clownish salesman,
symbol of human pettiness, who tries to sell her a useless household gimmick. His spiel is interrupted by the entrance of Alvaro,
an angry truck driver whom the salesman forced off the road a
little way back, yelling "Wop" and "Dago" at him as he roared by.
To the angry young driver, the salesman sneers, "Is something
giving you gas pains, Macaroni?" then knees Alvaro in the groin,
reports him to the company, and gets him fired.

Frustration and pain drive Alvaro into Serafina's house where
he bursts into sobs, and Serafina joins him. The sufferers find
rapport in their common misery and a childlike warmth grows
between them. Serafina offers to mend Alvaro's torn jacket while
he washes up. When he takes off his shirt, she gasps. Here is her
husband's torso supporting the head of a half-wit. When she discovers that he, too, drives a banana truck, like Rosario, she believes that he is a sign she has prayed for. He, in turn, having lost
his job, evaluates the security, comfort, and satisfaction that this
little widow could afford him and makes arrangements to return
that night.

By evening, the transformation in Serafina is remarkable. With
the prospect of a fresh love in her life, she lays aside her despair
over Rosario and dresses for her visitor. So again we see her sitting
primly, as in the first scene, looking plump and ready for love.

Alvaro proves to be a fumbling lover. From the time he arrives,
all his comments are suggestive. While groping in his pocket, he
drops a contraceptive on the floor. Serafina orders him out. Before
he goes, he shows Serafina the rose tattooed on his chest. The
effect startles the wary widow only briefly: Alvaro's efforts are too
clumsy. Poor Alvaro is in the family tradition—his grandfather
was the village idiot, and his father was the product of the idiot's
union with a woman who stumbled on a rock while running away

from him. Alvaro has none of the aristocracy and *savoir faire* of the lamented Rosario. So the seduction scene collapses into a slapstick chase and ends in Alvaro's childish and complete abashment. He is so honestly ashamed of his behavior that Serafina pities him. Relenting toward her boobish lover, she explains that her day has gone entirely wrong and that she has reason to suspect her late husband of infidelity.

Serafina, with her dream blasted, is left without any reason for pride or purity. She sends Alvaro out the front door noisily and welcomes him in the back door secretly, turns out the lights, and relaxes for the first time in three years.

In the early hours of the morning, Rosa and Jack return from their picnic. The evening has apparently been a frustrating one for both. Rosa, as passionate a female as her mother, has made it difficult for Jack to live up to the promise he made before the shrine. When Jack leaves, Rosa comes into the house and falls asleep on the couch, looking like Botticelli's "Birth of Venus." Alvaro, showing the signs of a night of drinking and loving, stumbles into the living room and discovers Rosa. Kneeling, he mutters in naive delight, "Che bella!" This wakes Rosa, who screams with fright. Serafina rushes in, angry at the village idiot's grandson, and ashamed before Rosa. Trying desperately to face it out, she pretends Alvaro is a housebreaker, but she doesn't fool Rosa.

The daughter dresses hastily, intent now on joining Jack and fulfilling their love before he sails away. Then Alvaro races out of the house, thus disclosing their affair to the entire neighborhood. Serafina no longer has any secrets, or pride, or daughter. Even the ashes of Rosario have blown away during the night. The play ends with Alvaro standing at the top of a hill, displaying his bare, tattooed chest to the laughing community and shouting his love for Serafina, while Serafina, gives him the rose-satin shirt she has sewn for Rosario as Estelle's gift.

Although the story is comic, it certainly has the components of tragedy—the violence of Serafina's emotion, the death of her idol, the destruction of her ideal. However, the character of the Sicilian, as Williams sees it, is such as to bring a rediscovery of happiness. The passion we see in Serafina is too vital to be obliterated or perverted. These people can love again, be happy and fruitful even after disaster. The death of the dream does not hurt Serafina as it does Blanche because Serafina is made of more resilient stuff. These Mediterraneans know how to satisfy their lust for life.

Yet the story is one of Williams' weakest, largely because his feeling for comedy is in conflict with his stronger sense of tragedy. The Latin point of view is as foreign to him as is the Lawrencian. Neither ideal has any true relationship with either his emotional nature or his personal experience. He remains irrevocably Anglo-Saxon, looking with longing and frustration at the Latin answer to life.

Though the plot has the speed and complications of ideal comedy, it is obviously contrived; the strings are visible by which puppet-master Williams manipulates his characters.

Then there is the admixture of tragedy. Just as Tennessee Williams cannot conform to Aristotelian tragedy, so he also departs from classical comedy. There is real vice and anguish in this story. Rosario's death is a tragic event and the revelations that follow are no trivial "follies." There are, nevertheless, a greater consistency of character and of mood and a more natural humor in *The Rose Tattoo* than in *You Touched Me!* whose comedy was expressed mainly in wit and touches of satire. In *Rose Tattoo* he shows a robust, earthy humor.

The principal characters, Serafina, her daughter Rosa, and Alvaro, have an animal vitality. The minor characters, the sailor Jack, the doctor, the priest, Estelle, or the neighborhood women are developed no further than their functions call for; and the neighborhood women are restricted to their Greek-chorus role.

The Strega (witch), however, is lively. And the oafish Alvaro is endowed with a clownish charm, though he hardly seems the man to accomplish the redemption of the glory-seeking Serafina.

Some aspects of Serafina are overdrawn, especially her immolation in slovenliness. Yet she does have personality—her pride, her equally passionate asceticism and sensuality, and her quick and sincere sympathy with Alvaro. These give her warmth and frequent charm. She lacks the reality of the fragile moth women who are Williams' forte, but she is the best of his Mediterranean earth mothers.

The departure from the native South is not altogether successful either. Granted that Williams discovers an analogous lyrical background where the natural speech patterns are colorful and rich in metaphor, it also leads him to excess. He overdoes the rose motif, which soon becomes cloying as it is obtruded in the names, tattoos, and dialogue.

His intent in *The Rose Tattoo* is clear—to sound a paean to natural love, to sunlight and children and gaiety, to Mediterranean warmth and expressiveness. The idyll is light, gay, gaudy, bawdy, and funny. But it does not compare with *The Glass Menagerie* or *A Streetcar Named Desire*.

In this and in his future work Tennessee Williams faced a new problem. Everything after *Streetcar* was to seem anti-climactic.

The author himself admits weaknesses in *The Rose Tattoo* that he should have cleared up. Since he let the play go from its Chicago tryout on to Hollywood without sufficient revision, he should not have been surprised at its comparative lack of success. When it opened in Chicago, he wasn't satisfied with it. He made many changes, some of them after having read and pondered the critics, but these changes were not enough.

This time, the director, Daniel Mann, was more in awe of the playwright than the playwright was of him. Instead of demanding a stronger, tighter script as Elia Kazan would have done, Mr. Mann was "willing to take a chance on the script submitted." But Williams sees the fault as entirely his own, not the director's. After all, he had been nettled by critics who gave equal credit to the director, as to the playwright, for previous successes. He insists that Mr. Mann did a "beautiful job" on both the stage and film versions of *The Rose Tattoo*.

The acting was again superb. Although the part of Serafina was designed for Anna Magnani, whom Williams had met in Europe, Maureen Stapleton did a "wonderful" job, according to both the critics and the author. The film did have Miss Magnani as its star, and Williams said of her, "I never saw a more beautiful woman; enormous eyes; skin the color of Devonshire cream." The charm and warmth of Maureen Stapleton, however, made her one of Tennessee Williams' favorite leading ladies. She, in turn, felt that "Tennesse's characters are rewarding for an actor because they're not simple black and white, or just good guys and bad guys, not always your best foot forward because you're the hero or the heroine." Eli Wallach, who won unanimous applause for his portrayal of Alvaro, became another member of the growing Williams troupe, appearing later in *Camino Real* and *Baby Doll*.

The minority of critics who applauded *The Rose Tattoo* included Harold Clurman. He considered Serafina "a rich and lyric portrait of an Italian peasant." The new subject freed Williams of tensions and allowed him to write a "hymn of praise to the unfettered sexual instinct." In it Williams again displays "unusual ingenuity in the manipulation of cliché for humorous purposes."

Generally, however, the critical report was negative. Walter Kerr saw in it fresh evidence of a fundamental flaw in Tennessee Williams' work—the author can't conclude anything. Short stories frequently dissolve into fantasy; plays just stop; Blanche's madness washes out a struggle that needs to be resolved; Serafina's response to the revelation of her husband's infidelity and crime is an inadequate sexual gesture. She has developed as a "quicksilver compound of physical passion, intense idealism, and hysterical religiosity. That a single sexual act should reduce these qualities to a happy harmony is implausible; it tends to suggest that there was no conflict in the first place." This criticism is actually double-edged: first, Tennessee Williams is an unfailing sentimentalist about sex, invariably believing that the psychological aberrations of the universe can be settled on one big bed; and second, that he has no disciplined sense of form. The first is a failure in realistic understanding; the second is a failure in artistic control.

John Mason Brown found Williams a wasteful writer without any real ability in structure. The villagers, for example, never become the chorus they are plainly intended to be. This structural inadequacy derives from an intellectual inadequacy. "He sees, he hears, he feels," Mr. Brown says, "but he does not appear to think."

The chief target for the critic's arrows was the symbolism. Some called it "muddled" and some "feeble"; everyone insisted that Williams should have rationed his roses. John Mason Brown commented: "Do not ask me to describe the meaning of all the roses, real or imaginary, with which several of Mr. Williams' characters are tattooed. Let me only confess that not since the Houses of York and Lancaster feuded long and publicly have roses been used more lavishly than by Mr. Williams. . . . To Gertrude Stein a rose was a rose was a rose. But to Mr. Williams roses are mystic signs, proofs of passion, symbols of devotion, and buds no less than thorns in the flesh. . . . Mr. Williams' roses, moreover, are not real blooms. Instead, they are dramatically the equivalents of so many cheap paper flowers used to fancy up a lot of downright foolishness."

Generally, the critics considered the play mediocre and saw a pretentiousness in the production and direction that destroyed such simple beauty as it might have contained. Conceding it to be a non-patronizing folk comedy, beautifully and tenderly written in parts, that demonstrated Williams to be no formula playwright, they nevertheless saw it as a departure rather than a development. Running only 133 performances, *Rose Tattoo* joined the plays that Tennessee Williams considers his failures. It was not a failure in the material sense, however, for the sale of the movie rights fully compensated for its comparatively short Broadway run.

Another failure purchased by Hollywood also came out of Williams' Roman experience—*The Roman Spring of Mrs. Stone*, a short, stream-of-consciousness novel. This solitary Williams attempt at the novel, unlike *The Rose Tattoo*, is a study of Anglo-Saxon decadence. Its heroine is a retired actress who has just experienced change of life and who has also just lost her husband. It is a chronicle of her life after death, largely told in reminiscences over a childhood spent playing King-on-the-Mountain; an adolescence devoted to rebuffing the advances of a Lesbian friend; and a womanhood dedicated to avoiding motherhood by her marriage to an Easter bunny of a man who needed her for a mother-substitute. Her stage career, which was built on carefully disguised craftsmanship rather than real art, was triumphant largely because she always managed to demolish her competition. Now wealthy but lonely and old, the beauty that had made her King of the Mountain is fading, and she must buy substitutes for it.

In the lush Roman springtime, she sees both a commentary on her wasteland life and a key to her rejuvenation. The story concerns her relations with successive gigolos. When the crass demands for money of the first hurt her pride too much, she dismisses him and her problem gets another temporary solution, in a more animalistic sexuality with a new gigolo. It is a study of the human tragedy of age without fulfillment, and of the contrast of the barren materialist American outlook with the vital Roman outlook.

Typical Williamsian symbolism abounds—springs of renascence and fertility, phallic obelisks, predatory birds of American materialism. But the heroine is a new type for Williams. She apparently is a sketch of the aging actresses who have come to fascinate him as he comes to know more and more of them, and whose portrait he was to complete in the sordid-splendid heroine of *Sweet Bird of Youth*.

The novel was weak in structure. Williams does better with the spoken word; the more stringent requirements of drama subject him to a control that failed him in the looser fictional form. Nor does the characterization have the power Williams showed himself capable of in his plays. We have only to contrast Karen Stone of the novel with Serafina della Rosa to see how much more satisfying, human, and consistent is the heroine in his dramatic work.

Although Rome failed to inspire Williams to the heights he had reached in his earlier plays, it served some purpose: it developed Serafina and planted the seed for the Princess (in *Sweet Bird*), it revealed talent for folk comedy, and it made Tennessee Williams a happier, more optimistic human being.

CHAPTER X

Camino Real

The earliest group of Tennessee Williams' published plays, *American Blues,* includes several ultra-poetic efforts. "Moony's Kid Don't Cry" has florid speeches about stars as seen from the forest. The precise flower symbolism of "The Case of the Crushed Petunias" anticipates the dreaful lyrical flights of *You Touched Me!* "The Unsatisfactory Supper" uses the rose and the rosebush to stand for the innocent lovers of the world, the standard Williamsian rose symbol. In each of the plays since that time, the same symbols and the same poeticizing have appeared.

Williams' critics have never been quite comfortable with this poetic tone in his work. Sometimes, as in *The Glass Menagerie* or *A Streetcar Named Desire,* they justify it as in character with those who speak the lines or they applaud it for itself. Brooks Atkinson has consistently acclaimed the lyric beauty of the playwright's work.

Streetcar was the first Williams work whose poeticizing seemed natural. It is consistent with Blanche's anachronistic ideals that she speak in the style of Southern sonneteers; and then too, she's an English teacher. The same rhetoric, when used earlier in the introductory comments of *Menagerie,* had struck most critics as pretentious, although again, Tom, being a poet with a "poet's weakness for symbols," his speech was in character. *You Touched Me!*, however, had no such justification for its avoidance of ordinary speech, and *Battle of Angels* was full of over-wrought imagery which, in the mouth of a shopkeeper's wife and an unschooled wanderer, were out of character. Whether effective or not, a striking feature of Tennessee Williams' prose is its frequent lapses into free verse, that are responsible for both his moments of greatest power and of greatest weakness.

One analyst, Henry Popkin, writing in the *Tulane Drama Review*, separated Williams' dialogue into two categories: the respectful and the disrespectful. The respectful is in the Southern oratorical tradition: flowery, lofty, and verbose. It can appear in hauntingly poetic scenes, such as Blanche's musing on death in *Streetcar* and Tom's farewell to Laura in *Glass Menagerie;* or it can be used with sympathetic irony, as in Alma's nervously stilted speeches in *Summer and Smoke* and Blanche's frightened efforts to charm Stanley. The disrespectful speech, on the other hand, is usually given to the more animalistic nature-men, who have the bluntness of Damon Runyon characters. If they use long words, it is with an unfamiliarity that brings a laugh. This disrespectful dialogue usually runs contrapuntally to the respectful.

One might surmise from this that Williams' formal verse is of high quality. On the contrary, it is far inferior to his drama. It is full of lush imagery, rather like a bowl of overripe fruit. John Woods, who reviewed *In the Winter of Cities,* a collection of Williams' most cherished lyrics, found them oddly unsettling. Though much in them was genuinely poetic, there were unpoetic pedantry, staginess, extensions, resumptions, and false moves. The most effective pieces are "The Blue Mountain Ballads," in which the poet is natural and comic and delightful. The "Gold Tooth Blues," for example:

> *Now there's many fool things a woman will do*
> *To catch a man's eye, she'll wear a tight shoe,*
> *She'll wear a light dress and catch a bad cold*
> *And have a tooth pulled for a tooth of gold.*

> *I'm a gold tooth woman with the gold tooth blues*
> *'Cause a gold tooth makes a woman look old!*

This poet-dramatist needs the restriction of the dramatic form. Even his short stories tend to get out of hand largely because of their loose form. A story may end up preaching or singing, the tale forgotten.

In any event, Tennessee Williams' most devastating dramatic failure grew out of the poetic drama "Ten Blocks on the Camino Real," one of the short plays in *American Blues*. The expanded version is not essentially different from the original, adding some lines from his poetry, some ideas from a verse play "The Purification" and from "Lord Byron's Love Letter." A dramatic poem in prose, it makes no greater demands on the imagination than Wilder's *Skin of Our Teeth* or Eliot's *The Cocktail Party*, which were successes in the same season. Elia Kazan saw enough in it to be delighted to produce it; a year after it flopped, Harold Clurman was still defending it, and a revision of it appeared in *Theatre Arts*. Clurman made the point that Christopher Fry, T. S. Eliot and Thornton Wilder are more acceptable as playwrights of fantasy simply because they sound more intellectual and thus appeal to the snob instinct, whereas Tennessee Williams is admittedly and consistently lowbrow. Undoubtedly much of the difficulty lies in personal taste. No one, after all, can prescribe the precise degree of reserve that the dramatist must retain to be acceptable. *Camino Real,* exposing the naked, quivering romantic, will stand or fall with personal taste. For Tennessee Williams, it will probably remain his favorite child. Like *Battle of Angels,* he loves it for its expression of his basic faith, for the labor devoted to its creation, and for its public rejection.

The idea for "Ten Blocks on the Camino Real" first came to Williams when he was sick in a desolate corner of Mexico. Ill and friendless and penniless, it seemed to him he would never escape. His fears recalled terrifying visions he had had as a child. They came like a pageant before his eyes. When he had sufficiently recovered he spent two months recording the spectacle. The story lay dormant for a number of years until another attack of despair re-evoked it. He wrote the full-length version "in a time of desolation: I thought, as I'd thought often before and often thought since, that my good work was done, that those 'huge cloudy symbols of high romance' that used to lift me up each morning (with the assistance of coffee so black you couldn't see through it even when you poured it before a fair-weather window), that all those mornings had gone like migatory birds that wouldn't fly back with any change of season. And so it was written to combat or to purify a despair that only another writer is likely to understand fully." Although Tennessee Williams considered *Camino Real* a purgation for his despair, audiences drew no relief from it.

The play exists in several versions, differing in details of construction. The version discussed here is the printed text, which varies somewhat from the Broadway production.

The play is a dream. As the house lights dim, a spot falls on an exhausted Don Quixote and his weary squire, Sancho. The scene into which the two wanderers step is a "tropical seaport that bears a confusing, but somehow harmonious resemblance to such widely scattered ports as Tangiers, Hawaii, Vera Cruz, Casablanca, Shanghai, New Orleans"—a scene which, although indeterminate, looks like Mexico. The village is divided into the rich and the poor sections by an ancient fountain in the plaza. On one side is the deluxe Siete Mares Hotel, that supplies its wealthy clientele with waters from a natural spring while the city outside dies of thirst. The cracked fountain in the plaza that supplies the poor people has gone dry. On the poverty side are a fleabag flophouse, "Ritz Men Only," a pawnshop, and a gypsy fortune teller's booth.

Don Quixote immediately recognizes the town as the one he has been warned against, "a walled town which is the end of the Camino Real and the beginning of the Camino Real." The admonition he recalls was, "Halt there and turn back, Traveler, for the spring of humanity has gone dry in this place. . . ." Suddenly, we notice at one side a crumbling triumphal arch leading off into a wasteland. In the distance are snow-capped mountains and possible purity, the way out that few have the courage to take. Sancho, after one look at this glum future, dumps his master's belongings on the pavement and retreats to La Mancha. Don Quixote, true to his tradition, stays, refusing to be deterred from his quest for "that green country he lived in which was the youth of his heart, before such singing words as *Truth! Valor! Devoir!* turned into the meaningless mumble of some old monk hunched over cold mutton at supper!" Before starting this last and most perilous of his adventures, the old knight lies down for a nap and a dream. His dream, he says, "will be a pageant, a masque in which old meanings will be remembered and possibly new ones discovered." From the shadows in his dream, he will choose a companion to replace the cowardly Sancho.

Don Quixote's words are interrupted by the shrill cries of a white cockatoo, Aurora. Then we notice the man holding her, Gutman, the proprietor of the luxury hotel, who has been watching Don Quixote, mockingly. Gutman picks up the narration from here, giving it a sardonic tone, until the last scene, when the perennial romantic once more takes over. With Gutman we watch some of his symbolic hotel clients, strayed here from history and literature: a penniless Casanova; Marguerite Gautier (Camille), who can no longer afford to reject rich old men for poor, handsome young lovers; Prudence Duvernoy, Camille's companion, searching for her dead lap dog; and Lord Byron, who has lost his gifts among the potted palms of the luxury hotel.

Gossiping with Casanova, Prudence speaks of Camille, whose "candle is burning low." Camille has run away from the narrow white bed of sickness, escaping from the reality of disease and age to the dreams of the past. Prudence, in keeping with her name, insists that the moment has come for prudence; it is now time to put away beautiful lovers as one would put away "white gloves meant only for summer, and pick up a pair of black ones suitable for winter."

A hoarse cry breaks through their conversation. A survivor, black from the sun on the wasteland, stumbles crazily into the square, gasping for water at the dried-up fountain. As he lurches toward the luxury hotel to beg for a drink from its spring, an officer shoots him in the stomach, and he reels back to die like a "pariah dog in a starving country." Gutman, smirking, calls our attention to the apathy of his guests. Confused and exhausted, they sometimes pass questions "amongst themselves like something illicit and shameful, like counterfeit money or drugs or indecent postcards." At this hour of the day, they "pull themselves together, and drift downstairs on the wings of gin . . . and exchange notes again on fashionable couturiers." Casanova, to drown his revulsion at the sight of the dying man, orders a cognac, but Gutman refuses because Casanova's remittance has failed to arrive.

Soon we realize that Gutman is also a politician. He calls the local dictator to warn him that the blind woman they call "La Madrecita" and the guitarist called "The Dreamer" have taken up the dead man's body. He sees danger in the Madrecita's madonna-like sympathy and the musician's anarchy. "Revolution only needs good dreamers who remember their dreams, and the love of the people belongs safely only to you—their Generalissimo!" The brutal treatment of the survivor has stirred up the crowd; the cry of "Brother" is beginning to circulate—the most dangerous word in any tongue, Gutman tells the Generalissimo. To divert the aroused people, Gutman proclaims the Gypsy Fiesta. The bogus fortune teller announces over the loudspeaker: "Tonight the moon will restore the virginity of my daughter." As Esmeralda, the Gypsy's daughter, appears to a blast of trumpets, Kilroy, hero of the piece, enters.

Kilroy is an ex-prize fighter who still has his golden gloves and his jeweled belt with CHAMP on it, and whose heart has cost him his career and his wife. It is as large as the head of a baby and, we later discover, made of solid gold. The doctors have ordered him to give up liquor, fighting, smoking, and sex. Although his "real true woman" would have stuck by him, he deserted her out of kindness. Now, having left his ship with a pocketful of wages, Kilroy finds himself in a crazy town in which no one will tell him where he is or help him find the telegraph office. Within a matter of minutes, he is jabbed in the stomach by a policeman, accosted by a filthy prostitute, and robbed. When no one will believe that he ever had any money, he becomes desperate, threatening to report to the American Consul.

As he makes this threat, some white-jacketed, snickering street cleaners come, dump the survivor's body into a trash can, and trundle it off, looking back at Kilroy, giggling and whispering. Frightened and broke, he decides to hock his ruby-and-emerald-studded belt. "This is not necessary to hold on my pants," he says, "but this is a precious reminder of the sweet used-to-be. Oh, well. Sometimes a man has got to hock his sweet used-to-be in order to finance his present situation." The loan shark, however, wants his golden gloves instead of the belt. Kilroy insists he'd hustle his heart on the street, peddle his heart's true blood before he'd leave his gloves at the loan shark's.

Back on the street, Kilroy meets the dissipated, effete Baron, whom he greets with delight as "a normal American. In a clean white suit." To which the Baron replies, "My suit is pale yellow.

My nationality is French, and my normality has often been subject to question." But at least, Kilroy observes, the suit is clean. Also, the Baron might direct him to the "Y," which he explains is "Sort of a Protestant Church with a swimmin' pool in it." Camino Real, of course, has no "Y" or any other decent communal facility. As they talk, the Baron confesses that he too once asked questions. Now he has turned to what others consider corruption, but he prefers to call "simplification." While they are talking, the street cleaners return, dump the Baron into their can, snicker at Kilroy again, and leave. He knows now that he will die in this town.

Now Casanova drifts onto the scene to answer Kilroy's questions. He tells Kilroy that the street cleaners take the bodies of the indigent to the laboratory where they are reduced to their chemical components. Unique organs are displayed in jars of formaldehyde at the museum. Their shared revulsion reveals Kilroy and Casanova to be brothers in spirit—both travellers and romantic lovers. Casanova describes the arch that is the dangerous exit from Camino Real, which he cannot use because he is "sweetly encumbered with a lady." But Kilroy is eager to attempt the escape from this walled city of desperation. Before he can attempt it, the local police apprehend him on a charge of vagrancy, the penalty for which is to wear the fright wig, electric nose, and clown suit of a patsy. Kilroy tries to escape in a mad chase scene, but is caught and becomes the patsy; he doesn't talk any more, he just lights his nose. Casanova explains: "You have a spark of anarchy in your spirit, and that's not to be tolerated. Nothing wild or honest is tolerated here!"

Casanova then leaves the abused Kilroy and joins Camille for dinner in the hotel dining room. These aging lovers represent Bohemia to their drab middle-class neighbors. Irritated by the snobbery, Casanova talks flamboyantly about carrying the banner of Bohemia into the enemy camp. Camille, however, recognizes that "Bohemia has no banner. It survives by discretion." This woman is a legend, Gutman tells the audience, the legend of the sentimental whore. Once her flower's color announced to her lovers whether the moon was favorable for love. Now the camellia is always white. Gutman goes to their table and insults Casanova, with the public announcement that his baggage has been removed from his room. Camille softens the public humiliation by offering to pay the bill. In their resumed conversation, Camille reveals that she is not yet resigned to the retired life that the aged Casanova accepts as the inevitable end for worn-out lovers.

As if in answer to her dreams, the Fugitivo, a plane with unscheduled flights, lands to pick up passengers. But Camille's money, papers, and effects are in too much confusion to permit her departure in the five minutes allotted. Thus she remains trapped in Camino Real, missing what she suspects was her last hope for escape.

But Casanova is pleased. This life is better, in his view, than the dangers incurred by an escape. "The only country, known or unknown, that I can breathe in, or care to, is the country in which we breathe together, as we are now at this table. And later, a little while later, even closer than this, the sole inhabitants of a tiny world whose limits are those of the light from a rose-colored lamp —beside the sweetly, completely known country of your cool bed."

In a protesting gesture of vitality, Marguerite (Camille) tosses her ring to a gigolo and rushes off for a degrading night that ends in the bitter realization that her youth and charm *have* slipped away.

In the meantime, we witness another departure from Camino Real—that of Lord Byron. "The metal point's gone from my pen, there's nothing left but the feather." Remembering the cremation of Shelley on the beach at Viareggio, he thinks of the bubbling brain, the awful stench, and comments: "A man's burning *ought* to be pure!—*not* like mine—(a crepe suzette—burned in brandy . . .)." His vocation is to influence the heart of man, to bring order out of the chaos of the universe. So he must make a voyage back to the self he used to be, back to Athens—"If not purity, at least its recollection." Byron then walks through the Triumphal Arch, out into the Terra Incognita.

At the festival of the virgin, instead of a king of fools, a king of cuckolds is elected. Casanova is chosen and now wears horns to symbolize his election. Kilroy, still in his fright-wig and neon nose, embraces him as a brother and both turn to watch the festival. This gypsy festival is a parody of fertility rites mixed incongruously with the veneration of the Virgin Mary. The moon rises, and the Gypsy announces that her daughter has again become a virgin. Now she must choose her hero for the night.

Using the excitement of the celebration to cover his actions, Kilroy has slipped into the pawn shop and hocked his golden gloves for ten dollars. He plans to use the money for his escape, but when he comes out of the pawn shop he finds himself the center of the festival, Esmeralda's choice for the night. Fearing for his weak heart and desperate to escape, he tries to beg off, but his resistance collapses. By the time he reaches the point of lifting her veil, he is too exhausted, however, to go any farther. Leaving Esmeralda, Kilroy joins his fellow failure in love, Casanova. The two discuss their prospects for the night. Casanova, unable to pay for his room at Gutman's hotel, turns with a sigh to the single "pads" across the street; Kilroy chooses to sleep under the stars, though knowing that the street cleaners will catch him tonight. After Casanova leaves, Kilroy awaits his last battle. The returning Camille, whose degradation at the hands of her brutal young gigolo has been as complete as Kilroy's, sits with him, holding his hand as the street cleaners approach. Kilroy makes a wild effort to fight off his death, but the figures encircle him and stuff him into their can.

But unlike the others, Kilroy doesn't die when ordered to do so. His body is simultaneously across the knees of the keening Madrecita and in the dissecting hands of the medical students. When the students discover that Kilroy's huge heart is of pure gold, the ghost of the prizefighter jumps up, snatches the heart from the students, and repeats his frantic race of the earlier scene across the stage and through the audience. Esmeralda utters a prayer for him, but her mother throws a slop bucket in his face. The disheveled Kilroy sums up his brief career in this mad town: "Had for a button! Stewed, screwed and tattooed on the Camino Real! Baptized, finally, with the contents of a slop jar; Did anybody say the deal was rugged?"

At these words, Don Quixote stirs from his dream and walks over to the dry fountain. As he approaches it, it begins to flow. The disillusioned Kilroy stands beside the old knight, repeating that the deal is rugged, a truth that the Knight of the Mournful Countenance readily acknowledges before he advises, *"Don't! Pity! Your! Self!"* As Kilroy takes Sancho's place beside him, Don Quixote says, "The violets have broken the rocks!" And the two fighters go off through the Triumphal Arch into the Terra Incognita.

The play, as is apparent from this recapitulation of its action, is completely expressionistic. As a dream play, it makes no attempt to conform to the waking world of reality. Moreover, the dream it narrates is that of a madman, Don Quixote, seeking a successor to Sancho Panza, one who will also abandon himself to the quest for the ideal. Reality is further challenged by the choice of its characters, who are drawn from different centuries and from both history and literature. By permitting lush symbolic allusions, the characters do enrich the poetry of the play. Most of them are the "fugitive kind," who have arrived at the end of a royal road of imagination to meet with reality—age, disease, cruelty, disillusionment, and death. Kilroy joins them as the quintessential modern American dreamer, its comic-strip myth. Esmeralda sums up Tennessee Williams' love for them in her final prayer:

God bless all con men and hustlers and pitch-men who hawk their hearts on the street, all two-time losers who're likely to lose once more, the courtesan who made the mistake of love, the greatest of lovers crowned with the longest horns, the poet who wandered from his heart's green country and possibly will and possibly won't be able to find his way back, look down with a smile tonight on the last cavaliers, the ones with the rusty armor and soiled white plumes, and visit with understanding and something that's almost tender those fading legends that come and go in this plaza like songs not clearly remembered. Oh, sometime and somewhere, let there be something to mean the word *honor* again!

Camino Real, more than any of his other plays, sums up Tennessee Williams' creed, which he takes from *The Doctor's Dilemma:* "I believe in Michelangelo, Velasquez and Rembrandt; in the might of design, the mystery of color, the redemption of all things by beauty everlasting and the message of art that has made these hands blessed. Amen." Any hope for redemption from the world of the Camino Real lies, Williams says, in the violets' breaking through the rocks. Beauty, imagination, and love must triumph over cruelty, ugliness, and fascism. The soft can win out over the fierce.

Most critics missed this and saw only the monstrous in its fantasy. They characterized it as "horrifying and repellant," a "malign world . . . of corruption, cruelty, disease and death" where the characters are "doomed by the viciousness of human beings, too weak and indolent to escape from the contaminations of their kind." Brooks Atkinson said that Williams' world "is going out with neither a bang nor a whimper but with a leer and a grimace of disgust. . . . There is no health in it. With rare exceptions everyone succumbs to depravity. The Camino Real is a jailyard of vice." Unlike the Puritans, who were not much more cheerful about wordly pleasures, at least they had faith in a power that would redeem them. "They had a way out and dreams of future glory. But Mr. Williams has nothing in reserve. . . . It is a shock to realize that Mr. Williams' conception of the world is so steeped in corruption."

Yet, as in *Streetcar,* though the dominant forces are the brute ones, the spent loveliness of the Camino Real fugitives does imply that men are not all Gutmans. Nor are they left without hope of escape from the walled city of despair. Williams insists that the drama is not a document of despair, but of eternal idealism. It served for him, he says, and possibly for others during its brief run in 1953, "as a spiritual purgation of that abyss of confusion and lost sense of reality that I, and those others, had somehow wandered into. . . . What the play says through this unashamed old romanticist, Don Quixote, is just this, 'Life is an unanswered question, but let's still believe in the dignity and importance of the question.' "

Unfortunately, the problem is more distinct than the hope. As Dante found, Hell is easier to conceive than Heaven. Against the dynamic and material corruptions of Camino Real, the idealism apears frail and vague.

Camino Real is virtually an anthology of Williamsian themes, symbols, characters, and favorite phrases. The wasteland in the background is a standard symbol and the foundation in the center of the setting (with water here directly equated with human kindness) has appeared in other Williams plays. The Gypsy paradise echoes the Paradise dance hall in *Menagerie.* The phony religion of the fortuneteller serves as distraction and opiate for the masses; Madame Sosistrotis replaces God and His prophets; Casanova impotently thumps his phallic cane while Camille tosses her Freudian ring to an eager gigolo—these and similar common symbols stud this rococo play.

Williams acknowledges the elaborate use of symbolism in *Camino Real* and tries to explain its value to him. Symbols, he says, "are nothing but the natural speech of drama." He insists that dreams and communication are both based on these images that lie in our conscious and unconscious minds. "A symbol in a play has only one legitimate purpose which is to say a thing more directly and simply and beautifully than it could be said in words." He cannot endure writing that is a "parade of images for the sake of images," and closes a book in disgust when it keeps on saying one thing is like another. Nevertheless, "symbols, when used respectfully, are the purest language of plays. Sometimes it would take page after tedious page of exposition to put across an idea that can be said with an object or a gesture on the lighted stage." As an example, he cites the battered portmanteau of Jacques Casanova which is hurled from the balcony of the Siete Mares hotel. "While the portmanteau is still in the air, he shouts: 'Careful, I have—' and when it has crashed to the street he continues—'fragile —mementoes . . . ' I suppose that is a symbol, at least it is an object used to express as directly and vividly as possible certain things which could be said in pages of dull talk."

Besides the standard symbols, the author also uses archetypes for characters. Some of his earlier characters had had an archetypal nature—Val as Christ, Myra as Mary, but none of those were so obvious as these in *Camino Real*. Now, rather than building a character to reflect a universal attitude, Williams simply uses a known character and relies on allusions to do the work for him. But this immobilizes one of his chief talents—the ability to create believable, colorful characters. His archetypes, when analyzed, conform to the standard Williams' adversaries—the materialists and the idealists; and their opposition is less ambiguous than in his other plays.

The themes are equally typical of Williams—hatred of power, of inhumanity, of materialism; the love and sympathy for the mutilated, diseased, poor, and confused. And they are stated with a directness unprecedented in Tennessee Williams' drama.

In *Camino Real*, fantasy takes over too completely, and it requires too great a "suspension of disbelief," so that the audience considered the play a self-indulgence. Williams, in a way, endorsed this judgment by his statement that the play's appeal to him "was its unusual degree of freedom." Recording his own reaction to the form, he said, "When it began to get under way I felt a new sensation of release, as if I could 'ride out' like a tenor sax taking the breaks in a Dixieland combo or a piano in a bop session. You may call it self-indulgence, but I was not doing it merely for myself. I could not have felt a purely private thrill of release unless I had hope of sharing this experience with lots and lots of audiences to come." His desire, he insisted, "was to give these audiences my own sense of something wild and unrestricted that ran like water in the mountains, or clouds changing shape in a gale, or the continually dissolving and transforming images of a dream." Such freedom, he insists, is not chaos or anarchy. "On the contrary, it is the result of painstaking design, and in this work I have given more conscious attention to form and construction than I have in any work before. Freedom is not achieved simply by working freely."

Critics also disliked its poetry. Typical was the comment by Anthony Hartley, who said, in an article appearing in the *Spectator,* that it was quite impossible to become interested in the characters of *Camino Real,* either the actual or the historical ones. "Since Mr. Williams is making a shot at communicating the incommunicable, he takes a kind of poetical language which has ravaged the modern American theatre. This begins with the stage directions . . . and it becomes much worse later on. . . . His lyricism is as flabby as his dialogue is taut."

From the very beginning, *Camino Real* had been a troublesome play. The author had originally had a difficult time getting a backer. Elia Kazan offered to work with him on *Camino Real,* but even Mr. Kazan's wife, a Williams fan, didn't like the play. Twice Williams read it to unresponsive backers.

The first night had a large and enthusiastic audience. "One can be taken in by this," the author generalizes ruefully. "I went home

and as the hours wore on and I got no congratulatory calls, I became panicky. Then Kazan arrived with his wife and the John
Steinbecks. He had brought them to present their condolences. I
guess I flipped my lid. I shouted to Kazan: 'How dare you bring
these people!' "

When he slammed into his bedroom, leaving his embarrassed
guests alone in the living room, "A friend of mine explained to the
Kazans and the Steinbecks that I was hysterical and served them
a round of drinks; then they left. It was terrible. I did love that
play so much."

Writing about its reception Williams records that "At each performance a number of people have stamped out of the auditorium
with little regard for those whom they have had to crawl over,
almost as if the building had caught on fire, and there have been
sibilant noises on the way out and demands for money back if the
cashier was foolish enough to remain in his box." Just as he had
been unable to understand why Boston had thought *Battle of
Angels* obscene, so now he could not understand why audiences
found *Camino Real* obscure. "I had never for one minute supposed
that the play would seem obscure and confusing to anyone who
was willing to meet it even less than halfway."

Tennessee Williams himself thought that the audiences were
lazy. The expressionistic presentation outraged them. Willing to
go as far as impressionism with him, they balked at the complete
abandonment of objective reality. He attacked the theatre-goers'
conservative taste in this image: "A cage represents security as well
as confinement to a bird that has grown used to being in it; and
when a theatrical work kicks over the traces with such apparent
insouciance, security seems challenged and, instead of participat-
ing in its sense of freedom, one out of a certain number of playgoers will rush back out to the more accustomed implausibility of
the street he lives on."

Camino Real closed almost immediately. After mulling over

the failure for a time, the author settled down to rewriting the play. The revision was published in *Theatre Arts*, October, 1953, with an introductory article by William Hawkins, who listed the major changes, saying he considered them "all to the good." Depending less on suggestive fantasy, the play was now tighter and clearer.

But the play remained vulnerable to the two main criticisms. The symbolism, which one critic had found all too obvious, became more obvious in the revision. It also remained, in the view of critics like John Mason Brown and Brooks Atkinson, a "sick" play. Unwilling to accept the fantastic epilogue of Kilroy's revival and escape, believing instead that Kilroy's death was the actual end of the play, most critics agreed that, "Mr. Williams' is an insect rather than a human comedy. Unlike William Faulkner at Stockholm, he does not decline to accept the end of man. In his cosmos, man is finished and unworthy of redemption. Having lost all faith in himself, and all reason for us to have faith in him, man, as Mr. Williams sees him, deserves nothing except oblivion."

The next few years found Tennessee Williams writing half a dozen new plays, but always turning back to this rejected favorite, changing, polishing, loving it. Then, in 1960, he again saw a chance for a stage production. By then off-Broadway had come to his rescue twice—once with *Garden District* and again with the highly successful Quintero revival of *Summer and Smoke*. Jose Quintero was enthusiastic about *Camino Real* in spite of its Broadway failure, and thought the same therapy that had worked on *Summer and Smoke* might be the cure—and so it proved. On May 17, 1960, at St. Marks Playhouse, *Camino Real*, at last, met with success.

Quintero went even further than Kazan to visualize the black phantasmagoria of the Camino Real world, though it meant muting the note of hope. The horror is so effective as to make the audience feel that Camino Real is hell rather than purgatory. Yet a means of escape remains. There is no eternal damnation portrayed in the script, but rather a punishment for failure of positive, courageous action. The Quintero production, by neglecting the note of hope, is more to blame than the author for critical attacks on the negativism in *Camino Real*.

Despite this and other defects, such as poor acoustics and a mumbling of the lines that spoiled their poetry, the off-Broadway production was a comparative success. This may be attributed partly to revision and partly, perhaps, to the new climate of acceptance in the Beatnik era.

Camino Real embodies the two artistic criteria that Tennessee Williams values most. He insists that his work must be dynamic and organic. According to his definitions, *Camino Real* is both. But we are thankful that the public rebuke following its production forced him back into creations that were more disciplined and realistic. Luckily, in his next play, he turned back to his area of artistic strength, the love and hatred, aristocracy and barbarism of the Delta dwellers.

CHAPTER XI

Cat on a Hot Tin Roof

The play that Tennessee Williams had been working on for the two years before, during, and after *Camino Real* was to prove one of his most satisfying. It rose from the fountainhead of his creative talent.

Cat on a Hot Tin Roof came as a relief to Williams fans who had begun to fear that his talent was limited to the portrayal of psychopathic Southern belles. In *Cat* they discovered that he also knew and could communicate about men. He could understand and love normal, sensuous, dynamic human beings. *Cat*, for all its burden of perversion, disease, mendacity, and death, is nonetheless a healthy play—startlingly so for the work of one whom everyone had come to consider a "sick" playwright. His sympathy is broader here; he does not reserve his love for doomed misfits.

The theme is one that Williams had sketched briefly in a short story called "Three Players of A Summer Game." It is a charming little mood piece about a game of croquet played on some summer evenings by a plump little girl, her thin, lovely mother, and Brick Pollitt a tall, slim, graceful man with a fiery thatch of hair.

A Delta planter, formerly a celebrated athlete at Swanee, but now at the end of his youth, Brick has married a debutante Mardi

197

Gras Queen named Maggie. The "perfect couple," blessed with all the advantages—youth, beauty, riches, intelligence, health—had gradually gone into a mystifying decline. Two years after their marriage, "Brick had started falling in love with his liquor, and Margaret, his wife, began to be praised for her patience and loyalty to him." For some unknown reason, Brick began to see his life as something disgusting. As his interest ebbed in life and work, Margaret took over. She did his work, she drove the car, finally she virtually assumed his masculinity. "She abruptly stopped being quiet and dainty. She was now apt to have dirty fingernails. . . . Her hair was now cut short so that she didn't have to 'mess with it.' " Her laugh boomed out as she waved a brown, muscular arm at the people on the street.

All of this has taken place before the summer and the croquet games. Then, Margaret had been called away for the summer and death had presented Brick another opportunity for manhood. A young doctor who had been treating him for his alcoholism suddenly developed a horrible brain tumor that grew like a fierce geranium that soon shattered the pot. The doctor's young wife stood beside the deathbed tight-lipped, able only to reiterate the word *God*, until Brick took a hypodermic needle and ended the doctor's anguish. Then he took over the management of the widow's life. He settled the estate, bought the house, repainted it a splendid white, set up a game of croquet on the lawn, which he sometimes played with the orphaned daughter; he took the widow as his mistress and, for a time, appeared to have recovered his masculinity.

But when he also resumed his drinking, the croquet game became an excuse for clowning, and he grew more and more irregular in his visits. Now, when he visited, it was usually with a group of strangers from out of town whose wild parties had to be halted by the local constable. His affair came to an end in jail where he mumbled incoherently the name of his wife, "Margaret." The widow moved to another city; Brick Pollitt again lost his driver's license and his masculinity; and Margaret looked stronger and more manly than ever as she carted her captive through the streets.

"He was a man," comments the author, "who had been, and even at that time still was the handsomest you were likely to remember, physical beauty being of all human attributes the most incontinently used and wasted, as if whoever made it despised it, since it is made so often only to be disgraced by painful degrees and drawn through the street in chains . . . the way some ancient conqueror, such as Caesar or Alexander the Great or Hannibal, might have led in chains through a capital city the prince of a state newly conquered."

The widow and the orphan Mary Louise disappear from *Cat on a Hot Tin Roof,* leaving the story to Brick and Maggie. Allusions to football largely replace the allusious to croquet. The marriage of the virile woman and the effeminate man, one sucking the strength out of the other, turns into the more subtle relationship of the less manly Maggie and the less feminine Brick. The trauma that precipitated Brick's fall is now spelled out. The best addition is the Pollitt family, included to provide a comprehensive case history of the destructive effect of a predatory family on a sensitive man. The change from a summer of adultery to a day of revelation is also good, focussing everything on the point of the story, the emasculation of Brick. This is the moment of truth for Brick, and incidentally for his father. Each has lived with his life-lies, and each wants, in a passionately loving and yet destructive way, to rip the veil of illusion from the other.

Brick is still slim and firm; liquor has not yet visibly wrecked him. But he feels disillusioned and spent. His athletic fame and his friendship with Skipper, another football star, have been his only reasons for living. Now both are gone, and Brick is left with his bottle. "He has the additional charm of that cool air of detachment that people have who have given up the struggle." The coolness is a pose, though; he envies the moon for its ability to be a "cool son of a bitch," and drinks until he hears the click that allows him to escape from the heat of life. Beneath this calm exterior is a banked fire that flashes out when disturbed.

His father, Big Daddy, is a large man of violent emotions. Profanity is his natural vocabulary. His lust for riches, for food, for love are enormous even after sixty-five years of rich living. His wife disgusts him, perhaps because as a justification for his infidelities, he has never really believed in her love for him. For his other son, disparagingly nicknamed "Gooper," he feels only irritation, disliking his greed and his hypocritical obsequiousness, and even the fact that he has a large brood of children, because it points up Brick's barrenness. Brick is the only person he really loves, and the love takes in Brick's wife, Maggie, whom he admires for her practicality and her spirit. Big Daddy is a magnificent portrait. In spite of his gross humor and profane speech, his integrity in what he is makes him the hero of the piece.

The play is set on Big Daddy's birthday, which becomes ironically, the time for announcing his approaching death. We find ourselves caring for Brick largely because of his father, and loving Brick when he in turn loves Big Daddy. If this is, as it appears to be, a recollection of Williams' own father, then we can see a deep admiration for the man replacing the earlier hatred. Big Daddy, like C. C. Williams, is too completely antithetical to the quiet, delicate personality of the son for any hope of rapport; but he is capable of stirring a love so strong it can be confused with hate. Big Daddy and Brick do love each other. That is why each can so hurt the other.

The subsidiary tragic relationships in the household are between these men and their wives. Big Mama, like Williams' good-hearted, simple-minded, ample-bosomed, loving, sensual women, has given a lifetime of devotion to Big Daddy, laughing at herself for it and smilingly condoning his hatefulness. She has slept with him for forty years without convincing him of her love for him. Her frustrated lifelong love of this man is deflected to Brick, her favorite son also, in whom she sees much of Big Daddy's charm. But even here she is frustrated; Brick shrinks from her fondling as from all bonds of human affection. The pain discernible through her practical jokes and boisterous spirits makes this coarse old woman a beautiful, strong study in unfulfilled love.

Only Maggie understands Big Mamma. She should; she shares her problem. Maggie also loves an unresponding man. The most important thing in Brick's life was his friendship with Skipper, not his love for Maggie. Maggie showed Skipper to be a homosexual (in the *Tea and Sympathy* manner of giving him a single opportunity in bed to prove his virility). When thus exposed, Skipper had taken suicidal refuge in alcohol and narcotics. Brick, knowing how Maggie forced this intolerable self-realization on Skipper, sees her as his enemy, while Maggie feels that this, like everything she does, was a testimony of her all-embracing love for Brick. Sleeping with Skipper was thus an effort to break what she considered an unhealthy friendship that threatened their marriage.

But Brick has recoiled from sexual relations with her and she feels as tense as a cat on a hot tin roof. In Williams' words, Maggie's tormented face, "her anxious voice, strident in the heat of combat, is unpleasantly, sometimes even odiously, disturbing" to Brick. Too tenacious to jump off the roof although miserable on it, too passionate to leave the unspeakable unspoken, she becomes shrill and hysterical. She tries to force Brick to discuss Skipper, to make him understand the hold he had on Brick, and then to come to bed with her.

Mixed with this love, lust, self-justification, and strength are Maggie's charm, wit, vitality, and common sense. She is catty about Mae and Gooper, whom she despises; she suspects their greed; but she envies them their hideous, no-neck children.

Maggie loves Brick and Big Daddy, but she also loves money.

Having once been as "poor as a church mouse," she sees no romance in poverty. Also, it takes money to support a drinker. It is easy to see why Big Daddy admires her. "Yes, this girl has life in her," he says.

Gooper, or Brother Man, is an officious little lawyer who has always had to take second place to the favored brother. In Williams' categorizing, he is one of the unfortunate men who "sweat"—whose curse is that they try too hard at everything, seeking approval and receiving rebuffs, while the beautiful ones of the world, with effortless grace, rank as heroes.

Nevertheless, Gooper has married into society. His wife is Mae, once a Mardi Gras Queen, an honor for which Maggie despises her. Her chief virtue, now, is her fertility. She has borne a horde of monster-children almost as if to emphasize Maggie's barrenness. Meaner and still more materialistic than Maggie, Mae provides further reasons for Maggie the Cat to stay on the roof, spitting and clawing to protect Brick's property rights.

Mae has an animal instinct for spotting the weakness of her opponent, and once she sights the tender spot, she prods it unceasingly. She and her husband are more caricatures that complete portraits, as is the hypocritical little parson who comes with the hope of getting an air conditioner for the church as a memorial to Big Daddy.

The action, contained in the single day of Big Daddy's birthday celebration, centers around the reports from the cancer clinic. Only Big Daddy and Big Mama have no idea that the old man has a cancer. Mae and Gooper have brought their progeny to impress Big Daddy with the desirability of leaving his estate to a sensible family man rather than a no-good, drinking homosexual. To counter their maneuver, Maggie tries to get Brick to take hold of himself and put up a fight for the inheritance, but since Brick has broken an ankle, he is in no condition to leave his bedroom,

While everyone courts Big Daddy's attention, Brick shows no interest. Much of the after-dinner conversation has Big Daddy's robust appearance for its theme. The family congratulates him that the clinic's reports cited only a spastic colon. And Big Daddy, certain now that he will live for years, accuses Big Mama of trying to take over the plantation during his illness; then he clears the room so that he can talk with Brick.

Brick, as usual, is at the bottle, waiting for the magic click that signifies a few hours of alcoholic peace. Big Daddy, having heard from Gooper and Mae, who have been eavesdropping on the nocturnal quarrels between Brick and Maggie, wants to know: (1) why Brick doesn't sleep with Maggie, (2) why Brick quit his job as sports announcer, and (3) why Brick is so intent on throwing his life away. Before allowing Brick to reply, Big Daddy defines his own values. For all of his wealth, he knows that he can't buy life, and he knows that life is all there is. Man, he says, is an animal, without pity for his fellows and cursed with the knowledge of mortality. Now that he has a new lease on life, he intends to stop driving himself and enjoy luxury, gentleness, and women for the remainder of his days. He might as well enjoy this life, since there is no other. "When you are gone from here, boy," he tells Brick, "you are long gone and nowhere!"

Brick is disgusted. He knows this is all founded on the lie about the clinical report. Besides, with Big Daddy's oratory going on, he won't hear the click that signals the alcoholic release from reality. Their talks, he says, always end up painful and irrelevant; communication is impossible. Big Daddy, however, insists on some answers, and to force an answer he grabs Brick's crutch and will not give him a drink until Brick will explain why he drinks. Brick's reason can be summed up in a single word—*mendacity*. Big Daddy, outraged that a son of his should be too frail to face lies and live with them, shouts, "I've lived with mendacity!—Why

can't *you* live with it? Hell, you've got to live with it, there's nothing else to live with except mendacity, is there?" But Brick replies
there is an alternative—liquor.

The old man refuses to let this talk end like all their other conversations, with the truth left unspoken. At this moment, we see
that these two men have a deep affection for one another. They
cannot lie to one another; unfortunately, they have never been
able to talk openly either. Forced to be explicit about his reasons
for giving up his job, Brick explains: "Sit in a glass box watching games I can't play? Describing what I can't do while players do
it? . . . Drinkin' a coke, half bourbon, so I can stand it? That's
no goddam good any more, no help—time just outran me, Big
Daddy."

Brick's answer still seems too vague for the practical old man.
Insisting on a physical rather than a metaphysical reason, Big
Daddy says bluntly, "You started drinkin' when your friend Skipper died." The implied accusation of homosexuality rips through
Brick's detachment, and he is horrified at the suggestion. Brick is
a Puritan. While his father is willing to treat the problem with
open-minded tolerance, Brick is repelled. Using all the vulgar
names the insinuation connotes to him, he finally sputters, "Big
Daddy, you shock me. . . ." He recalls that a pledge in their fraternity at Old Miss who was discovered attempting an "unnatural
thing" was driven off the campus. He and Skipper never went
further than a handshake. "Why can't exceptional friendship, *real,
real, deep, deep friendship!* between two men be respected as
something clean and decent without being thought of as—
fairies. . . ."

But, once the dam is breached, the whole story floods out: the
aerial passes that made Brick and Skipper football stars, the attempt at pro football with Maggie tagging along, Skipper's sickness, then Brick's, and finally Maggie's destruction of Skipper—
forcing him to admit what he felt toward Brick so that Brick would

be free to love her. "He, poor Skipper, went to bed with Maggie to prove it wasn't true, and when it didn't work out, he thought it was true!—Skipper broke in two like a rotten stick—nobody ever turned so fast to a lush—or died of it so quick. . . ."

Big Daddy still isn't satisfied, sensing that some clinching facts have been left out. The main omission turns out to be a long-distance call from Skipper, who confessed everything to his friend, hoping for assurance. Brick hung up. This was the last time the two ever spoke. Pouncing on this, Big Daddy sees that Brick is passing the buck. "This disgust with mendacity is disgust with yourself. *You!*—dug the grave of your friend and kicked him in it! —before you'd face truth with him!"—to which Brick blurts out, "*His* truth, not *mine!*"

Then, lashing out to hurt the man who has now taken his psychic as well as physical crutch from him, Brick tells Big Daddy that he is dying of cancer. They've been friends, he rationalizes, "and being friends is telling each other the truth. . . . You told *me!* I told *you!*"

Slowly and passionately Big Daddy blasts out in a final rage against the dying of the light, "CHRIST—DAMN—ALL—LYING SONS OF—LYING BITCHES!" He too is now finally and completely disgusted with mendacity.

The concluding scene of the play is the disclosure of Big Daddy's devastating truth to the only member of the household still unaware of the death sentence—Big Mama. Her shattering misery at losing this huge, vulgar, hateful man reveals "the history of her forty-five years with Big Daddy, her great, almost embarrassingly true-hearted and simple-minded devotion to Big Daddy, who must have had something Brick has, who made himself loved so much by the 'simple expedient' of not loving enough to disturb his charming detachment, also once coupled, like Brick's, with virile male beauty." Her loving reaction endues the elephant of a woman with dignity and beauty. As Williams says of her, "She almost stops being fat.' It is the same sort of tragic beauty to be seen in the foolish Amanda of *The Glass Menagerie* at the moment when all her hopes collapse.

In her misery, Big Mama calls for the only other person she loves, telling Brick he must take over the plantation for Big Daddy. In the plea, she calls Brick her only son, and insists that he now take hold of himself. Gooper and Mae sputter in fury. They have already drawn up plans for the estate, but Big Mamma, displaying unexpected dominance and composure, excoriates their greed.

Maggie, seizing the opportune moment, announces that she is going to have a child. Her determination makes the lie believable, and Brick's not contradicting it seems a confirmation. Big Mama believes the story and goes off to tell Big Daddy. Maggie's story is merely premature—not false. She locks up Brick's liquor that night and refuses to give it back until he has slept with her. Brick acquiesces. Maggie, as she turns out the rose-silk lamp declares, "Oh, you weak people, you weak, beautiful people!—who give up. —What you want is someone to—take hold of you.—gently, gently, with love! And—I *do* love you, Brick, I do!"

His resigned, sad, ironic reply is, "Wouldn't it be funny if that was true?"

This final echo of Big Daddy's commentary on Big Mama's avowal of love leaves the problems of the story unresolved. In this original version of the story, Maggie is almost as aggressively triumphant as she was in the short story. The difference is that we are glad of her victory. Because of the cat's determination, they will have children and win their share of the inheritance. The future, however, remains dim. Brick will continue to drink and to believe that Maggie soiled the only beautiful thing in his life, his friendship with Skipper; and he will also probably continue to deny Skipper's homosexuality and his own responsibility for Skipper's death.

Williams, answering the familiar charge of ambiguity, explains this relationship in greater detail for those who demand absolute clarity on such issues: "He [Brick] will go back to Maggie for the sheer animal comfort of sexual release, even if she did not make him dependent on her for such creature-comforts as only a devoted slave can provide, a devoted slave who is also a devoted master, even if she had not smashed all his liquor bottles and only she would 'drive him in town for more.' He is her dependent. As Strindberg said: 'They call it love-hatred, and it hails from the pit....' "

Elia Kazan, on seeing the first version, had reservations about this third act. As summarized by Williams, they "can be listed as three points: one, he felt that Big Daddy was too vivid and important a character to disappear from the play except as an offstage cry after the second act curtain; two, he felt that the character of Brick should undergo some apparent mutation as a result of the virtual vivisection that he undergoes in his interview with his father in Act Two. Three, he felt that the character of Margaret, while he understood that I sympathized with her and liked her myself, should be, if possible, more clearly sympathetic to an audience."

Only the suggestion about Maggie could Williams embrace wholeheartedly, "because it so happened that Maggie the Cat had become steadily more charming to me as I worked on her characterization." The other two suggestions were less palatable. "I didn't want Big Daddy to reappear in Act Three, and I felt that the moral paralysis of Brick was the root thing in his tragedy, and to show a dramatic progression would obscure the meaning of that tragedy in him and because I don't believe that a conversation, however revelatory, ever effects so immediate a change in the heart or even conduct of a person in Brick's state of spiritual disrepair."

Certainly sympathy for Maggie is a good point. A woman of such wit and tenacity merits a sympathetic presentation of her victory. Dramatically, it is an enormous loss to drop Big Daddy so early in

the play. Since the audience can almost imagine his reaction to
Gooper's premature funeral arrangements and Maggie's announcement, we might as well see and enjoy his colorful responses to
them. But the third point is germane.

Because of this unwilling surrender to Kazan's opinion, Williams has been roundly criticized. The Williamsian naturalistic
universe works unrelentingly toward the destruction of beauty,
purity, and youth. The author bases his determinism on the assumption that people are incapable of change even to avert disaster. Blanche or Stella or Amanda might each realize that she is
wrong, but she must lie or go mad rather than take the alternative
path. Only *Summer and Smoke* allows the characters to change;
but the change is actually only the discovery of their hidden real
natures. Whether this static concept of human will is true or not,
it is basic to Tennessee Williams' thought and work. He must
conform to it if he is to maintain his artistic integrity and to communicate, truthfully, his personal vision of truth.

Williams' excuse for including his director's third act rather
than his own is practical if not ideal: "I wanted Kazan to direct
the play, and though these suggestions were not made in the form
of an ultimatum, I was fearful that I would lose his interest if
I didn't re-examine the script from his point of view. I did."
Then the success-seeking author continues, "The reception of the
playing-script has more than justified, in my opinion, the adjust-
ments made to that influence. A failure reaches fewer people, and
touches fewer, than does a play that succeeds."

The disturbing thing about this explanation is its implication
that the author lacks artistic integrity. This spokesman for an
organic theatre that honestly interprets human experience, puts
success first and changes his plays to please a director. As a noviti-
ate, deference to others was understandable; but after ten years of
comparatively phenomenal success, he should have accepted the
responsibility for his work all the way. It is unfair to put the blame

on Mr. Kazan. Wihtout intending it, Williams reinforces the general impression that his directors shape his plays for him.

Actually, the new third act is not so very different from the old. A storm is added to reflect the violent passions on-stage; Maggie and Brick talk a little longer and it is made clearer that Maggie loves her husband and that he, in turn, is developing some feeling for her. His tacit agreement to Maggie's announcement is changed to a defense of her against Gooper's malice. Some people, he observes, make love without huffing and puffing.

"An' now," he concludes to Gooper and Mae, "if you will stop actin' as if Brick Pollitt was dead an' buried, invisible, not heard, an' go back to your peep-hole in the wall—I'm drunk, and sleepy— not as alive as Maggie, but still alive. . . ."

When they are alone, he tells Maggie that he admires her. Her triumphant maneuver to get him to bed is the same, but his ironic answer to her avowal of love is deleted.

The effect of these changes is that Brick seems a stronger person. And, though he doesn't sweep his wife off to bed as Stanley Kowalski would have done, it now seems plausible that (in Williams' words), "he was warmed and charmed by this delightful girl, with her vivacity, her humor, her very admirable courage and pluckiness and tenacity, which are almost the essence of life itself." Their future may appear a shade happier than in the first version, but no sensual paradise can be anticipated.

Big Daddy's re-entrance into the play is interesting. He has softened considerably since the horrifying revelation. He comes back in the new cashmere robe that Maggie and Brick gave him for his birthday, his "soft birthday," he now calls the occasion. The surprise entrance catches Gooper clutching his "pregnant-looking" briefcase full of legal papers, much to his embarrassment. This serves the old man as a pretext for a rotten joke (eventually removed from the acting version for fear of the censor's wrath). Maggie's anouncement is made as she kneels before Big Daddy, and the lie seems an act of love. Big Daddy raises her to her feet, calls his lawyer for the drawing of a new will, and takes Big Mama off to the belvedere. The scene is in character as we have come to know the old gentleman. The rebellion has subsided; he finds peace in the hope offered by Maggie; and in his gentle act toward Big Mama, we sense that their last days together will be a brief sunset of love.

But this second more hopeful and consoling conclusion is out of character for the author. One point for which Tennessee Williams has been admired is that his empathy for his characters does not lead him to deflect their inevitable and disastrous courses. The changes in both Big Daddy and Brick, well written though they may be, are not consistent with what the author has prepared us to expect. The audience may now leave the theatre with a sigh of relief, but suspecting, perhaps, that the whole truth has not been told.

The play raised still another issue. Some critics felt that Williams had at last come to grips with the problem of homosexuality, but others felt that the author had evaded it. Is Brick a homosexual and, if he is, can he be cured?

Williams replied that he considered ambiguities sometimes artistic and always defensible, but that he had not intended to be ambiguous or evasive in Brick's case. Quoting from the play's text, he says of Big Daddy and Brick: "The thing they're discussing, timidly and painfully on the side of Big Daddy, fiercely, violently on Brick's side, is the inadmissable thing that Skipper and Brick would rather die than live with. The fact that if it existed it had to be disavowed to 'keep face' in the world they lived in, a world of popular heroes, may be at the heart of the 'mendacity' that Brick drinks to kill his disgust with. It may be the root of his collapse. Or it may be only a single manifestation of it, not even the most important." After all, there should be some mystery left in the revelation of character. "You may prefer to be told precisely what to believe about every character in a play, you may prefer to know precisely what will be the future course of their lives, happy or disastrous or anywhere in between. Then I am not your playwright." As for Brick and the possibility of homosexuality—"He probably,—no, I would even say quite certainly,—went no further in physical expression than clasping Skipper's hand across the space between their twin-beds in hotel-rooms and yet—his sexual nature was not innately 'normal.'" He certainly loved Skipper much more that he will ever love Maggie. But Brick's sexual adjustment, says Williams, "was, and must always remain, a heterosexual one."

Other points came under attack as well. Even without the deleted obscene joke, audiences thought the play inordinately dirty. Williams insisted that the four-letter words helped to establish some of the characters. A man like Big Daddy could hardly speak without them.

When Williams heard that the word was getting around town that this was a dirty play, he was disturbed. He did not want a success gained by smut. Some of the profanity was cut from the acting version and more from the film version. Tennessee Williams never seems to be quite aware of the sensationalism of his language and ideas. Mr. Bentley objected to the recurrent question, "How good is he (or she) in bed?" People generally do not ask this question, especially of people near and dear to them. He insists that the script is dirty, only the production is "aggressively clean."

Most critics felt, nevertheless, that *Cat on a Hot Tin Roof* was the work of a mature artist. Brooks Atkinson hailed Williams' emergence as a competent craftsman from his period of experimentation. "Seldom has there been a play in which the expression of thought and feeling has been so complete." *Cat* swept the honors for the year, winning Tennessee Williams his second Pulitzer prize and his third Critics' award.

Much of the praise again went to Elia Kazan for his direction and to Jo Mielziner for his scenery. Burl Ives' robust portrayal of Big Daddy pleased the critics, too. Barbara Bel Geddes was slightly less pleasing as Maggie; Ben Gazzara was a credible, charming Brick. Pat Hingle as Gooper and Mildred Dunnock as Big Mama demonstrated, said one critic, "that to a real actor there is no such thing as an ungrateful part."

Cat's European reception resembled that of William's earlier triumphs. The critics gave it a cool reception, but it was a box-office success.

Cat also reached Hollywood. M.G.M. purchased the script of its former employee as a vehicle for Grace Kelly; but its eventual star was Elizabeth Taylor, as Maggie; this, her first Williams role, won her a dramatic triumph.

Cat on a Hot Tin Roof deserved its awards and the half-million dollars that Hollywood paid for it. It is a mature and beautiful work of art. Perhaps some of its depth derived from the freedom the author now felt. For the first time, he was able to use his father in his art. In *The Glass Menagerie,* he had left the father out as if he were no part of the family. In *Streetcar,* if the father is seen at all, it is in the image of the apelike Stanley. But in *Cat,* the father becomes a central, powerful, colorful, sympathetic study. Big Daddy far transcends any other Williams male portrait. He has more individuality and depth than the ex-Captain in *You Touched Me!* and more understanding and tolerance than the old salesman in "The Last of My Solid Gold Watches." On a purely personal basis, we must judge Big Daddy a remarkable achievement. Williams' lifelong hatred of this masculine tyrant had finally softened after the old man's death, to understanding, respect, and even love.

The relationship between Brick and Big Daddy is, in many ways, the one Williams and his father had had, the brick wall isolating them from one another so that all their talks ended in misunderstanding. The masculinity of the domineering father who finds it hard to understand the idealistic, yielding sensitiveness of the son is an echo of that earlier, impossible relationship. To this the author now adds real affection. Now each would love to be able to communicate with the other. For Big Daddy Brick has become the most important being in his life. He would like to mold him with those huge hands of his into the commanding heir who will efficiently manage the Pollitt estate. But he simply can't see the delicate shadings of truth and falsehood that flicker through Brick's mind. Yet his inability to understand Brick's nature and difficulties in no way lessens his love for him. The relationship has subtlety and truth.

And, for the first time in a major Williams play, latent homosexuality in a protagonist is acknowledged. In *Streetcar* the key to Blanche's problems was a homosexual husband. We suspect, however, that in her case and in others, the puritanical, idealistic, confused females are really only female impersonators. Stanley Hyman, the critic, discusses this possibility in an article on the Williams short story "Rubio y Morena." He calls the trick the "Albertine" strategy (from the Albert-Albertine reference in Proust): the sexes change places, especially in love affairs so that the female becomes the aggressive; the male the passive party, as in Maggie's and Brick's relationship in *Cat*. When the story deals with homosexuality and the author is employing the Albertine strategy, the male is pictured as a female, like the gaunt, masculine girl in "Rubio y Morena."

Williams, apparently, has been discussing his own situation in most of his plays. The female who claims his sympathy is an expression of many of his own needs and blocks. His idealism is constantly outraged by the carnality of the physical. When, like Alma, he tries to reject his Puritanism, he is trapped in an equally unrealistic anti-Puritanism.

The same conflict immobilizes Brick. He can't help his friend Skipper or himself because he is too prudish to discuss homosexuality. Big Daddy sees the problem in cruder terms but with

more sympathy; no nice idealism veils his matter-of-fact vision. The
way to help Skipper, Big Daddy feels, would have been not to break
the friendship but to talk with him. To Brick, however, the whole
thing is dirty. He is so afraid of his latent homosexuality and so
much a victim of his own conflicting drives that he can't help
Skipper, and becomes, thereby, an unintentional accomplice in
Skipper's death. This is no evasion on Williams' part. Brick simply
can't acknowledge the homosexual tendency within himself because he accepts the world's judgment upon it. It is an honest study
of a man's reaction to an inadmissible truth.

The little boy in St. Louis, chased home by bullies shouting
"Sissy!" and taunted at home by a father who called him "Miss
Nancy," could certainly understand Brick's feelings. *Cat,* unlike
so many of the short stories which sympathize with homosexuality
(see "One Arm" for an interesting variant) is no defense of perversion. It calls for understanding, even possibly for a cure, or at
least for an adjustment. This is another healthy point in the play.
For once Williams discusses perversion and idealism sensibly and
honestly without any apparent need to shock or hide behind a
female mask.

Another healthy new element is the characterization of Maggie.
She has more fibre and vitality than Stella, more reality than Rosa
Gonzales, more practicality and sense than Serafina. Tennessee
Williams believes in her. She is an American girl drawn from those
he could know, not a Latin whom he romanticizes. If Brick's salvation is possible, she will be the means to effect it. She loves him de-
votedly, but she is also sensual, like Big Daddy, though not prom-
iscuous. We see her frustrated and unhappy now, but we sense
that she has the tenacity and strength to triumph. Tennessee Williams is no longer the artist exclusively of decadent Southern misfits. Maggie is a real and charming human being. It is a pleasure to
see Williams so infatuated with her.

Sex is more varied in this play than in most Williams dramas.

The author seems to have a maturer view of the possible combinations of love and lust: ideal love of friends (spoiled by Skipper's intrusion of the sexual), love of parent for child (which Big Mama feels to an almost incestuous degree for Brick), lust between the sexes (which Gooper and Mae experience, producing their children in litters), and love-lust between the sexes (which Big Mama feels for Big Daddy and Maggie feels for Brick). The last of these combines sex with respect and devotion. It is certainly a more ideal possibility than Stella's surrender to Stanley or Serafina's use of Alvaro. Williams seems to have realized that Lawrence needs tempering; all the world's problems are not to be solved in the sexual embrace. There are organs functioning above the waist. At last, he combines the need for ideals with a reasonable evaluation of physical hungers. Williams' men and women still fail to come together satisfactorily, probably because the author's own love was so cruelly frustrated, and because his observation has not led him to alter his belief that a malignant universe keeps lovers apart. But at least, even though it remains hypothetical, the ideal proposed is becoming more normal and optimistic.

The old themes are also there. *Cat* again explores the problem of life-lies. The truth, though necessary, is invariably painful and occasionally fatal. The masks that men wear allow them to respect themselves, but bar them from self-realization. This play's only movement is the uncovering of truths. The decisive airing comes in the scene between Big Daddy and Brick, when revelations are exchanged like blows. But, the storm over, the last act can be quiet, if not happy. Unlike O'Neill, Tennessee Williams is beginning to believe that men can live without "pipe dreams." At least briefly, each man can and should look clearly at the dismaying truth in his own heart. Paradoxically, the view will reveal different things to each man. Like Pirandello, Williams believes that "'Truth' has a protean nature, that its face changes in the eyes of each beholder."

There is also the recurrent theme of shattered ideals—Big Daddy's hope of a robust old age and Brick's spiritualized friendship for Skipper. Brick is foolish to feel disillusioned; to come to satisfactory terms with life he need only modify his dreams. But we know that Brick won't change.

Another theme is the family hostility, pointed up, here, in the viciousness of Gooper's and Mae's jibes at Brick and their callousness to the news of Big Daddy's approaching death. Even when mutual needs force the family into temporary unity, it lacks sympathy. The family unites to secure individual benefits but not in mutual affection, though Big Mama does love deeply and selflessly.

Another theme, linked to this, is man's inability to communicate with his fellows. "Each of us is sentenced to solitary confinement in our own skins," says the shy author. Unable to speak without painful embarrassment, he assumes his problem to be a universal one. He confesses, in the prefatory essay to this play, "A morbid shyness once prevented me from having much direct communication with people, and possibly that is why I began to write to them plays and stories. But even now when that tongue-locking, face-flushing, silent and crouching timidity has worn off with the passage of the troublesome youth that it sprang from, I still find it somehow easier to 'level with' crowds of strangers in the hushed twilight of orchestra and balcony sections of the theatres than with individuals across a table from me." People discuss the surface of life, afraid to reveal their inner thoughts to the scathing scrutiny of their fellows. And even when they can count on the sympathy of the listener, words cannot convey all they wish to say. Williams feels that it is because of this "thwarted effort to break through walls to each other" that we talk and write and wire, clasp hands, fight, and even destroy one another. "It is a lonely idea, a lonely condition, so terrifying to think of that we usually don't." Since man confuses himself with his masks and lies, he can't make another understand what he, himself, shrinks from understanding. Here, too, Williams is working with the ideas of the subtle Pirandello, the philosopher-dramatist who explored the problem of the many faces of truth and of personality.

In spite of the violence of much of its language and the sensational appeal of many of its human difficulties and expressions, *Cat on a Hot Tin Roof* is more subdued and more real than either *Summer and Smoke* or *A Streetcar Named Desire*. There is no doom like the brothel or the madhouse for its characters. *Cat* has one of the precious few successful conclusions Williams has been able to find for any story.

The direction in which *Cat* appeared to be carrying Tennessee Williams was a healthy and optimistic one. Then, suddenly two disasters struck to reverse this trend. One was a shattering Broadway failure; the other was the death of his grandfather.

Mrs. Dakin, his loving, concerned, generous grandmother, had died a few months before the success of *The Glass Menagerie,* a triumph that would have given her immeasurable pride and pleasure. Later, Tennessee Williams invited his grandfather to come and stay with him. The old gentleman, straight-backed and courtly, agreed to live with his grandson for several years in New York and Florida. Despite his clerical collar, the retired clergyman enjoyed his cocktails, loved meeting the celebrated people who gathered around his grandson, and remained unshocked by anything Williams wrote. He enjoyed reading and reciting Shakespeare. He and the author were a close and devoted pair. They made a game of seeing to it that he lived to be a hundred. The Reverend Walter E. Dakin died two years short of the goal, in 1955.

Recalling the old gentleman's memories of the English violets he had seen in his first parish in South Pittsburgh, Tennessee Williams transported a blanket of the lovely blooms from New York to the funeral in St. Louis. In his grandfather died the embodiment of a beauty that Williams had envisioned as the classical elegance of the aristocratic South, symbols of which recur in his dramas, though he never used Walter Dakin, himself.

Tennessee Williams' next works were uninspired rehashes of older stories. When once again he was able to create original new dramas, they had turned back to violence, disease, hatred, and disintegration.

CHAPTER XII

Williams Warmed Over

While still riding the wave of popularity that followed *Cat*, Tennessee Williams decided to use it to the advantage of some old favorites in his trunk. Williams does not abandon an unsuccesssful or incomplete work, but reshapes it in different forms. Short stories and one-act plays develop into fuller, more complex ideas, and finally full-length plays. "Portrait of A Girl in Glass" ripened into *The Glass Menagerie*, "The Yellow Bird" became *Summer and Smoke*, "Ten Blocks on the Camino Real" lengthened into *Camino Real*, "Three Players of a Summer Game" turned into *Cat on a Hot Tin Roof*, and after *Cat* two one-acters, "The Long Stay Cut Short" or "The Unsatisfactory Supper" and "27 Wagons Full of Cotton" were merged in *Baby Doll*.

This fusion took little creative effort. Williams had used the same characters in both; so he needed only to unite the plots. He didn't even do this with any thoroughness. The finished product still contains a double plot, joined by a single solution. Its germ had been in Williams' mind since that summer in McBurney's attic when he had laughed over an idea he had for a story: a huge woman's seduction by an undersized man wielding a whip. Most of the writing had been done years before; he had completed the scenario by the time *Cat* was securely launched on Broadway, and Elia Kazan had filmed most of it before February, 1956.

Both sketches are studies in human malevolence, set in an Erskine Caldwell-type South. "The Unsatisfactory Supper," which had appeared in the *American Blues* collection of one-acters, has only three characters. The two major characters are Baby Doll, a large, indolent, stupid, mean woman; and her husband, the equally hateful, crass Archie Lee. This particular evening, their wrangle is over the supper of uncooked greens offered by Baby Doll's Aunt Rose, a sweet, senile spinster, who inadvertently forgot to light the stove. "She is the type of old lady, about eighty-five years old, that resembles a delicate white-headed monkey." With frightened humility, she tries to make up for it by offering to fix them Eggs Birmingham. Having run through the relatives who might let her stay with them, she is desperate not to lose her last refuge before the country poorhouse.

But Archie Lee has decided to get rid of her, fearing that she might catch a lingering disease that would require expensive medicine. Knowing that none of Baby Doll's kin would help finance even a funeral, Archie Lee meanly threatens Baby Doll ". . . if she breaks down an' dies on us here, I'm giving you fair warning—I'll have her burned up and her ashes put in an old Coca-Cola bottle." When Aunt Rose reappears with an arm load of roses, which she calls "poems of nature," he meets her with a blunt question about her future plans. Trying to avoid the inevitable, she turns the discussion to Jesus and hopes of heaven. But Archie Lee flatly demands that she leave first thing in the morning.

Suddenly a twister appears. While the others rush into the house, "Aunt Rose remains in the yard, her face still somberly but quietly thoughtful. The loose gray calico of her dress begins to whip and tug at the skeleton lines of her figure." As the tornado nears, "she looks wonderingly at the sky, then back at the house beginning to shrink into darkness, then back at the sky from which the darkness is coming, at each with the same unflinching but troubled expression. . . . Nieces and nephews and cousins, like pages of an album, are rapidly turned through her mind, some of them loved as children but none of them really her children and all of them curiously unneedful of the devotion that she had offered so freely as if she had always carried an armful of roses that no one had offered a vase to receive." The play ends with the twister's catching the old woman and whipping her toward the rosebush.

The story, especially in its final stage directions, mingles a fragile and sweet poignancy with a biting cruelty. It has characteristic Williamsian characters and touches, including the rose symbol and the broken moth-woman.

The characters of the other story, "27 Wagons Full of Cotton," include Baby Doll (now called Flora) and Archie Lee (now named Jake). Baby Doll has evolved into a stupider, but somewhat more benign elephant lady and Jake is older and more brutal toward his wife. The story revolves around a case of arson and its aftermath. Jake burns down a business rival's cotton gin and forces Baby Doll to provide his alibi. His simple-minded wife apparently enjoys Jake's sadistic love making, as he alternates between baby-talk and arm-twisting. The morning after the fire, Silva Vicarro, owner of the burned gin, brings his twenty-seven wagons full of cotton to Jake's mill for ginning. Jake leaves Silva, a "small and wry man of dark Latin looks and nature," with Flora while he goes off to work. Vicarro traps Flora in her witless lies about the previous night. Determined to take his revenge on her ample flesh, he moves with quiet mastery through a rape-seduction scene.

When Flora emerges on the porch that evening, "Her appearance is ravaged. Her eyes have a vacant limpidity in the moonlight, her lips are slightly apart." Moving with her hands stretched gropingly before her till she reaches the pillar of the house, she stops and stands moaning. "Her hair hangs loose and disordered.

The upper part of her body is unclothed except for a torn pink band about her breasts. Dark streaks are visible on the bare shoulders and arms and there is a large discoloration along one cheek. A dark trickle, now congealed, descends from one corner of her mouth."

When Jake returns from his day's work he is so elated by his profitable day that he is unaware of anything peculiar except for her idiotic laughter. That, he assumes, is the result of her being on a "goddam jag." Although Flora tries to tell him what his crime has cost her, he is oblivious to her hints. He sees no irony in the "good neighbor policy" Vicarro proposes: that Jake will gin all of his cotton while Vicarro will spend the long afternoons of the ginning being entertained by Flora. The play ends with Flora considering herself, for the first time, "mama" rather than "baby," sitting idiotically rocking her white kid purse, and singing a lullaby of the sinister possibilities ahead: "Down will come Baby—cradle—an' —all;"

The inhuman, racialist Jake is a symbol of the decadent Southerner, and the Italian newcomer's peculiar vengeance—taking over the woman of the vanquished—is symbolic of the replacement of the decaying strain by a new stock.

Baby Doll is the unique example of a Williams drama written exclusively for films. The published version of the film script lacks his characteristic poetic commentaries on people and setting.

The film version develops the Baby Doll-Archie Lee marital difficulties by adding a note of frustration. Baby Doll married Archie Lee when her father died, but on condition that she remain a virgin until her twentieth birthday, two years off. The time of the story is immediately before the long-awaited birthday and consummation of the marriage. At this point Baby Doll exacts further conditions. Before she will be, as she delicately expresses it, "ready," she must have a fully furnished house. When Archie Lee can't meet payments and the furniture company comes to repossess the furniture, Baby Doll pouts and announces the deal is off. Archie then demands that Baby Doll's Aunt Rose leave to reduce their expenses, but Baby Doll insists that she stay. Then Archie Lee has one of his rare glimmers of thought. He decides to recoup his financial losses by burning out the competition.

During a community gathering for the celebration of the rival plantation's first aniversary, Archie sets fire to the gin. Since the natives resent the meteoric rise of the foreigner, no neighbor makes a move to help Silva put out the fire. The firemen are worse than ineffectual, and closeups of their expressions disclose pleasure as the flames mount. The desperate Silva rushes into the fire for evidence of arson, and finds a kerosene can, which he shows to the marshal but does not give it to him, knowing better than to trust the law in this hostile community. But when he gives the can to one of his farmhands, the man is set upon and the can taken from him. With no evidence, and nothing in his heart but rage, Vicarro threatens to take his cotton elsewhere to have it ginned. The marshal, in a voice that speaks for the community, hints that this would be unwise: "You take the advice of an old man who knows this country like the back of his hand. It's true you made a lot of enemies here. You happen to be a man with foreign blood. That's a disadvantage in this country. A disadvantage at least to begin with. But you added stubbornness and suspicion and resentment." Silva, calmer now, reconsiders. He quietly surveys the group, noting the absence of one gin-owner, Archie Lee Meighan. Archie Lee, he says quietly, will be the one to gin his cotton for him.

The narrative of "27 Wagons Full of Cotton" completes the story. Silva brings the cotton to Archie, whose antiquated gin soon breaks down. While Archie goes off to Memphis for new parts, Silva has one of his men replace the broken cylinder from his own stock and continue the work. With Archie away and Aunt Rose off to the county hospital, Silva has Baby Doll all to himself. He immediately traps her into contradictory statements about the pre-

vious evening, then chases her through the yard and into the
house, where he corners her in the attic. Silva then has her sign
an affidavit certifying Archie's guilt of arson. With the paper in
his pocket, Silva slides down the banister and prepares to leave
the house—to Baby Doll's intense disappointment. During the
chase she had first feared, then anticipated, being raped, and is
disappointed now that he wanted only the signature. Understanding her thoughts, Silva says gently, "You're a child, Mrs. Meighan.
That's why we played hide-and-seek, a game for children. . . ."
Now, he wants only to go home and take a nap. Baby Doll shyly
suggests that he stay and rest in the crib where she usually sleeps.
Suddenly, there is the effect of two timid children trying to strike
up a friendship. He smiles and accepts, requesting that she sing
him to sleep.

At the end of the day, Archie charges breathlessly into town only
to find everyone sniggering at him. When Baby Doll appears on
the porch in a silk wrapper, and Silva follows, looking cocky and
rested, Archie becomes suspicious. The lazy afternoon, which we
are to assume did not include a seduction, has taught her the truth
about her husband. He belongs to the ineffectual and destructive
sort who blow things up and burn things down. When they cannot
meet fair competition, they commit arson. With this display of
new wisdom and atypical vocabulary, Baby Doll saunters off to
ask Vicarro for a drink of the fresh, sweet well water that only he
has been able to pump. The new maturity, softness, femininity that
Baby Doll displays infuriate the suspicious husband.

Just then Aunt Rose calls them in to an unsatisfactory supper of
uncooked greens, for which Archie would have had no appetite no
matter how appetizing. Although Archie is interested when Silva
offers to let him gin his cotton from now on, he suspect's Vicarro's
motives. Not man enough to confront Silva, Archie picks on a
weaker person, threatening to throw Aunt Rose out of the house.
His brutality elicits Silva's dry comment, "Mr. Meighan, when a

man is feeling uncomfortable over something it often happens that he takes out his annoyance on some completely innocent person just because he has to make somebody suffer." Then, with old country dignity and courtesy, he offers to drive Aunt Rose wherever she chooses to go. To her reply that she hasn't anywhere else to go, Silva answers gallantly, "Yes, you do. I need someone to cook for me at my place. I'm tired of my own cooking and I am anxious to try those Eggs Birmingham you mentioned." Thus he helps her maintain her self-respect and leave the Meighan house with dignity. By this gesture, Vicarro also shames Archie Lee.

His anger at this and at Baby Doll's new attitude, fed by drink, builds to an explosion. When he hurls accusations at the couple, Silva first deflates him by a quiet medical diagnosis of his livid coloring and then demolishes him with a summary of the facts, including his knowledge of the arson, his possession of the signed affidavit, and a candid statement of his relationship with Mrs. Meighan. "Well, all I can say is, a certain attraction—exists! Mutually, I believe! But nothing's been rushed. I needed a little shut-eye after last night's—excitement. I took a nap upstairs in the nursery crib with the slats let down to accommodate my fairly small frame, and I have faint recollections of being sung to by someone—a lullaby song that was—sweet . . . and the touch of— cool fingers, but that's all, absolutely!" He is foreign, he admits, but not revengeful—"at least not more than is rightful."

Baby Doll, by now thoroughly disgusted with her husband and frightened of his growing violence, decides she will leave with Aunt Rose. At this, Archie goes berserk. Vicarro climbs a pecan tree and pulls Baby Doll up behind him. Before there is any real harm, the chief of police arrives to lead off a sobbing, staggering Archie. Baby Doll, chewing a pecan, looks down at her aunt and says, "I feel sorry for poor old Aunt Rose Comfort. She doesn't know where to go or what to do. . . ."

But Silva asks in reply, "Does anyone know where to go, or what to do?"

The play ends with the sound of Aunt Rose's singing "Rock of Ages."

Though this film script is an improvement upon the one-acters out of which it grew, it is undistinguished in characterization, plotting, and theme. Its people are closer to the "Tobacco Road" half-wits than to the more interesting, intelligent, cultured, but confused members of the usual Tennessee Williams world. The absence of allegory, novel stage effects, and poeticizing should please Williams' critics, but its uninspired account of subnormal people is an unappetizing substitute. More realistic and believable than *Battle of Angels,* it lacks the fire and excitement of the latter.

Even so, as in *The Rose Tattoo,* Williams proves himself superb at comedy. He writes from inside his characters to whom arson, adultery, and lynching are the resources and diversions of a drab and impotent existence, not actions with moral significance. His sympathy for the fiery little, whip-carrying, Lawrencian Vicarro and Baby Doll's accusation of her husband's malevolence are the only hints that this is the same author who generally takes a much soberer view of such problems. Perhaps it is good for Tennessee Williams to write an occasional comedy, even though it fails to measure up to his tragedies. It gives him perspective and objectivity, forcing him to restrain the anger that wells up in him over prejudice, cruelty and deceit. Unfortunately, he was not able to carry this over to his next tragedy, as he had done in moving from *The Rose Tattoo* to *Cat on a Hot Tin Roof.*

Baby Doll had great popular appeal. Kazan's production intensified the vitality, color, mood, and even symbolism in the script. Carroll Baker's portrayal of Baby Doll had sweetness and warmth. Refusing to put on the fat necessary to the part as written, she added physical beauty to it. Karl Malden, as in *Streetcar,* gave an authentic impression of sweating frustration; and Eli Wallach, in his first film appearance, made an excellent Vicarro. Here acting and direction were indisputably decisive for the success of the picture. Kazan's direction shows genius.

Kazan's new company, Newtown Productions, filmed the picture at Benoit, Mississippi. Except for the lead parts, the members of the cast were townspeople. He was pleasantly surprised by the townspeople's reactions. Since there were no hotels for miles, he and his cast roomed with them. He recalls the town's changing responses: "At first we were received warily. They were on guard. But you know a lot of human differences are solved when people are thrown together. People really basically want to be liked."

Sensing this, he decided to make them want to join in the movie making. "We had a personal story. We went around getting acquainted. I let them watch me shoot. I attended a wedding—the son of the man in whose house we stayed. Mildred Dunnock could have been elected Mayor; they adored her." By the time they finished, the troupe felt they had gained the acceptance of the town.

"We got more open-heartedness, more genuine hospitality there than in any other location I've worked at," Kazan said. One day, he mentioned casually that he would like to have a mule for one of the scenes. Before he had noticed what was happening, a man had left and had returned with three mules—so that he could choose the best among them. "One cold night, when we filmed the burning of the gin mill, the whole town was rooting that everything would come off right." In ten weeks, they had filmed eighty percent of the picture. Summarizing the experience, Kazan said, "They had a ball. So did we."

When the picture was finally wound up in New York, the cast staged an impromptu party with a single bottle of whiskey serving for toasts all around. After the hand-shaking and back-slapping Kazan felt the inevitable pang at the breaking up of a team. "You feel so wedded to a crew," he commented. There's so much sentiment—"It's one of the strongest bonds I know."

His actors felt and still feel the same way about him. Eli Wallach is one of many who have testified to Kazan's genius for directing. He's "wonderful, disarmingly simple. . . . He knows how to wind you up, stimulate you, make you want to do things."

This small, cat-footed, agile man is about Williams' age. Soft-spoken, but fast-thinking, Elia Kazan has a brilliant critical mind that influences playwrights to do more revisions for him than for any other director they know; and he has a similar knack for drawing inspired performances from his actors. Like Williams, he despises city clothes and party manners. Most often he appears in a lumber jacket, open shirt, and wrinkled slacks. Vivien Leigh once said of him, "Gadge is the kind of man who sends a suit out to be cleaned and rumpled." Clifford Odets has called him a man of "natural responses." If he is bored by an individual or a group, "he simply departs without apology or explanation."

There have also been abundant complaints about him. Eric Bentley comments that Kazan "goes to work on the actors' nerves like an egg beater. His orgasmic organization of scenes has become a mannerism: time after time, the slow to-and-fro of dialogue works itself up to a frenetic climax."

The most frequently used adjective for a Kazan production is *nervous*. His concern over detail keeps the action in continuous flux. His own intensity communicates to the players, who almost invariably do a superior job for him. Many believe that his work with the Actors' Studio, where he applied the Stanislovskian techniques of the Moscow Art Theatre, helped redeem acting from the low state into which it was falling. He had a large part in the training of many fine new actors who perform with a truth and expressiveness unparalleled in theatre history.

When he turned to films, Kazan added to the naturalistic acting and stylized and symbolized direction he was famous for, a new treatment of cinema resources—new uses of lighting and camera—off-angle shots, intense closeups, and daring long shots. In *Streetcar*'s filming, he reproduced the stage scrim effect by photograph-

ing Blanche in filtered lights until her moment of truth, then
flashed the naked light harshly on her face; in the rape scene, he
recorded her reaction by darting the camera's eye crazily over the
room. His script changes have brought both approbation and
condemnation. His creative work in helping Arthur Miller develop
Willie Loman's character, or in getting Tennessee Williams to
bring Big Daddy back into the final scene of *Cat* illustrates his
view of what a good director must do.

In some cases where Tennessee Williams calls for realistic settings, Kazan has influenced him to accept, instead, the poetic
setting and the stylized presentation associated with Williams.
Kazan has done so in the belief that these changes better express
the author's personality. Henry Hewes is one of the many critics
who feel that the director was expressing his own personality instead of Williams', thereby creating ambiguous works. Much of
Williams' sober laughter at the world's falsity appeared to have
been elicited by Kazan. Strangely enough, while seeming to pull
the author away from his own inner discipline and emphasizing
anti-social attitudes, the director has seemed intent on making
the characters more likeable and the actions less harsh. For example, he suggested the alternate ending for *Cat,* and the changes
in Vicarro's and Baby Doll's characterizations, as well as the softened conclusion for the film.

The new, un-Williamsian conclusion to *Baby Doll* made critics
wonder just how good Kazan actually was for Williams. He could
make him popular, but could he allow him to be great in his own
way? Many felt that the relationship was beginning to show the
strain of two powerful, creative minds tugging in different directions. Mr. Hewes noted that, "Kazan and Williams both make the
strongest possible effort to remain great friends," implying hidden
or unspoken conflicts. There was never any open break as there
had been between Kazan and Arthur Miller. (During the Congressional investigations of Communist activities, Kazan admitted his

one-time membership in the Communist Party and named other members. Miller, on the other hand, said in 1956 that he had never been a Communist Party member, and had steadfastly balked at implicating others; he considered Kazan wrong for having done so.) But the beginnings of a quieter schism in the Williams-Kazan axis were visible.

Baby Doll made a sensational entrance into New York City. Two artists, Robert Everhart and Jim Pasquin, were commissioned to paint Carroll Baker's picture on a block-long billboard over Times Square, delighting passersby with the 75-foot legs and 8-foot eyebrows of the thumb-sucking heroine. Then, when the fifty-dollar-a-ticket premier (for the Actors' Benefit) was publicized, the red-headed hussy was denounced by Mayor Wagner, whose name had appeared by mistake as a sponsor. Right after this snub, although the picture had passed the Motion Picture Industry's board of censors under the old Hays Code, and the New York State Board of Censors, it got a "condemned for all" rating from the Roman Catholic Legion of Decency.

Not content with the Legion's blacklisting it, Cardinal Spellman made it the subject of his first public condemnation since his attack on the Communists for jailing the Hungarian Cardinal Mindszenty in 1949. He took the pulpit of St. Patrick's Cathedral on December 16, 1956, to warn American Roman Catholics away from the film. He voiced his horror at *Baby Doll*'s "revolting theme," the brazen advertising promotion, and the film's contemptuous defiance of natural law. He called *Baby Doll* an "obvious violation" of the motion-picture code, referred to the "conscienceless venal attitude" of its promoters, and insisted that it would have a "definite corruptive moral influence" on the American public.

Most magazine critics agreed with the Cardinal that the movie exhibited sex to a disgusting degree. To the *Saturday Review* it was "one of the most unhealthy and amoral pictures ever made in this country." To *Time* it was "the dirtiest American-made motion picture that has ever been legally exhibited." It is amusing to speculate on what these critics would have said if Messrs. Williams and Kazan had used the original script of "27 Wagons Full of Cotton" instead of the comparatively innocuous rewrite. Kazan replied to Cardinal Spellman that the film was not immoral and "I am outraged at the charge that it is unpatriotic. . . . But in this country judgments on matters of thought and taste are not handed down ironclad from an unchallenged authority. People see for themselves and finally judge for themselves. That's as it should be. It's our tradition and our practice. In the court of public opinion I'll take my chances."

Tennessee Williams was puzzled. "I can't believe that an ancient and august branch of the Christian faith is not larger in heart and mind than those who set themselves up as censors of a medium of expression that reaches all sections and parts of our country and extends the world over," he said wistfully. Years later, when he had had time to consider, he supposed it was the long seduction scene that bothered the clergy. It apparently didn't occur to him that *Baby Doll* expressed some unusual thoughts on marriage, to wit: that people may marry to secure themselves legal guardians until they reach the age of consent, that consummation may be delayed for years and may be used as one of the terms of a business contract, and if the marriage partner rouses disgust, it is commendable to take a lover. The ending of *Baby Doll* may be happy, but it is hardly orthodox. Williams admitted parts of the movie made him cringe. When asked to specify them, he answered, "The girl in it did a little too much licking of ice cream and too much sucking of her thumb, I think," apparently wondering if this could have been what upset the prelate and the Roman Catholic Church. He was never seen any conceivable way in which this comedy could contribute to delinquency of either adults or juveniles. The story never struck him as anything but funny. Possibly, he conceded, admittance to the film might be limited to adults. But after all, few children would understand or enjoy the Freudian symbolism and meaningful looks anyway.

In the meantime, Tennessee Williams had returned to his first love—*Battle of Angels*. He felt that, in spite of Boston, the play had more value than most plays that had won acceptance. If his public could now take the obscenity in *Cat*, the violence in *Streetcar*, and the sexuality in *The Rose Tattoo*, they would now be more sympathetic to the *Battle of Angels* than that opening night audience had been.

When it opened in 1957 in a new city, Washington, under a new title, *Orpheus Descending*, *Battle of Angels* was a thoroughly revised play. During the seventeen years since its catastrophic failure, Williams commented, "It never went into the trunk; it always stayed on the work bench." He decided to offer it, not "because I have run out of ideas or material for completely new work," but because he finally thought it finished. Of the revision, which he had decided would be his last, he said, "About 75 per cent of it is new writing, but what is much more important, I believe that I have now finally managed to say in it what I wanted to say, and I feel that it now has in it a sort of emotional bridge between those early years . . . and my present state of existence as a playwright. . . . Nothing is more precious to anybody than the emotional record of his youth, and you will find the trail of my sleeve-worn heart in this completed play that I now call *Orpheus Descending*." Also, he insists that the story of the "wild-spirited boy who wanders into a conventional community of the South and creates the commotion of a fox in a chicken coop" expresses the "unanswered questions that haunt the hearts of people and the difference between continuing to ask them, a difference represented by the four major protagonists of the play, and the acceptance of prescribed answers that are not answers at all, but expedient adaptations or surrender to a state of quandary."

One of the revisions of the original play had used a frame-device. Instead of a straight narrative, the author had set the first and last scenes after the events of the play. The drygoods store had been turned into a museum where tourists examined the relics of these tragic events. But the museum idea, although it lent perspective to the story, had further confused the already-confusing plot. The opening scene had scarcely been intelligible, with its unexplained allusions and its ironic treatment of the spinster sisters who had inherited the store after the mass tragedy. The direct treatment, to which Williams reverted, is quieter and more realistic. Yet, although the direct method is an improvement, it seems regrettable that the author felt obliged to discard his beloved flashback, as if realizing that his audience was impatient for him to get on with the story and skip the poeticizing.

Whenever Williams starts to revise, he seems to hit upon the same frame-device. His reason for this is the effect that time has on life. "It is the continual rush of time, so violent that it appears to be screaming," he observes, "that deprives our actual lives of so much dignity and meaning, and it is, perhaps more than anything else, the *arrest of time* which has taken place in a completed work of art that gives certain plays their feeling of depth and significance." Drama allows us to view people in a selective static world. By this means, the dramatist can give to characters and to their actions "a dimension and a dignity that they would likewise have in real existence, if only the shattering intrusion of time could be locked out."

Sometimes Tennessee Williams can give the chaotic world he sees about him a repose through a static presentation, leaving most of the action to memory. It allows, as in the Greeks' use of off-stage action, verbal beauty and excitement to replace the more vulgar reality. Frequently, though, he finds it impossible to give his stories the beauty of repose and restraint that he considers essential to the purest art. At such times, he creates his world outside of time in an artificial way. In *The Rose Tattoo*, for example, a folk

singer plays his guitar at the opening of the play, at each major
division, and at the final curtain, to suggest that the drama, like
its sister art, music, systematizes the chaotic world, giving it pattern and nobility. The frame of the revised *Camino Real* is Don
Quixote's dream. In the frame revision of *Battle of Angels* the
museum had made the action a part of the immortalized past.

Certainly Tennessee Williams has a valid point in using such
frames. They do fulfill his needs. But they are also a sort of
self-plagiarizing, repeating the same device for the same effect.
Even *The Glass Menagerie* seemed weakest at those moments
when the frame became noticeable, when Tom was admitting that
the story was all a part of his own romanticized memory. The
problem is that the frame allows Williams to escape the restriction
imposed by the dramatic situation and indulge his poeticizing. It
also gives him a deceptively warm feeling inside that he has constructed a neater work, not vulnerable to the usual critical harping
on weak plotting.

With the deletion of the museum scene, how was the exposition
to be handled? Much of Myra's background must be explained
before the audience can understand what the fuss is all about.
Rejecting a realistic solution, the author puts two outsiders on the
stage who, for the first half-hour of the play, talk about the
heroine's background and nature. Such a talky first act could succeed in *Cat,* because the talking was done by the main characters
and its subject was the dilemma of their relationship. But the
talking women in *Orpheus* are merely small-town gossips who
cannot engage our sympathy, and they play no real part in the
story. The author might as well have returned to the formal
Elizabethan prologue for his exposition.

Myra, renamed "Lady," to make her symbolic role as the Virgin
Mary a bit clearer, is given more background than previously. We
learn that her father, a Sicilian, had been an organ-grinder with
a monkey when he first came to this country and had had to find

some other livelihood when the monkey died. Jabe, now more a personification of evil than of death, becomes the focus of the local racialist prejudice. His cancer is now the symbol of communal corruption. Society, as a whole, is now the villain, rotten with hypocrisy, its church-supper religion covering malice and blood-lust and hatred of anything alien or free. *Orpheus* becomes a protest against the cruelty of humans, not of the gods. The same theme dominates *Sweet Bird of Youth*, a product of the same creative period.

Another innovation in *Orpheus* also echoes *Sweet Bird*, the picture of lost innocence. Val is less of a primitive, Lawrencian Christ figure than a variant of Chance Wayne, (in *Sweet Bird*) who has lost his youth and his purity. Val insists that, although he has lived amidst corruption, he is not corrupted. "Heavy drinking and smoking the weed and shacking with strangers is okay for kids in their twenties but this is my thirtieth birthday and I'm all through with that route." However, this semi-gigolo, semi-youth finds that reforming is not so easy as he had anticipated, and he decides on the gradual approach. The autographed guitar which he strums replaces the overly poetic, unfinished book of the earlier version. His search for purity rings true, and it is easier to sympathise with this shamed and disillusioned idealist than with the allegorical animal of *Battle of Angels*. After his affair with Lady, he agrees to stay with her—as an act of love. He is interrupted in the middle of a gesture of devotion by Jabe's vengeful shot which kills Lady, as in the earlier story. Val's battle for integrity against the tempting comforts of conformity, the urge to replace the snake-skin jacket with a blue-serge coat, seems more real than the simple animal purity of the earlier story.

There is also greater depth in the new portrayal of Lady, though her gains are not so great as Val's. The horrible sequence of her losses—first of her young lover, then of her father, then of her aborted child, then of her freedom in the whoredom of marriage to

Jabe—these, as in the earlier story, have left her empty in a seemingly barren universe. She finds revival in Val, or rather in the
virility he represents. In the new version, she is less patient in her
relations with the gossips, more at odds with her community. This
isolation makes her love affair more a childlike groping for protection than a release of overpowering sexual drives (more Williamsian than Lawrencian).

The third pariah of the town is now named Carol, not Cassandra. She is more believable, though less heroic. (Williams
appears to start with classical or religious archetypes but gradually
modifies them into modern Americans.) Carol, the sister of Lady's
old love, is paid to stay away from home. This relationship and her
previous meeting with Val in New Orleans make her role a more
organic part of the story. Instead of wearing bedraggled evening
gowns of spotted white satin, she now appears barefoot, clothed in
a raincoat and a turned-down sailor's hat; her face is powdered
white and her eyes heavily shadowed. She has become a Vieux
Carré beatnik.

In her eccentricities, she becomes a case study of a social deviate.
"I used to be what they call a Christ-bitten reformer. . . . You
know what this is?—a kind of benign exhibitionist." In this role,
she protested the wrongs done to the Negroes: "I thought it
wrong for pellagra and slow starvation to cut them down when the
cotton crop failed from army worm or boll weevil or too much rain
in summer. I wanted to, tried to, put up free clinics. I squandered
the money my mother left me on it." Then came the culminating
point in her private crusade, the Willie McGee case. "He was
sent to the chair for having improper relations with a white whore.
I made a fuss about it. I put on a potato sack and set out for the
capital on foot. This was in winter." She walked barefoot in her
burlap sack to deliver a personal protest to the governor of the
state. "Oh, I suppose it was partly exhibitionism on my part, but
it wasn't completely exhibitionism; there was something else in

it, too." She got only six miles out of town—"hooted, jeered at, even spit on!—every step of the way—and then arrested! guess what for? Lewd vagrancy! Uh-huh, that was the charge, 'lewd vagrancy,' because they said that potato sack I had on was not a respectable garment." And she concludes: "All that was a pretty long time ago, and now I'm not a reformer any more. I'm just a 'lewd vagrant.' And I'm showing the S.O.B.'s how lewd a lewd vagrant can be. . . ." Rumor has it that Carol is a junky as well as a lush, and on the police records she is also down as a reckless driver. All this the audience is expected to recognize as manifestations of her anger against a stagnant world, and not as the antics of a filthy-rich brat. The mulatto chauffeur, who, in the older play, was rumored to be Carol's lover, has now been replaced by an abstraction—interest in the Negro race.

As in the first version, Carol tries to seduce Val, but is activated now, like Lady, by a childlike need for human companionship. This over-bred, aristocratic outcast is attracted to the outcast savage, being akin in their mutual anachronism. Val understands her needs, takes her delicate wrist, examines it, and tells her she isn't built for passion. He prefers lusty Mediterranean women for his mistresses. Startled by his perception, she admits that the act of lovemaking is, for her, "almost unbearably painful, and yet, of course, I do bear it, because to be not alone, even for a few moments, is worth the pain and the danger." Their understanding is mutual; she sees the danger for him just as he sees it for her. When he exchanges his snake-skin jacket for a blue serge coat, she protests. "You've taken off the jacket that said: 'I'm wild, I'm alone!' and put on the nice blue uniform of the convict." These two anachronisms, the savage and the aristocrat, along with Lady, the foreigner, are the alien elements that disturb the town. Williams considered titling the rewrite *Something Wild in the Country*. These people, like The Mummers, represent the creative ferment of anarchy in a conformist world.

The other characters change very little in the revision. Jabe represents death, but as Pluto rather than Jehovah, and carries a lighter load of allegory. Vee, the primitive-painter mystic is more sympathetic. She is relieved of her former burder of Freudian "religious" paintings. Her frustrations in her marriage are clearer, as is her repressed disgust with the horrors she sees in "lynch justice." Val understands her through his own love of music and his quest for primordial purity. Their friendship is innocent of the sexual implications in the first play.

The role of her husband, the sheriff, is strengthened, as he jealously stalks his wife, suspecting her of lusting after Val. When he catches Val kissing her hands, he takes it as the beginning of a seduction. Enraged at Val's "messin' " with his wife, the sheriff gathers an angry mob and orders Val out of the county by sun-up. This incites a communal hysteria of sex envy. Jabe murders Lady and the mob lynches Val. Hanging not being enough to sate their cruelty, the mob burns Val to death with a blowtorch—a dramatic flourish that outdoes the bloodiest Elizabethan tragedians.

There are fewer minor characters than in the original version, but except for David, Myra's old love, they are given no greater depth. He explains that life has punished him for abandoning her. His marriage has been a whoredom, too, and left him unmanned. One new character enters, a nurse, who symbolizes the sterility of the scientific attitude. As she confirms Lady's illicit pregnancy, she voices the community's condemnation.

Despite these revisions, the fable itself remains essentially unchanged. It has become somewhat more compact and probable, with the climax rising more naturally out of emotional tensions. It is much more likely that a suspicious husband would attack a man like Val than that a blond from Waco would charge over the countryside screaming "Rape!" and the encounter between Lady and her old love is made more believable by his relationship to

Carol. The relationship between Val and Lady is developed more subtly and convincingly. In place of the alternations of open antagonism and embarrassed self-consciousness, there is a wary searching out of one another's personality. The physical part of the love affair has the hesitations natural to people who have been hurt, seeking to protect their pride.

Perhaps the most basic change is in the turn from the theme of a totalitarian God destroying those who break His petty rules and challenge His arbitrary judgments, to the theme of a totalitarian society destroying non-conformists. Here Williams is apparently moving toward society's castration of Chance in *Sweet Bird* and its cannibalistic martyrdom of Sebastian in *Suddenly Last Summer*. The sub-theme of legal versus real relationships echoes *Baby Doll*. The whoredom of Jabe's and Lady's marriage is "legal" while the decent love between her and Val is "adulterous."

The shift to Greek mythology spared Williams much controversy. Not only is it an interesting use of the Greek fables, but it also rouses no ire, since there is no pressure group of ancient Greeks to protest. Christianity, too, may be merely a beautiful allegory to Tennessee Williams, but he has been made painfully aware of Judeo-Christian sensibilities.

Although *Orpheus* may not "mix up sex and religion" like *Battle of Angels,* it is a much grimmer story. As the characters are made more understandable, they become less heroic. The underlying theory appears to be that we live in a world of psychopaths, not heroes. They have lost their dreams and their purity. Rather than plan an escape to the open life under the stars, Val contemplates a return to the "all-night bars with B-girls and raffish entertainers." He has given up the hope of discovering anything important. Lady is less of a lady in the new version. She appears as interested in the successful opening of a new department for the store as in this chance love affair, whose aim appears to be to prove her fertility. And Carol is not the beautiful wild aristocrat,

but a disillusioned reformer who recognizes the ugliness of people's lives, her own included.

In this tragedy, society as a whole is the villain, and there is no
salvation for anybody. The horror is thereby intensified. Myra
Mannes has said of Williams that he writes in the tragic tradition,
but he does not write tragedies. A play should leave the audience
cleansed and illuminated, not emotionally exhausted. *Orpheus
Descending* left a good many theatre-goers with "the feeling of
having been stretched on a rack for two hours." However, Williams
had previously written several gloom-and-doom plays that were
box-office successes. The blackness of the mood, therefore, does not
wholly account for *Orpheus'* failure.

Although Maureen Stapleton again proved herself an inspired
Williams' heroine, and that unfailing Williams' champion, Harold
Clurman, directed the play enthusiastically, *Orpheus* ran only
sixty-eight performances in New York. Most critics found it struc-
turally weak, theatrical, and obsessive in its thinking. But though
they considered it below Williams' standard, they considered a
second-rate Williams' play "more exhilarating than most of the
plays that turn up on Broadway."

Nonetheless, the reaction to it signalled a significant metamor-
phosis in public taste. Seventeen years after its original failure,
Orpheus raised hardly a single Puritan murmur. Brooks Atkinson
commented that *Orpheus Descending* was one of "Mr. Williams'
pleasantest plays" and went on to wonder what its original trouble
spots had been. Tennessee Williams had persuaded playgoers to
examine his exhibits of social ugliness without revulsion. They
still weren't comfortable about his generalizations, but now, at
least, they sat through the recitation of them and were frequently
touched by what they saw and heard. He had accomplished a
major task in educating theatregoers to accept determinedly *avant
garde* art.

Nevertheless, *Orpheus* failed. The author is not sufficiently objective about his own work to realize when he sounds like a parody of himself, as *Orpheus* unfortunately sometimes does. The audience rejected not the point of view, but the clumsiness of the play. As one critic pointed out, it is not so much whether the writer is an optimist or a pessimist, it is whether he presents his vision with artistry. The critical consensus was that *Orpheus* lacked the beauty that such a grim view must have in order to convince. Audiences took the critics' word for it and stayed away from the play.

European critics and audiences gave it a similar reception. Paris' *Orpheus* received mixed reviews, but no enthusiastic endorsement; the London reviews were "kindly but unenthusiastic," too. The play was an international failure—and the downcast playwright thought he had reached the end of his theatrical career.

"Possibly," he said, "I exaggerated the reactions; however, I became a little frightened. I've always been startled by people who are antagonized by plays for reasons other than the quality of the work. Some of my plays, I think, have suffered from a reaction of ethical bias and an imposed and conventional morality."

Hollywood bought *Orpheus,* retitling the photoplay *The Fugitive Kind,* and although it had a modest success as such, this did not, for Williams, mitigate the catastrophe of its failure on Broadway.

In addition, the increased production cost made the author feel responsible to those who suffered financial losses. "The obvious and biggest millstone," said Williams, commenting on the difficulties involved in Broadway productions, "is expense. That's why fresh plays don't get put on. . . . It took only about $20,000, if I remember, to stage, *Battle of Angels. Streetcar* cost at least three times that." *Orpheus* cost ten times as much as *Menagerie.* He became frightened of Broadway and of the critics who could so easily make or break a reputation. The next play, he determined, would be produced off-Broadway, in the relaxed atmosphere of the little theatres which he had always loved and in which he always felt comfortable. "I couldn't cope at this time with doing another controversial play on Broadway," he said. He also felt that he couldn't cope with the creative turmoil of another year like 1957. He had reached a breaking point. For the first time, he thought seriously of taking his personal and consequently his artistic problems to a psychiatrist.

There is a postscript to *Orpheus*'s history. In spite of its Broadway failure, Hollywood thought it would have box-office appeal. It was produced with Anna Magnani and Marlon Brando in the lead roles. These two temperamental stars made almost impossible demands. Mr. Brando wanted his part fattened and Miss Magnani insisted on Sidney Lumet's directing it. The production was delayed over a year. For the part of Carol, or Cassandra, they picked another Academy Award winner—Joanne Woodward—whose husband, Paul Newman, had appeared in the stage and film versions of *Cat* and later in *Sweet Bird*.

Williams did some work on the film script, but felt that he had almost no influence on the movie. Most of the time it was being shot, he was away on a four-month tour of Asia and Europe. He later admitted that he didn't enjoy his work with movies because when the author does his own screen adaptation he has little control over the final product. "Unfortunately, once a movie gets rolling, there's not much the author can do. Too many people are involved. And it's too difficult to keep checking up on it." He decided, after *Fugitive Kind,* that he would never do another movie adaptation, and he let someone else do the film work for *Roman Spring.* "There comes a time in life," he explained, sounding very old and very weary of it all, "when you have got to conserve your energy for what's most important to you. And the theatre is what's most important to me."

When he returned from his trip abroad, he was in time to make an unannounced appearance at a rough-cut showing of the film, put on as a sneak preview, after *The F.B.I. Story*. The theatre was crowded with teenagers who had come for the main attraction and did not appreciate the extra treat. As Tennessee Williams was leaving the theatre, someone spotted him. "There's Tennessee Williams!" came the shout, followed by a chorus of boos. Asked later what his response to the public insult had been, Williams said, cheerfully, "I turned and booed them back." The audience, he said, "looked like the juvenile delinquent kind." Since he has never aimed his stories at a juvenile audience, even non-delinquents, he was not the least perturbed. "It was pretty ridiculous to show *The Fugitive Kind* to that sort of audience."

Reporters wondered if he was pleased with the film, but he was restrained in his answer. He said thoughtfully, trying to avoid commitment that might prove bad publicity for the movie, "I would like to have seen it adhere more closely to the script." But he quickly added that he was too close to the situation to judge objectively.

At the time the not-altogether-satisfying film version appeared, a completely satisfying off-Broadway version was also opening. Tennessee Williams was finally to see the play win modest success. Two and a half years after its Broadway failure, a critic was to comment on the Gramercy Arts Theatre production of *Orpheus* that, like wine, the play improves with age. John Ramondetta and Ann Hamilton played the leads. The part of Carol went to Diane Ladd, a kin of Tennessee Williams', also a descendant of Sidney Lanier. She had not been chosen for that reason, the reviewers agreed, but for her talent. Williams considered the production superior to the film; after all, it followed the script better. "I was thoroughly delighted with it," he said happily. "I think Adrian Hall's brilliant staging has found the key to what I believe is my most difficult work." Once again, off-Broadway had come to the rescue.

CHAPTER XIII

Garden District

When *Orpheus* descended, one of Tennessee Williams' close friends suggested that he try a less violent subject for his next play. "Well," he answered, "the only way I can do that is go to an analyst." The idea amused him. He had been aware of the increasing horror in his plays. In an article written before the Washington opening of *Orpheus,* he protested that the developing tension and anger and violence of the plays were also those of the world in which we live. However, he admitted to an increasing tension in himself as a writer and as a person and that his writings did border on the psychotic. "I guess my work has always been a kind of psychotherapy for me." Perhaps, he mused, his popularity came from his sharing this therapy with his audience. To the startled query, "You think the world's going mad?" he replied, "Going? I'd say nearly gone! As the gypsy said in *Camino Real,* the world is a funny paper read backwards. And that way it isn't so funny." He felt that he had the right and the responsibility as a writer to express the tortured condition of his world, hoping that his plays could serve as a release for others as for himself.

Later, though, he acknowledged that he doesn't write about the world, but simply and exclusively about Tennessee Williams. "I

don't pretend to write about a world that has become increasingly
violent," he said, "I may write about troubled people, but I write
from my own tensions." He really has very little choice—he writes
as he must and can. Writing is the only secure and constant value
for this author. "I write," he says, "because I love writing." He
doesn't choose his themes; they obsess him. "Frankly," he said in
a moment of devastating self-analysis, "there must be some limitations in me as a dramatist. I can't handle people in routine situations. I must find characters who correspond to my own tensions.
If these people are excessively melodramatic . . . well, a play must
concentrate the events of a lifetime in the short span of a three-act
play. Of necessity these events must be more violent than life."
But the recognition that his art springs from his inner turmoil
makes psychiatric treatment hazardous. What if a successful adjustment were to seal off the fountainhead of his art?

But problems had accumulated that made psychiatric help ad-
visable. Among them were: claustrophobia, wanderlust, hypochondria, unpunctuality, alcoholism, and fear of suffocation. "It
was so bad," Williams commented, "that for a long time, when I
went for a walk, I couldn't walk down a street unless I could see a
bar—not because I wanted a drink, but because I wanted the
security of knowing it was there." He has been known to flee a
restaurant on finding its bar closed, and rush home to be where
the liquor was, even though he didn't especially want a drink. His
claustrophobia was similarly overpowering. Once, driving home
through New York's Brooklyn-Battery Tunnel, he became so
frightened that he almost leaped from the car. He had to have a
calming drink as soon as he emerged into an open street. He believes that fantasied threats to personal security are the roots of
most human violence and hatred. Afraid of loving anything or
anyone for fear of tempting the gods to withdraw that love object,
he had become increasingly cool toward friends. Success had made
him wary of self-seekers, and suspicion led him to break with old

friends. It reached the point where he stiffened if touched, even by a close friend. The symptoms intensified when *Orpheus* collapsed, and panic about his writing ability was added to his other anxieties. He finally went to the analyst, Dr. Lawrence Kubie.

Dr. Kubie insisted on Williams' undergoing a complete physical checkup to cope with his hypochondria, but the examination did not much diminish it. Assured that he was in splendid physical condition, and there was no residual heart murmur from his childhood attack of diptheria, Williams said "I still don't believe him."

The analyst's next bit of advice was for Williams to take a rest, stop writing, "lie fallow" temporarily. Williams found the idea alarming. "I'm afraid if I quit work I'd never be able to start again." Except for a three-month vacation in 1944, just after he sold *The Glass Menagerie,* and just after he decided, as he does annually, that he might die at any moment, he has never had a real vacation from his work. Wherever he is, he spends three to four hours at the typewriter every day.

Then the analyst tried another approach. Being acquainted with Tennessee Williams' work and recognizing the "psychic wounds expressed in it," he asked, "Why are you so full of hate, anger, and envy?"

The patient contested the word *hate.* "Anger, oh yes! And envy, yes! But not hate. I think that hate is a thing, a feeling, that can only exist where there is no understanding." Picturing himself as a surgeon using the scalpel on corrupted human tissue, Tennessee Williams believes he can understand the problems without hating the patient. For a long while, five days a week, at $50 an hour, the two argued about hatred and Williams' attitude toward it. The playwright said he found the treatments "immensely stimulating" and believed they were helping him.

While under psychiatric treatment, Williams read many books on related subjects. All his work, even before this, had reflected psychic tensions; it was full of complexes, Freudian symbols, case studies, dreams, etc. It is a psychology student's paradise, with every character a ready subject for analysis. In his reading, Williams came across a term, of which his psychiatrist disapproved, but which Williams considered the key to his problems: infantile omnipotence. He explained this to the surprised Mike Wallace on a television interview: "We scream in the cradle, mother picks us up. She comforts us, she suckles us, she changes the diaper, whatever is giving us discomfort is tended to and through this she rocks us to sleep and all that. And whatever gives us discomfort, we find, is—is relieved in response to an outraged cry." As the child grows up, he discovers that the world no longer is so permissive, so tender, and so comforting, and the child "misses the maternal arms." Then, reverting to the protests that had won such effective response in childhood, the enraged adult starts screaming. "And that's what most of our neuroses spring from," triumphantly summarized the analytical Mr. Williams. "We meet a more indifferent world, and then we become angry." To him this explained the outraged cry is his own writing.

As he thought back over the early years of his life, searching for the seeds of the "passion, hatred, frustration, bitterness, and violence" that bubbled to the surface in his plays, he agreed with his psychiatrist that his childhood and youth had left him resentful and enraged. St. Louis had obviously been the crucial point. There, for the first time, he had felt an outcast at home and at school. There, too, he took his first tentative steps into creative writing which was violent from the beginning.

Besides, St. Louis was where he had lost Rose. Even now, she was seldom out of his thoughts. She had been committed to a mental hospital—an incurable schizophrenic. To quiet her, the doctors had performed a pre-frontal lobotomy, which had restored lucidity but left her unable to live without supervision. When Williams became affluent enough, he put her in a private sanitarium in Westchester. Throughout the years, he has visited her unfailingly and loved her unceasingly. Always wondering what it is like in her world, the "beanstalk country" as he calls it, he feels that he and she are akin—she in her glass menagerie; he in his writing. Both are attempts to forget the jungle in which man lives.

Because of Rose, of himself, and of his reading, he started work on a short play about psychiatry. The concept had come early in the period of his psychiatric treatment. The new play, *Suddenly Last Summer,* set in New Orleans' fashionable "garden district," proved to be his most shocking play.

To avert a repetition of the stresses *Orpheus* had incurred, he decided on an off-Broadway production. "I couldn't cope at this time with doing another controversial play on Broadway," he told a reporter. "The financial risk off Broadway is not so great and the conditions, therefore, are less of a life and death matter."

The new theme being cannibalism, he was afraid of arousing unpleasant comments. Yet he was pleasantly surprised at the first reading by the cast. "Now that I've heard it read, I find it isn't as shocking as I thought, at first, it would be. The total effect, I feel, is not distasteful, but it does involve material that will arouse some controversy.

As an opener for the program, Williams picked a one-act play from the *27 Wagons Full of Cotton* collection, "Something Unspoken," which also deals obliquely with Rose and is also set in the Garden District of New Orleans. The joint production was called *Garden District.*

"Something Unspoken" gave the evening of theatre a quietly restrained beginning. In it, a woman of social prominence, Cornelia, and her secretary, Grace, outwardly discuss the day's mail while inwardly fuming over their tense love-hate relationship. In phone calls that interrupt their conversation, Cornelia reveals her snobbery, arrogance, and prejudice as she reacts to news of her

unsuccessful campagin for the presidency of the local Confederate
Daughters Chapter. Resentful that a newcomer, "a dark horse,"
wins, and mumbling that "nothing succeeds like mediocrity,"
she resigns to join other societies where she expects her worth
will win recognition—the Colonial Dames, the Huguenot Society,
and the Daughters of the Barons of Runymede. Meanwhile her
secretary is bearing the brunt of her disappointment.

Gradually their history together is revealed. Cornelia had invited Grace for a visit after the latter's frail, young, professorial
husband had died and after Cornelia had lost her mother. Fifteen
years ago, this day, Grace had brought springtime and roses to the
house with her gentle beauty. Cornelia, although domineering, has
been devoted to this secretary, and has been frustrated by the
latter's inability to return her outspoken affection. They have a
way of cutting at one another, although a bond of real love exists.
Part of Grace's irony and restraint is the recognition of her wasted
life here. Now she is turning a soft grey, the color of cobwebs, while
Cornelia turns the invincible grey of iron. There is a suggestion of
Lesbianism in their feelings, with Cornelia in the masculine role,
Grace in the weaker and feminine role. At the end there is more
than a hint of the sinister Strindbergian concept of human relationships. As Grace hears Cornelia's disappointing news, "a slight,
equivocal smile appears momentarily on her face; not quite malicious but not really sympathetic." As the curtain falls, she turns to
exclaim over the fifteen beautiful roses Cornelia has given her—
one for each year of their life together.

Tennessee Williams has said that the love-hatred of these two,
the dominating and the dominated, is somewhat the relationship
that existed between Rose and Mrs. Williams. "Something Unspoken" may be a clearer presentation of it than was given in
Menagerie, but *Menagerie* was a tenderer and more subtle play.

"Something Unspoken" is virtually plotless. It is simply a sketch
of the interplay of contrasted personalities. As such, it has nice

control, balance, and economy. The dialogue is sharp and sparkling, showing how cleverly Williams can do satirical characterization. *Garden District* would not have been the most talked-about off-Broadway production of the 1957–1958 season if it had not been for the second and longer play *Suddenly Last Summer*, which had all the tension and horror that "Something Unspoken" lacked. While the mansion of Mrs. Violet Venable, another socially prominent New Orleans matron, could be the same as Cornelia's, the garden is something else again. There, the atmosphere is more like that of a "tropical jungle, or forest, in the prehistoric age of giant fern-forests when living creatures had flippers turning to limbs and scales to skin. The colors of the jungle are violent, especially since it is steaming with heat after rain. There are massive tree-flowers that suggest organs of the body, torn out, still blistering with undried blood; there are harsh cries and sibilant hissings and thrashing sounds in the garden as if it were inhabited by beasts, serpents, and birds, all of savage nature. . . ." The garden, which contains carnivorous flowers that lure and devour insects, is the creation of Mrs. Venable's recently deceased son, Sebastian, and she preserves it as a monument to him.

She explains this to a coolly professional young psychiatric surgeon, Dr. Cukrowicz (Polish for *sugar*), whom she is showing through it. Besides this eccentric interest in botany, she tells him, Sebastian was a poet—not famous, because he *"dreaded, abhorred! false values that come from being publicly known, from fame, from personal—exploitation."* Every summer, Sebastian wrote one poem. The other nine months of the year (the length of a pregnancy) he lived in preparation for that exquisite effort. In the meanwhile, Sebastian searched for God. The search had ended with his discovery in the Encantadas, on a volcanic island.

There massive sea-turtles crawl laboriously onto the sand for their annual egg-laying. Sebastian and his mother watched the animals deposit their eggs and then crawl, exhausted, back to the sea. Sebastian and Mrs. Venable returned, when the eggs hatched, to see the sand alive with the tiny sea turtles making their dash for the sea, while predatory birds dived upon them, turned them over to expose their soft undersides, and tore and ate their flesh. Sebastian's guess was that only one in a thousand survived to reach the sea. This was Sebastian's vision of God.

The doctor counters that such a vision could be equated with much of life experience, but not with God. Although a good Episcopalian, Mrs. Venable insists that "God shows a savage face to people and shouts some fierce things at them, it's all we see or hear of him."

As she continues her reminiscences, we learn of the years she spent following her son, whom she worshipped, and neglecting her prosaic husband. While she was off to a Tibetan Buddhist monastery after Sebastian, who was on one of his God hunts, her husband died. After that, she and Sebastian sought to surround themselves with beautiful, talented people, judging them by their degree of "personal charm." Over the years, Sebastian refused to grow old . . . using abstinence and discipline as a means of preserving his youth. His chastity was his mother's most treasured memory of the adored son. He was still a celibate at forty, when he died, she says—almost as if in fulfillment of a vow. Not realizing what this might reveal, she brags, "I was actually the only one in his life that satisfied the demands he made of people." But the life that he and she built together like a work of Renaissance art is being destroyed by an unthinking vandal.

The reason Mrs. Venable has been confiding all this to the good Doctor Sugar is to persuade him to undertake brain surgery on that unthinking barbarian—her niece, Catherine—who was with Sebastian when he died and has been insane with fright and horror ever since. Bits of her story have gotten back to Mrs. Venable, enough to convince the jealous guardian of her son's memory that Catherine could destroy it. Her "obscenities and babblings" should be cured, insists Violet Venable, by a frontal lobotomy. The doctor tells her that Catherine's mind would be relieved by such an operation, but its capacities would be curtailed. To which Mrs. Venable replies, "Oh, but what a blessing to them, Doctor, to be just peaceful, to be just suddenly—peaceful. . . ." Almost as if desiring a retreat into mindlessness herself, she contemplates the blessedness of being able to look up without seeing the savage birds of the Encantadas.

The doctor will not commit himself about the operation until he has examined the patient—in spite of the handsome endowment the rich Mrs. Venable has promised his hospital. As he starts to leave, his patient, Catherine Holly, enters. The beautiful girl is accompanied by a hospital nurse. Mrs. Venable rushes into the house to fortify herself with her five o'clock daiquiri before meeting the vandal whose psychosis, she believes, is chipping away at the monument of Sebastian's memory.

The doctor retreats to an upstairs window from which he can observe Catherine's vain efforts to steal a cigarette under the eyes of the watchful nurse. Catherine can see the doctor in the window, and his blondness reminds her of Sebastian. She begins to blurt out incoherences about her love for him, her inability to save him, her memory of running down the steep, white street in Cabeza de Lobo.

At this point, her mother and brother come to tell her that they need the money that Sebastian willed them, but which is withheld until she changes her story about his death. Unless Catherine does that, Aunt Violet will keep the will in probate forever. Besides, they argue, the story simply couldn't be true.

But Catherine affirms, "I *didn't* invent it. I know it's a hideous story but it's a true story of our time and the world we live in and what did truly happen to Cousin Sebastian in Cabeza de Lobo. . . ."

Since Catherine was the only witness to his death, her aunt has brought her to the house to hear the story from her, hoping that she will change it.

As the whole family gathers, there is general confusion. The character grouping is curiously like the jungle setting—people preying upon each other like jungle beasts. The doctor takes Catherine aside, talks to her, and gives her an injection of truth serum. Aroused by his sympathetic interest, she gives him a passionate embrace which he accepts with clinical calm. She then tells the story of the events of the previous summer.

The winter before, she had been seduced by a married man, a traumatic experience that had left her depersonalized. She had begun to refer to herself in the third person—a schizophrenic reaction. Sebastian decided to take her with him to Europe on his annual holiday, partially to help her overcome this reaction, and partially because he could no longer be accompanied by his mother, who had suffered a stroke that had paralyzed part of her face. Catherine hints that Sebastian was a homosexual who used his mother's incestuous love and good looks to lure young men to him. Her age and her illness having made her useless for this purpose, he had turned to Catherine as fresher bait.

Because Catherine didn't understand her function at first, and because she never quite understood her companion, she failed him. She had not been able to give him, as his mother had, the controlled support he needed in order to write his annual poem. As Mrs. Venable described it, "A poet's vocation is something that rests on something as thin and fine as a web of a spider, Doctor. That's all that holds him *over!*—out of destruction."

Catherine amplified the image, "Yes, something had broken, that string of pearls that old mothers hold their sons by like a—sort of a—sort of—*umbilical* cord. . . ."

Suddenly, last summer, Sebastian felt his youth gone, could not write his poem, became restless, and took Catherine to Cabeza de

Lobo, where he ignored the fashionable set, and spent his afternoon at a public beach. He bought Catherine a white lisle bathing
suit that was practically transparent when wet, and she realized
that she was procuring for him. Now surrounded by the homeless,
hungry young people who spent their days on the public beach,
Sebastian dispensed with Catherine's services. But, as the crowd
around him became bigger and greedier, Sebastian grew frightened
and stopped going to the beach.

One blazing white day, Catherine and Sebastian had lunch at an
open-air restaurant. Weakened by the heat and his ascetic diet,
Sebastian kept touching his damp face with his handkerchief and
popping white pills into his mouth. Catherine and he discussed
going north—since they had *done* Cabeza de Lobo. As they talked,
behind the fence separating the restaurant from the beach naked
black children swarmed up, making strange noises and begging for
bread. "Don't look at those little monsters," said Sebastian. "Beggars are a social disease in this country." The waiters drove the
children away with sticks. But the little beggars returned with
homemade percussion instruments and began an eerie serenade.
Sebastian, recognizing some of the musicians, became terrified.

He told the waiter he had a heart condition and that the noise
was making him sick. As the waiters began chasing the band away,
Sebastian rushed out into the street, into a day so blazing white it
looked as if "a huge white bone had caught on fire in the sky and
blazed so bright it was white and turned the sky and everything
under the sky white with it!" Instead of returning to the shaded
restaurant, Sebastian started up a steep hill. His hand was in his
jacket; Catherine knew that his heart was bothering him. But the
music followed him. He walked faster, then started to run. The
children screamed, pursued and overtook him. Catherine heard
Sebastian scream just once "before this flock of black plucked little
birds that pursued him" overtook him halfway up the white hill.
Catherine called for help, but by the time the waiters, police, and

others reached the scene Sebastian's body was naked, parts of it devoured by the children, who had "Torn or cut parts of him away with their hands or knives or maybe those jagged tin cans they made music with, they had torn bits of him away and stuffed them into those gobbling fierce little empty black mouths of theirs." Sebastian's body looked "like a big white-paper-wrapped bunch of red roses."

At this point in Catherine's narrative, Mrs. Venable rushes at the girl, tries to strike her, and screams, "Lion's View! State asylum, cut this hideous story out of her brain!" As the old lady is led out, Catherine's brother decides that Catherine might be telling the truth, and the doctor quietly agrees that it could be.

When this shocker was produced, Williams gritted his teeth, preparing for a storm. "I thought I would be critically tarred and feathered and ridden on a fence rail out of the New York theatre, with no future except in translation for theatres abroad, who might mistakenly construe my work as a castigation of American morals, not understanding that I write about violence in American life only because I am not so well acquainted with the society of other countries."

Strangely enough, the play won considerable praise. The critics recorded their reaction to the horrors in this bitterest of the Williams' plays, and their annoyance over the repeated Williamsian jolt to their sensibilities. But they acknowledged that in this new study in hatred, Williams showed amazing control of his craft.

The play, again, has almost no action. It is a long but effectively broken monologue. Never had Tennessee Williams created so much by words alone. Hauntingly beautiful, though corrosively decadent, they suit the steaming jungle background. Man is both the artist and the beast. Brooks Atkinson felt that in the measured sadness of this requiem, Williams had attained the peak of his talent as "the poet of the damned." In his annihilation of the basic assumptions of society, his denial of the values by which most people live, in the horrible beauty of his dreadful speeches (Mr. Atkinson calls the descriptions of Sebastian's mutilated corpse "rose-perfumed") Tennessee Williams had made art out of malignance and maleficence.

To have this story told by a distraught eyewitness, rather than acted out, was a wise decision since the latter would have been more than even a sophisticated audience could take. And the intimate small theatre was better than a big Broadway stage for such id-to-id talks. In its off-Broadway setting *Garden District* became the most hotly discussed production of the season.

The London production, later in the year, met with a "restrained" reception. The pair of plays gave Mr. Darlington of *The Daily Telegraph* shivers down his spine.

When the play was made into a movie (the screen version by Gore Vidal), Williams felt there were "unfortunate concessions to the realism that Hollywood is too often afraid to discard. And so a short morality play, in a lyrical style, was turned into a sensationally successful film that the public thinks was a literal study of such things as cannibalism, madness and sexual deviation." Its real message, he felt, should have been "all human confusion and its consequence: violence."

He also believed that the film was miscast, although he is a great admirer of both Katherine Hepburn and Elizabeth Taylor. He sensed that Hepburn was unhappy with her part; and of Miss Taylor he said, "If it did nothing else, it demonstrated her ability to rise above miscasting. She was marvelously well cast as Maggie in *Cat on a Hot Tin Roof,* and that's when she should have got her Oscar. But it stretched my credulity to believe that such a 'hip' doll as our Liz wouldn't know at once in the film that she was 'being used for something evil.' I think that Liz would have dragged Sebastian home by his ears, and so saved them both from considerable embarrassment that summer."

The movie has some interesting changes from the play. Catherine gains in sympathy—largely because she is shown in the sanitarium, being bullied and abused. We are given a glimpse of a frontal lobotomy, and the state asylum in shown in its snake-pit aspects. In an escape attempt, Catherine blunders into the male "tank," where the drooling, groaning, grinning maniacs, as they become aware of a woman's presence, start lurching toward her; then as she rushes into the female "tank" we get a view of grimacing, pointing, shrieking women. Catherine's family is made worse, more fatuous and actually evil; they consent to the operation in a bargain for the inheritance. Nor is there any final redeeming through improbable change of heart for them. The violet (Violet Venable) trying to break through the rocks of reality in the effort to preserve the veneration of her son is played by Katherine Hepburn. Looking younger than her stage counterpart makes her son's use of her more believable. She goes quite mad at the end, following the pattern of Blanche in *Streetcar*. Also, with the greater flexibility of the camera, the audience can watch the human sacrifice. Thus, the movie is not so static as the play. Finally, Catherine and her doctor (played by Montgomery Clift, who appeared earlier in *You Touched Me!*) link arms at the close of the film and walk off into the sunset of love and happiness together—in the standard Hollywood and soap-opera tradition.

The old Williams' theme of the soft being destroyed by the hard gets its most didactic expression in *Suddenly Last Summer*. The horrible image of the sea-turtles and the birds, reiterated in Sebastian's final race from the children, is a variant of his standard symbol of the idealist, the artist, the ascetic, and the aesthetic being destroyed by the callous world. Robert Rice draws together this play and *Menagerie* in this lucid comment: "The world is a jungle," he seems to say, "and the alternative to living in it as a wild animal is to withdraw into one's own musings and fantasies, a menagerie where the animals are no longer threatening because they are made out of glass. Clearly, either choice is a sorry one, and just as clearly the everyday attempt of ordinary people to avoid the choice, to try to live a little in both the jungle and the glass menagerie, is sorry too; it is an eternal compromise and there-fore eternal frustration. There is no way out." The jungle is always on the scene to remind us that we live in a predatory world. Williams has said that the cannibalism episode is no more than a transcription in physical terms of what people do to one another emotionally every day.

The play restates themes expressed in earlier plays. The speech D. H. Lawrence makes in *I Rise in Flame, Cried the Phoenix*, about the harlot of darkness devouring the blond god of the sun contains the same statement. Another, more direct use of the cannibalism theme had been made in his short story "Desire and the Black Masseur," chronicling the perverted relationship of a little blond masochist and a hulking Negro sadist. Pounding the fragile white body until its bones are crushed and the flesh purple, the Negro finally kills his white partner in perversion and, then, to the accompaniment of a Good Friday revival service in the church across the street, devours the flesh. The allusion to the crucifixion story, as archetypal of this need for human sacrifice, is clear. Even the sacrament of the mass is suggested—with the transubstanti-ation, the eating of the actual flesh of the Savior. Nevertheless, Tennessee Williams appears to believe that our future is not al-together hopeless. "Slowly, with barely a thought of so doing," the story concludes, "the earth's whole population twisted and writhed beneath the manipulation of night's black fingers and the white ones of day with skeletons splintered and flesh reduced to pulp, as out of this unlikely problem, the answer, perfection, was slowly evolved through torture."

Apparently, Sebastian is a primitive sacrifice to the cruel car-nivorous God of his own vision, martyred like his sainted name-sake, supposedly in conformity with the unfathomable will of this terrible god. His death in the blinding white of revealed truth is his fulfillment. He has been searching all over the world for God. In the moment of his death, as in the vision of the turtle massacre, he sees his God face-to-face. If we agree with this metaphysical concept, we can choose to wait, like Sebastian, for the moment of sacrifice; or turn, like Mrs. Venable, to a desired world of unreality and go mad. Both the sacrifice of Sebastian and the willingness of her family to sacrifice Catherine, another saint, elaborate the theme of cannibalism. There is no immediate hope for escape, but the continuing sacrifices lead to an eventual solution. Williams just isn't clear what that solution will be.

Sebastian is the corrupted idealist—an example of what Williams calls "matured evil." His fellow humans are to be used for his amusement and discarded at will. His corruption, in violation of his extreme idealism and yearning for purity (notice his and his mother's obsession with white) make him search for the opportunity to sacrifice himself in expiation of his own sins.

His mother is the more innocent of the two. Her concept of Sebastian is their mutual ideal. They believe that if they deny the physical part of themselves, it will cease to exist. The emphasis on chastity and asceticism, unfortunately, works for a more distorted physicality than normality would have demanded: It has made her unconsciously incestuous, and him homosexual. Yet her abnormality never reaches the surface; his does.

Tennessee Williams is consistently dualistic in his thought. He assumes that deep-feeling and deep-thinking humans will fail to reconcile the flesh and the spirit. His Puritanism, in this corrupted form, reappears as he insists on the filth of man's physical nature. Like Cassandra in *Battle of Angels,* he wants no bones that have flesh still clinging to them—he wants them clean and sun-bleached before he touches them.

Typically, the characters with the less vulnerable underbellies are the fittest to survive sane and cleansed. Catherine, like Stella (in *Streetcar*), can recognize truth and yet lead an acceptable life. She is sensitive, enough to be shocked into schizophrenia by her seduction, and to have a relapse after witnessing Sebastian's horrifying death; but she has the strength and practicality to survive and recover her sanity.

The objective viewer, the doctor, of course manages well, too. Williams' doctors are almost invariably cold, impartial observers, who function as choruses, their clinical views usually reflecting Godlike omniscience. Of all Williams' doctors, only John Buchanan (in *Summer and Smoke*) had much personality—and that largely in the expression of a youthful rebellion; and as this subsides, his personality dwindles. In *Suddenly Last Summer,* the doctor is almost wholly impersonal—a virtue in a psychiatrist.

Naturally, the crude materialists also survive. The flesh-eaters always prevail in Williams' world. Sometimes they reform, but usually they just go their selfish ways, ignoring and trampling the moths along the path. Catherine's family follows this pattern.

Vivid though it is, *Suddenly Last Summer* falls short of Williams' best. His greatest power lies in characterization and dialogue. *Suddenly Last Summer* has little of either. Its best passages are Mrs. Venable's; they have wit, precision, and irony. We find ourselves caring less about Catherine and her traumas than about this refined purist and dreamer. But she is curiously unlike the other Williams idealists—she has not lost her dignity, her wealth, or her values. She goes mad when the merciful veil is stripped from the unendurable truth. Nevertheless, her degradation is less than Blanche's or Alma's. Her ideals are for her son rather than for herself. He and Catherine destroy the image she holds sacred; she herself is degraded only in so far as Sebastian is her creation. The shame, like the responsibility for the fall, lies almost entirely with him.

In a typically Williamsian sense, this is a morality play. Although gingerly touching on the problem of perversion, it nevertheless, insists on the inevitable punishment. Here Williams avoids the defensive attitude toward homosexuality taken in such short stories as "Two on a Party" and "Night of the Iguana." If not preaching against abnormality, he is pointing out the natural and social consequences. In *Cat* he dwelt on the dreadful awareness of social contempt for the homosexual; in the case of Sebastian, he points up the degradation and horror of using other people in violation of their human dignity.

But the real shock in *Suddenly Last Summer* is its reflection of neurosis. Obviously *Suddenly Last Summer* reflects the psychic imbalance the author experienced in this period. No other play by Tennessee Williams so directly calls for the adjective *sick*.

CHAPTER XIV

Sweet Bird of Youth

Tennessee Williams wrote *Suddenly Last Summer* at the beginning of his analysis. *Sweet Bird of Youth* is its midterm product. On this evidence alone, we could justifiably say that the psychiatric treatment helped. Psychiatry even cured his wanderlust for a time. Usually when he got restless he packed some bags and took off. During the year or so of his psychiatric treatment, he got over attacks of wanderlust by having violent arguments with his psychiatrist, which relieved the pressures. He was living in a modest apartment on East 58th Street, sharing his quarters with an English Bulldog called Brinda, and taking his daily swims. He did not seem much older than when he had first tasted the catastrophe of success. Plumper now, he looked healthy, and he sported a free-form mustache.

But certain changes were noticeable to his friends. For the first time in his life, he became punctual. Although there were traces of the old hypochondria, he listened with diminishing frequency for an uneven heartbeat. His claustrophobia had abated sufficiently to allow him to use a small self-service elevator to his apartment. Best of all was the change in his response to friends. Said one, "Tenn now has more warmth humanly. I remember a couple of years ago if anyone, even a dear friend like, say, Audrey Wood, kissed him on the cheek or put an arm around his shoulders, you could see him stiffen. Now if he likes somebody, it's more evident."

After he had spent his fury on *Suddenly Last Summer,* he started work on a less hostile play, *Sweet Bird of Youth.* But it was hardly the "happy play" he had been promising and that many were expecting.

Then, gradually, he lost interest in the sessions with his analyst, became restless, and "started hopping back and forth between the analyst's couch and Caribbean beaches." By the time he quit the sessions entirely, he had come to realize that the anger he felt with his fellow humans was also a self-condemnation. "Since I am a member of the human race," he asserted, "when I attack its behavior toward fellow members I am obviously including myself in the attack, unless I regard myself as not human but superior to humanity. I don't. In fact, I can't expose a human weakness on the stage unless I know it through having it myself. I have exposed a good many human weaknesses and brutalities and consequently I have them." At last the little Southern boy stopped running from the bullies and became aware of the repressed bully in himself.

His Puritan nature still remained the root of his being. For all of his Bohemianism, he was and is a Calvinist, preaching original sin—"Guilt is universal," he says. "I mean a strong sense of guilt. If there exists any area in which a man can rise above his moral condition, imposed upon him at birth and long before birth, by the nature of his breed, then I think it is only a willingness to know it, to face its existence in him, and I think that at least below the conscious level, we all face it. Hence the guilty feelings, and hence defiant aggressions, and hence the deep dark of despair that haunts our dreams, our creative work, and makes us distrust each other."

Violence is the earmark of the Williams' drama. It appeared in his very first published work, the story in *Weird Tales* about Queen Nitocris' subterranean dinner party. The shootings, burnings, lynchings, lunacies—and now cannibalism and castration—mark the trail of a tortured conscience seeking relief. Said Tennessee Williams, "If there is any truth in the Aristotelian idea that violence is purged by its poetic representation on the stage, then it may be that my cycle of violent plays has had a moral justification after all. I know that I have felt it. I have always felt a release from the sense of meaninglessness and death when a work of tragic intention has seemed to me to have achieved that intention, even if only approximately, nearly." This is the aesthetic justification for his screams of "infantile omnipotence."

Sweet Bird is set in a small Southern town on the Gulf of Mexico called St. Cloud. It is controlled by a hillbilly politician, Boss Finley, who claims to have been called there from the hills by the "Voice of God." Chance Wayne, a twenty-nine-year-old native who had left St. Cloud in search of fame, has returned with a pathetic substitute—he has become the gigolo of a faded movie queen, Alexandra del Lago, who styles herself "The Princess."

The two are a study in lost youth. Alexandra is tormented by the fear that her comeback after several years of premature death-in-retirement was an epic failure. At the premiere of her comeback picture, seeing how the close-ups recorded the marks of aging and overhearing what she took to be scornful murmurs from the audience, she had dashed away in terrified flight. She had found a release from tension and self-pity at Palm Beach in the company of a handsome beach-boy—Chance. Now they are travelling together, Chance acting as her sly servant-prostitute—and as male nurse much of the time, bringing her oxygen to relieve shortness of breath, preparing her hashish to settle her nerves, and catering to her sexual and other whims. Although egocentric and domineering, Alexandra is not all monster. She has compassion, understanding, and dignity.

But Chance is a weakling. His good looks have won him entry into circles for which neither his family background nor his talents would have qualified him. Unable to accept his mediocrity he still searches for a means to become the hero of St. Cloud. He hopes now that his association with Alexandra can win movie fame for him and his girl, Boss Finley's daughter, though both Heavenly (his girl) and he are losing their looks. He suspects, but suppresses from his consciousness, the futility of this American Cinderella dream.

On Easter Sunday morning, before Alexandra awakes, Chance has a caller in their hotel suite, Dr. Scudder, who has recently performed a hysterectomy on Heavenly because Chance infected her with V.D. Doctor Scudder warns him to leave town. Unable to speak out plainly, Scudder hints at the operation Heavenly has undergone and tells Chance she is no longer his girl—that her father has other plans. With another warning to Chance to leave St. Cloud, the little doctor withdraws—to see Boss Finley.

Just as Scudder goes, Alexandra awakes, gasps, takes oxygen, and slowly brings her day into focus. Chance, with the intention of blackmailing her, tapes their conversation as they smoke hashish, and asks her where she gets the narcotic. Her talk wanders into gloomy reminiscences. She had thought herself wise to retire at the right moment; but she discovered: "There's nowhere else to retire to when you retire from an art because, believe it or not, I really was once an artist. So I retired to the moon, but the atmosphere of the moon doesn't have any oxygen in it. I began to feel breathless, in that withered, withering country of time coming after time not meant to come after. . . ." Unable to turn to such resorts of retired stagers as giving lessons in acting or painting flowers on pots, she "wandered like a lost nomad" using drugs and sex to quiet the tiger within her. She had been persuaded by people who told her that she was an artist, "not just a star whose career depended on youth," to make another picture. But on watching her closeups at the preview, she decided that her legend could not be separated from the appearance of youth. Then had occurred her flight from the curious faces up the unbearably long theatre aisle, the fall over the regal white train of her gown, the nightmarish tumble down the marble stairs, rolling "like a sailor's drunk whore to the bottom," then the merciful hands without faces that helped her up, and . . . now this. . . .

Having finished her litany of sorrows, she becomes aware of Chance's transparent attempts to trap her into outright declarations that she uses and imports hashish. Suspicious, she questions him about their relationship. Chance says he is holding out for a Hollywood contract, a real one to replace a phony one she had given him earlier. When she inquired about his dramatic talent, he admits: "I'm not as positive of it as I once was. I've had more chances than I could count on my fingers and made the grade almost, but not quite, every time. Something always blocks me. . . ." He thinks success is a matter of luck and that not any gift of his own but being "discovered" and "promoted" will bring him success.

At this point Chance shows the tape recorder. In turn Alexandra makes a quick check of her valuables, finding nothing missing, however. Then she observes to the would-be blackmailer that he is trembling and sweating; obviously the part doesn't suit him. "It's so silly, it's touching, downright endearing, it makes me feel close to you, Chance." And she goes on, "When monster meets monster, one monster has to give way, AND IT NEVER WILL BE ME. . . ." Then she lists the terms of their future relationship. He is not to remind her of her heart trouble or mention death; he is to forget the legend of Alexandra del Largo; he is to satisfy her sexual demands when she makes them. "I have only one way to forget these things I don't want to remember and that's through the act of love-making," she explains. "That's the only dependable distraction so when I say now . . . it has to be now, not later."

Then, peremptorily, she demands his services in return for her signature on some travellers checks.

Later, as she is dressing for the day, Alexandra calls on him to entertain her with the story of his life. He begins by telling her that he was born with a "quantity X" in his blood, a wish or a need to be different. His good looks won him a place in the local snob set. While other youths went to college, he sang in the chorus of *Oklahoma!*, had his picture in *Life* and was entertained by social-register hostesses in New York. He got flattering attention on his trips home—until Korea came along. He joined the Navy because he looked good in the uniform. But battle fear, boredom, and panic over the approach of baldness precipitated a nervous breakdown and gained him a medical discharge. His homecoming was hardly the hero's return that he had anticipated. All the notice it got was a cursory mention on an inside page of the local paper. That was when Heavenly became the most important thing in his life. Love seemed the cure for failure.

Chance and Heavenly Finley had become lovers while both were in their teens. She remained the single permanent thing for him in a changing world. Her father, however, did not approve of their marrying. He had in mind a more useful political or financial alliance. Then, on Chance's last return to St. Cloud, not knowing that he had infected her on his previous visit, he had waited all afternoon at their trysting place; but she finally appeared only to say "Chance, go away.'

Alexandra softens as she hears the story and offers her help. Chance proposes that she stage a phony contest of youthful beauty, he and Heavenly, of course, to be the winners—the prize, a trip to the West coast together for movie tryouts. When Alexandra rejects this plan, Chance takes her refusal with the good grace of a person accustomed to disappointment. "I understand," he says, "Time does it. Hardens people. Time and the world you've lived in."

However, Alexandra assures him of her friendship, and he goes off to cash the travellers checks he has earned from her and to show off in her Cadillac.

The characters in the next scene are Boss Finley, his son, his daughter, Heavenly, her Aunt Nonnie, who has taken Chance's side in the courtship, and Dr. Scudder. Boss berates his son for conduct that has provoked unfavorable talk; he berates Aunt Nonnie for having encouraged Heavenly in the affair that has ended in her having to undergo a "whore's operation"; and he orders Heavenly to appear at the political rally that evening in order to squelch rumors about her and to wear a white dress to symbolize white chastity. When she protests, he makes threats against Chance which have a grim significance in view of the discussion with Dr. Scudder of the subject for the political rally— the recent castration of a young Negro as a demonstration of the determination of white racists to preserve their "blood purity."

The evil nature of Boss Finley is disclosed in references to a $12,000 brooch he bought for his dying wife and returned to the jeweler after her death; to an affair callously carried on in spite of his wife's knowledge; and to his plans for forcing Heavenly into a distasteful marriage. There is a tone of sadistic gloating in the discussion of these plans, and even a note of incestuous interest in his comments on his daughter.

That evening, before the rally, Miss Lucy, Boss's mistress, who has no respect or love for the old politician, warns Chance of the plans to castrate him and offers to help him get out of town. Aunt Nonnie also comes to give warning. Finally, Boss's son arrives to denounce him for having infected Heavenly and to threaten him with emasculation. As this evidence of the town's loathing of him piles up, Chance comes to loathe himself. In this crisis, Alexandra reels in, badly in need of his help; but he ignores her, handing her over to strangers. By this act, she feels that he has forfeited any emotional claim upon her.

Then Chance watches Boss escorting Heavenly and leading

white marchers to the rally called to defend the white woman's virtue and the Negro's emasculation. The horror advances toward its climax when a heckler is brutally beaten, and left for dead at Chance's feet. The mob is on the move now to run Chance himself out of town. In a desperate last effort to realize his dreams, Chance telephones a Hollywood columnist in Alexandra's name, hands the phone to Alexandra, and instructs her to tell the columnist that she is coming to Hollywood with a new discovery—a young man named Chance Wayne. But, when the call comes through, Alexandra talks about only herself.

She learns that her comeback was not the failure she had believed, but a triumph. Her morale and her dignity flow back into her, and she becomes "the Princess" again. She knows, says the author, "that her future course is not a progression of triumphs." But this knowledge that her reprieve is temporary in no way lessens her majesty at this moment. Then, with cruel accuracy, she analyzes Chance's situation. The laurel wreath was placed too early on his golden hair, and now "the gold is thinning and the laurel is withered. Face it—pitiful monster. . . . Of course, I know I'm one, too. But one with a difference. . . Out of the passion and torment of my existence I have created a thing that I can unveil, a sculpture, almost heroic, that I can unveil, which is true. But you? You've come back to the town you were born in, to a girl that won't see you because you put such rot in her body she had to be gutted and hung on a butcher's hook, like a chicken dressed for Sunday." Now the mob is preparing a similar fate for him. . . .

Alexandra offers to take him along with her, but as a lap dog on a golden chain. His alternative is castration. Chance, seeing himself clearly now, replies deliberately, "That can't be done to me twice. You did that to me this morning, here on this bed, where I had the honor, where I had the great honor. . . ." So nothing more can happen to him; everything has happened already. When asked what he's trying to prove by these last-minute heroics, he answers,

"Something's got to mean something, don't it, Princess? I mean like your life means nothing, except that you could never make it, always almost, never quite?"

As the Princess leaves, knowing that both are doomed by time, Chance hears the whistled signal of his executioners and turns to the audience in self-recognition, not self-pity, to request: "I don't ask for your pity, but just for your understanding—not even that no. Just for your recognition of me in you, and the enemy, time, in us all."

The play, in spite of some melodramatic confusion in its second act, is surprisingly potent drama. It conforms to the classical unities of time, place, and action, to provide the Aristotelian catharis. The first scene neatly balances with the last, which expands and illuminates its ideas. The futility of Chance's hopes, the degradation of his ideals, and the loss of his manhood were all expressed in those first moments. At the end, we understand their reality to this fading youth standing helplessly by while his fate overtakes him. The play carries us from delusion to truth. For the Princess, the truth has grandeur because she has had some creative part in it. For Chance the truth is devastating because it exposes his impotence. The balance in the play is sometimes as precise as that in *Summer and Smoke,* yet it seems less forced. Among other oppositions are Chance, whose genius, such as it is, is to give love; and Boss Finley, whose genius is hate. They are joined in their common need of Heavenly as the ideal whom they both besmirch. The theme of death is elaborated in every character; Boss's heart is failing; the Princess' breath is short; and both Heavenly and Chance experience sexual and emotional death.

The chief appeal of the drama, however, is the fascinating character of Alexandra. After all these years, the aging actress who sustained herself by periodic blood transfusions has come to life in art. All the aging stage beauties who have impressed Williams with their heroism and their talent are united in this magnificent composite portrait—Laurette Taylor and Helen Hayes through Tallulah Bankhead and Diana Barrymore. The part also integrates into one the fascinations of Williams' other feminine characters—the wit of Violet Venable, the tenacity of Maggie, the passion of Serafina, into a dignity and regal magnificence that outstrips them all. For the first time, a Williams heroine with a good mind and a degree of human sympathy is triumphant. The final scene, when she recognizes her value and draws herself up in a queenly pose, is the most significant recovery in any Williams play. It is an affirmation of human dignity. Her awareness that her triumph will be brief, soon to be cut off by her mortality, makes the gesture even grander.

Alexandra dwarfs every other figure in the play—including Chance. He has the same corrupted innocence that we saw in Sebastian, but lacks Sebastian's intelligence and taste. We can pity him; we can feel a certain dignity in his final gesture; but it is hard to respect him. His lost innocence and youth are certainly universal enough, but hardly heroic. Yet Chance, as an alter-ego of our rebellious Puritan author, has certain virtues besides his magnificent, and usually bare, torso. He is a comment on Williams' own discoveries about the hollowness of fame, and he is a better study than the early Lawrencian essays in phallic worship. He embodies the realization that sex without its vital connection to the rest of life is meaningless. Men castrate one another physically, as women do their men emotionally, because of sex envy. But man can also castrate himself by his prostitution of natural powers. And he comes to hate himself for what he sees in himself of the world's corruption.

It is significant of Tennessee Williams' more sympathetic virile heroes that they are worn out by the time we meet them. They've spent years on a party, and now the party is over. It is perhaps a metaphorical reference to our national party of the twenties and the disasters of the thirties—the period that set the dominant tone of Williams' drama.

Chance Wayne is an interesting combination of cheap values and real worth. In his infantile, braggart, brassy, exhibitionist personality there is a core of decency. This makes him see that his relationship with Alexandra is shameful and his values not worth defending. The author may be pointing to society as the monumental culprit, but Chance sees, whether or not Williams does, that society only carries out his own self-condemnation. He had castrated himself first.

Boss Finley is a combination of Big Daddy and Huey Long. He symbolizes fanaticism, fascism, and hatred. The father-image has regressed to its old distortions. His mistress is colorful—more than a mere variation of the old heart-of-gold-type prostitute. Heavenly is wan, lovely, and flat—as are most of the other minor characters. The heckler is interesting, if not entirely relevant, as the counterpart to Boss. Rather that the voice of God, which Boss proclaims over the loudspeaker, the heckler puts his faith in the silence of God—and is himself silenced.

The play has flaws other than the poverty of the minor parts, which is unusual in a Williams play. By concentrating the drama into the events of the culminating day, Williams intensifies his difficulties with exposition and has to resort to melodramatic violence. Also, the poetic passages, especially Chance's, glare with purple writing. The political-rally scene rings false, recalling, as Robert Brustein remarks in an article appearing in *Encounter,* the Big Effects of the old Federal Theatre days. And the plot complications are excessive. The play is tangled up in enough plots for three plays, and much of it is transparent contrivance.

But the chief weakness of the play is the social point it seeks to make—that society is responsible for Chance's tragedy. Had Chance been portrayed with qualities equal to his ambitions, then his failure could have been attributed to forces outside himself. We can be induced to pity Chance; but when the playwright demands more for him, he asks too much and, to that extent, shares the failure of his character. *Sweet Bird,* even more than *Streetcar,* which fell short of tragedy for the very same reason, but with a character more worthy of our respect and pity, underlines Tennessee Williams' inability to create pure tragedy.

The whole Williams' troupe united again to give *Sweet Bird* a great production—Elia Kazan doing a "heroic job" of directing, Jo Mielziner providing wide, open settings with his usual exotic lighting, and Paul Bowles contributing "spidery and tinkling music of exquisite texture." Geraldine Page, the star of the successful off-Broadway revival of *Summer and Smoke,* brought dignity, raucous humor, and sensitive virtuosity to the part of the Princess. Paul Newman—Brick of *Cat on a Hot Tin Roof*—was a perfect Chance, and Sidney Blackmer won plaudits as Boss Finley.

All seven of the New York drama critics found *Sweet Bird* an electrifying evening of theatre. With his success, Tennessee Williams' superstitions about the Martin Beck Theatre, the scene of the *Orpheus* failure, dissolved. The morning after the early March 1959 opening, five treasurers manned the box offices and seven others were kept busy filling mail orders. The advance sale stood at $390,000. M.G.M. had bought the screen rights with a deposit of $150,000 toward the ceiling price of $400,000. If he so desired, Williams could now retire and live well for the rest of his life. But he had no intention of retiring.

CHAPTER XV

Tennessee Williams—The Present and the "Perhaps"

When the success of *Sweet Bird* was assured, Tennessee Williams spent some time at Key West working on a new play, and then started on a trip around the world. In his extensive travels he has frequently been accompanied by his mother, though she arouses guilt feelings in him, since she disapproves of aspects of both his dramas and his life.

"Son," she asked him one day, "when there is so much unpleasantness in the world, why is it necessary to put it on the stage?" Yet, she does not allow the same criticism from others. When a visitor asked her the question she herself had earlier put to her son, she was quick to come to his defense:

"My son writes about life!" Williams notes with considerable pleasure that she said this "with the conviction of a rebel yell."

On his travels Williams never has stopped working. He spends his mornings at the typewriter, as if this were his link with reality. Tennessee Williams admits to being a poor sightseer. "I go to places and just absorb and I also must work."

This proved to be the pattern on his globetrot as it had been on the other trips. He went to Japan, Hong Kong, Bangkok—"I skipped India because by then I had had enough of human misery, heat, and yes, the flies."—Istanbul, Athens, Cairo, and, inevitably, Rome.

The Mediterranean Coast remains his favorite place for lingering. The critic Kenneth Tynan has said of him that there he takes on a protective coloring, looking more native than most of the natives. Only in London or New York is his appearance noticeable —some friends have likened it to that of a "retired bandit." He hates neckties and detests matching coats and trousers. This mark of the Bohemian is now taken as the mark of a wealthy eccentric.

Newsmen have estimated his total earnings at five million dollars but he denies this. "My annual income, even when I had a big hit on Broadway, never exceeded two hundred thousand and you must remember that I was in a very high tax-bracket."

Money admittedly means a lot to Williams as a measure of success. However, the actual figures only confuse him. He is one of the few people in his income bracket who give no serious thought to the fifteenth of April. Miss Wood takes care of it. For all of this lack of what his friends call "thingness," he is ever conscious of the need for money. His mother is now comfortably provided for, but his sister is another matter. Her sanitarium bills are high. (The reference in *Suddenly Last Summer* to hospital costs of $1,000 per month plus extras has an autobiographical ring.) He finds that, on present earnings, his income will drop to around $15,000 a year by 1966, and comments, "I'd better have something else ready by then." If he retired now, he would have to live "on a fairly modest scale," probably in his frame cottage at Key West.

He is a playwright forthrightly interested in success. When he is in a town where a play of his is on, he goes every night to count the house. A deeper reason for this than the money is the sense of communication that success affords him. His drama has been his one dependable means of breaking through the walls of his reticence. Even now, he freezes when he meets strangers. "Or I start stammering. So I take barbiturates." The little white pills that Alma, Sebastian, and Chance pop into their mouths in moments of upset are another autobiographical touch. These "phone numbers of God" help him squeeze through that dreadful enclosure separating him from others. Even writing is not an easy form of communication for him. He confesses, "Writing doesn't get any easier as you get older. And as I get older the wall between me and people seems to get tougher—harder to get through."

His daily rituals have not changed much over the years. At daybreak each morning, his English Bulldog, Baby Doll, patters into his bedroom to wake him. A few minutes later a huge black Belgian Shepherd, Satan, lumbers in, places one mammoth paw on Williams' chest, and refuses to remove it until his master gets up. By seven, every day of the year, he is in front of his typewriter—now a speedy electric model. He writes in his study, a little apartment separate from his main house, for three or four hours. While he writes, his phonograph plays his four favorite records over and over. If he should feel restless, there is a divan for relaxation, a refrigerator for refreshments, and an old upright portable organ for expressing those rare moments of happiness that might come his way. He has stopped drinking thick black coffee because of his heart, but he still smokes incessantly and frequently has a pitcher of martinis beside him.

The smoking habit is unwise for anyone so absent-minded as he. A friend once told him, "Every time I see you smoking, I start looking for a fire extinguisher." Williams confessed that he had scorched most of his shirts. In fact, even his skin bears scars from fallen red-hot cigarette ends. For such habits most of his friends consider him a "species of amiable baby." Robert Rice records their concern that, unless carefully watched, he will walk into open manholes or take a bite of his napkin and wipe his mouth with the steak.

This confusion extends to all his behavior. He once spent the night in a Southern jail because he had misplaced his draft card and was taken for a foreign spy. On another occasion, while escorting Maureen Stapleton to a rehearsal of *Orpheus,* she paused to lock her door and looked up in time to see the absent-minded author striding far down the hall. Calling him back to the elevator, which he had already passed, she asked, "Where are you going, Tennessee?"

"I don't know," he said cheerfully, and came back.

During that same period, he drove to the theatre from his hotel every day. The rehearsals were being held in Miami, a city which he frequents. Yet, on the fifth day, he couldn't remember how to get to the theatre.

This vagueness, needless to say, makes driving hazardous for himself, his passengers, and the world at large. His driving is usually cautious, but he has trouble keeping off the center line, which he also has trouble seeing. In addition, he usually forgets his driver's license—one issued in St. Louis which serves little purpose for a Florida resident. At one time Williams had three cars and a jeep. One was outside of New Orleans, one in Florida, and one in Oklahoma. All were left in garages for minor repairs and never reclaimed. While in Italy, he bought a white Jaguar. One evening he drove this car and his unsuspecting passenger, Noel Coward, into a tree along the Appian Way; since he was going slowly, neither of the men was hurt. But when Williams offered his friend a ride the following night, Mr. Coward declined saying, "I won't get into that death trap again." They took a taxi.

The Jaguar's end came some months later. Feeling depressed, Williams whipped up a thermos of martinis and took a spin in his car—at a much faster pace to relieve his mood. The crash nearly demolished the car. Amazingly, his only injuries were two black eyes and a lump on his head, inflicted by his portable typewriter. "I guess the typewriter was getting even with me," he quipped. His white Thunderbird caused less trouble largely because he drove it less often. These days he admits that the combination of poor eyesight, mechanical unhandiness, and wandering thoughts is not conducive to safe driving. Anyway, he can seldom find his way to his destination.

His unworldliness and vagueness put his agent in a state of frenzy whenever he has interviews or makes public appearances. He manages a relaxed appearance on television but he might at any moment commit *faux pas*. Delivering a lecture at Harvard he poured himself a whiskey bracer—and then forgot to set it down before walking onto the platform. Discovering his oversight, he managed quite urbanely. He put the offending glass on the lectern, pretending it was filled with water. On another occasion, he told the whole plot of an unfinished play to a reporter for the *Times*. When it appeared in the morning paper, Miss Wood was horrified. Her client was amazed; he hadn't thought that the reporter would print it.

With this vagueness it is no wonder that the author is no social critic. Occasionally, something in the paper or in his life upsets him; then he attacks the evil with full force. The childhood incident with his Negro nurse Ozzie sensitized him to discrimination; his love of Italians has made him bitter about Southern prejudice against foreigners, his attachment to the Mummers and other liberal art groups has left him slightly left-wing.

Although non-political, he says of himself in his earlier days, "I had all the makings of a Communist. I had all the impulses. I wanted to see everything overthrown." The only election he ever voted in was that of 1932. He cast his ballot for Norman Thomas. The Congressional investigations upset him by their possible infringement on human liberties, and he was appalled by the frenzied hostility toward Henry Wallace. But he decided, long ago, that his subject was man's inner life. His social criticism is usually limited to commentary on man's destructiveness; his politi-

cal stand is limited to anti-fascism. Other than these, he is unin-
terested in specific world issues. It came, therefore, as quite a
shock to his friends when he was interviewed on the Mike Wallace
show and suddenly launched into an attack on the Catholic
Church's attitude toward birth control.

His detachment from the world has led some of his friends to
consider him saintly. "Tenn sometimes reminds me of a saint who
is rebelling against his own saintliness, his own natural virtue,"
said one. His brother, Dakin, (now an Air Force officer) has indicated the same thing. He believes that Tennessee Williams, like
Chance Wayne, is searching for his lost innocence. Since Williams,
though he has no church affiliation, retains religious attitudes (he
prays for the success of his plays, and believes the prayers are
answered), his brother, a Catholic convert, hopes that he, too, will
accept that faith. They are, after all, related to St. Francis Xavier.
However, Tennessee Williams' affiliations with any organized
group have been rare and brief.

In fact, even affiliations with unorganized groups are brief. He
enjoys random hours of drinking, of swimming, and of conversation with friends, on afternoons and evenings, but he is most at
peace in the company of his typewriter and his imagination. Given
the choice between the jungle offered in the newspapers and the
glass menagerie of his own invention, his decision is obvious. Moreover, he is a writer who loves the actual process of writing.

Back from his globetrot, Williams felt refreshed and ready for
work on *Period of Adjustment* and three other plays. On his way
down to Key West, he stopped off to see Elia Kazan, who was in
Cleveland, Tennessee, filming *Wild River*. Williams wanted to
show Kazan the script of *Period of Adjustment* and discuss production plans. The play had appeared two winters before at Miami's
Coconut Grove Playhouse and was due to open on Broadway in
November. Williams characterized it as a "serious comedy" about

two couples "trying to make a go of marriages not made in Heaven."

The plot may be summarized as follows: On Christmas Eve, a newlywed couple drive up in a second-hand funeral limousine on a visit to Ralph Bates, one of the groom's wartime buddies. Bates' house is a Spanish-style stucco bungalow in a suburb of Memphis ironically called High-Point. The housing development has been built over a cavern and is sinking a little deeper each year into the ground. On this ever-uncertain earth, in a crumbling home, Ralph sits watching T.V. when the couple pull up to his door. When Isabel, the new bride, gets out of the car, expecting her husband to follow, he roars off, leaving her marooned with the stranger. She has been shaken by the experience of her wedding night at a motel, and this intensifies her distress.

As the friendly host comforts the pretty young woman and she warms to his kindness, her story spills out. She had been a student nurse when she met George, her husband, at the Veterans Hospital, where he was a patient. Her sympathy for the handsome young hero with the nervous tremor had turned into love before she could get to know him. Their marriage forced the realization upon her that they were complete strangers.

He had carried her off on the honeymoon in the second-hand funeral limousine he had bought, after announcing that he had quit his job. Since she had just lost her position at the hospital— for fainting at the sight of blood—she had felt alarmed over their insecure future and had insisted that George find work immediately. Infuriated, he had refused to have any discussion over it, turned the radio on full blast, and started drinking—to keep warm, he said.

By evening the tension had become unbearable. George had insisted on stopping by to see another friend, whose wife had sent them on their way with a minimum of ceremony. Then, they had ended up on their wedding night at a cheap motel, tired, angry, and—in George's case—drunk. When he leapt at his frightened bride like a satyr, she was so alarmed that she locked herself in the bathroom until she believed that he was asleep. Then she spent most of the night sitting up in a chair, pretending to be asleep herself.

The second day of their marriage having seen little improvement over the first, she is thinking of calling the whole farce off, and having the marriage annulled.

Her story, which leaks out gradually as she and Ralph sit talking in front of the fire, mingles with Ralph's. His marriage, too, has been far from ideal. Five years earlier, he had married a homely girl afflicted with psychic frigidity. Her father, a millionaire with diabetes, gallstones, and one kidney, was Ralph's boss. After the boss-father, McGillicuddy, had talked Ralph into marrying Dorothea, he had failed to show the grace to die and leave them his fortune. A typically greedy, materialistic businessman, he has given Ralph only one raise in the five years since the wedding—at the birth of Ralph's son. And now that Ralph has decided to quit the firm and the work for which he is eminently unsuited, the old man has talked Dorothea into leaving him.

Although absorbed in her own afflictions, Isabel gradually senses that Ralph and Dorothea have come to love each other. There is a warmth and sweetness to the house suggestive of mutual interest and affection.

By the time both stories are told, George reappears with a magnum of champagne. He manages to infuriate Isabel still more, driving her into the bathroom so that he can talk to Ralph in private. He accuses his bride of being frigid, of trying to castrate him, and of being an incurable papa's girl. Ralph comments that every marriage must have a period of adjustment, but George clings stubbornly to his pride. As they talk, it becomes apparent that, despite George's reputation as a ladies' man, he is actually a virgin, and fearful that his nervous tremor will make him a sexual failure. Ralph tries to explain that he needs to use some tenderness. The sexual violence, of which George's "shakes" are an indication, is frightening to women.

Overhearing this conversation, Isabel now understands that her husband is as inexperienced and as timid as she. She gives up her efforts to secure a room at a hotel and gradually warms to his need of her.

Meanwhile, Ralph has been preparing to take a plane to the Orient, when his in-laws appear with a laundry basket to carry off the china and the silver, and a revealing argument with his father-in-law ensues. Ralph holds on to the fur coat he has bought Dorothea for a Christmas present. He also refuses to allow the McGillicuddys to take his boy's Christmas presents. As the old couple leave, threatening a lawsuit, Dorothea enters, apologizes for her family, and expresses her intention to stay with Ralph. She isn't sure that Ralph loves her and he isn't sure whether she has not come back just for the beaver coat. Both have revealed so much of themselves that they can have little pride left. But they have survived their period of adjustment and they go to the bedroom to patch up their quarrel. So, too, do George and Isabel.

Thus the play ends with both couples going tenderly to bed. Tennessee Williams has said that he considers this a happy ending —at least, the couples stay together.

The four main characters in the play are all reminiscent of earlier Williamsian creations. The hero, Ralph Bates, has the cool understanding and mechanical talent of the Gentleman Caller (*Menagerie*). He is a man who has sold his life for security, and finds it not such a bargain. His wife, who barely enters the play, is a cardboard character. Her love for Ralph, recognition of her limitations, and ability to adapt when she must, are traits that she shares with Maggie, the heroine of *Cat*, but are not developed into a full and believable characterization.

The other couple are also familiar Williamsian studies, but much better drawn than Dorothea. George Haverstick is another Brick—the same alcoholic tendencies, the same confusion about the bedroom, the same love of the old hero-buddy, and the same impossible idealism. In place of Brick's broken ankle, we get George's "shakes"—an uncontrollable psychosomatic tremor that makes him act like a premature case of palsy. This indicates that, like Brick, he is not really cool; but, as we soon learn, unlike Brick, he is not the least bit inclined toward homosexuality. His hesitation at the marriage bed is based on a deep-seated fear of impotence.

His bride, on the other hand, is no Maggie. She is more like Blanche—sensitive, witty, stilted, sympathetic, and slightly hysterical. But, younger and more flexible than Blanche, she has her healthy sexuality under control. Her ideals center around a gentle father who yet has been moral and stern. She searched in vain for these qualities in her husband. (This study of Isabel and the earlier picture of Heavenly in *Sweet Bird* both point to Williams' growing interest in the Electra complex. Even Dorothea's hatred of the McGillicuddys could be exploration in this area.)

In *Period of Adjustment,* Williams is again pursuing his old theories—the problem of idealism in conflict with reality, of sex and love, of loneliness and the crying need for communication, of age and broken pride and the malignant effect of money—and of life.

Basic to the play is Isabel's conclusion that: "We are all of us born, live and die in the shadow of a giant question mark that refers to three questions: "Where do we *come* from? *Why? And where, oh, where are we going?*" The last of these questions seems to be answered by the setting—a house sinking, inch by inch, into a cavern. He seems to be saying—something there is in this world that loves abysses. By the end of the play, after exploring loneliness like that of the Infant Jesus (the symbolic reason for the timing of the story), and the temporary "obfuscations" of alcohol and sex, and discovering the need for compassion in a world of affliction, Isabel explains her lesson in these words: "Inside or outside, they've [men have] all got a nervous tremor of some kind, sweetheart. The world is a big hospital, a big neurological ward and I am a student nurse in it. I guess that's still my job!"

While we are on earth, awaiting our doom, there is communication and escape from loneliness in tenderness and sex—Lawrence is modified, but he still offers the key to the Williams world. So once again the grotesque comedy concludes with the sexual solution.

In the meantime man's hazy, impractical idealism drives him from the mendacity of marriage for wealth and the mendacity of work without meaning, and from the sight of blood; it makes him discontented with T.V. commercials, canned beer, and Spanish-type suburban stucco. George wants to raise Texas longhorns—beasts that are noble and almost extinct, creatures of beauty with no practical value. "There's dignity in the agrarian, the pastoral . . . way of existence! A dignity too long lost out of the . . . American dream. . . ."

The vision doesn't appeal to the women or to the more mechanical-minded Ralph, who longs to be "the first man in a moon rocket! No, not the moon, but Mars, Venus! Hell, I'd like to be transported and transplanted to colonize and fertilize, to be the Adam on a—star in a different galaxy, yeah, that far away even!—it's wonderful knowing that such a thing is no longer inconceivable, huh?"

Both men have quit their work for these visions. They are willing to go into some enterprise together, but it is clear that each will have to come back to earth and live with compromises and conformity and corruption in spite of his dreams. It is Brick's problem —the hero who wants to prolong his college-athlete heroism into an adult present that has no room for spectacular adventure. It is the plight of Tom in *Menagerie* and the vision of Hadrian in *You Touched Me!* Tennessee Williams has changed very little in the last fifteen years.

Other themes also remain unchanged—the pampered child growing into a sissy, the flight of the sweet bird of youth, the need for fellow-feeling rather than the understanding of psychiatry. Except for the attack on suburbia and T.V.—the latest symbols of status seeking and conformity—the play offers little dynamic, new material.

The form is also typical of Williams. The parallel patterns of the couples—one member of each pair with shakes, the jobless plight of each, the need for adjustment, the solution in sex. These make neat plotting reminiscent of *Summer and Smoke; Period of Adjustment* even shares a little of that older play's flatness and unreality resulting from the tidiness in structure. The virtually static patterns, the gradual unravelling of stories already completed, the exploitation of psychoanalysis, the symbolism of cars and shoes, sex and alcohol and death, the talky exposition, and the unsatisfactory conclusion,—these also repeat the old shortcomings.

Williams, however, insists that *Adjustment* is different from his other plays. "A little more upbeat, I'd say, and I didn't write it for 'big name' players. I hope that you will think there is considerable humor in it."

For a while, Williams thought of directing the play himself. Halfway through rehearsals he relinquished the reins, concluding sadly, "I can't direct my way out of a paper bag."

This directing impulse had been growing for some time. He had said, on his return from his world tour, "We have a little too much of a director's theatre on Broadway today, writers are too easily intimidated. As for myself, I have sometimes gotten panicked before a play reached Broadway, and have not stuck to my guns as I should have done, if things had not been so tense during the tryout." He realizes that it is senseless to freeze a script, regardless of the audience reaction, but he is also aware of the risks to one's integrity in allowing major changes with which he is not in full accord.

There had long been rumblings on the effect direction has on his work, rumblings which increased after critics saw the preface to the book version of *Cat*. Kazan found himself subject to "sniping" for which he thought the playwright responsible. Critics voiced suspicions that Kazan was responsible for the weakness of *Sweet Bird*'s second act. Finally, they started blaming Kazan for Williams' own drive for success. Kazan had stood up under the barrage and was all set to direct *Period of Adjustment;* but in the May before it was to open, he withdrew. His stated reason was that a movie engagement would tie him up until September. But Tennessee Williams did not credit this excuse. "Kazan," he said, "has suddenly gotten the crazy idea that he is not good for my work. We met Monday night for drinks. He showed up looking rather shaky and gray in the face, and told me definitely he couldn't do my new play. I tried my best to make him change his mind, but he was adamant."

Kazan tried to make the playwright see that timing, not anger, was the cause. "I offered to do the play when I was through with my movie, but Tennessee was not willing to wait till then. I consider him the greatest living playwright, and would certainly like to work with him again, if he will ask me."

But Williams insisted on the emotional explanation. Trying to account for it he said, "I think that Kazan has been upset by people who accuse him of looking for popular success—people who snipe at his so-called melodramatic interpretation of my plays." (Kazan admitted the sniping, but denied that it bothered him or had influenced his decision.)

"I was so preoccupied with my own work that I wasn't aware of how much sniping was going on," continued the distraught writer. Then he took up the standard criticisms of Kazan's effect on him and blasted them one by one: as for the success-seeking, he, rather than Kazan, was the one "terrified of failure. . . . It is quite true that I want to reach a mass audience. I feel it can dig what I have to say, perhaps better than a lot of intellectuals can. I'm not an intellectual, and perhaps, at times, I've exceeded the dignified limits in trying to hold an audience, but it's wrong to blame Kazan for this. My cornpone melodrama is all my own. I want excitement in the theatre. Wherever I've been excessive, it's due to a certain hysteria on my part that takes over." (Kazan commented wryly, "He should have said that earlier.")

As for the charge that Elia Kazan forced him to rewrite his plays, it's ridiculous, he insisted. "Nobody can budge me an inch. Kazan simply tried to interpret, honestly, what I have to say. He has helped me reach my audience, which is my aim in life—the bigger the audience, the better." As for the alternate ending for *Cat,* true, Williams wrote two different endings. "But both of these acts are mine. I wrote them, not Kazan." As for the poorly written second act of *Sweet Bird,* "I was in a terrible state of depression at the time, and just couldn't function, except on just a craftsmanship level. Kazan wanted a great second act, and I couldn't give it to him. I'm re-writing the act now, for the published version; I'm going to stick with my two main characters, whom I should never have left in the first place. The act is weak because I couldn't really identify with Boss Finley." In summary, he said of his favorite direction, with the emotional flourish typical of Williams, "His withdrawal has been shattering for me. I felt at home with him."

However, there are other good directors around, he noted, "as brilliant as Kazan." One is José Quintero, who directed the successful off-Broadway revivals of *Summer and Smoke* and *Camino Real.* Another is George Roy Hall, chosen to direct *Period of Adjustment* in Kazan's stead.

When *Period of Adjustment* appeared on Broadway, in November, 1960, the critical reaction was generally unenthusiastic.

Most admitted that the comedy had several quite funny spots and some that the entire play was "fairly amusing." Almost everyone praised Barbara Baxley's playing of Isabel. Howard Taubman, critic for *The New York Times,* further allowed that *Adjustment* showed Mr. Williams' sure craftsmanship—"He can make a familiar character yield moments of delicious humor, and he can employ old theatrical devices as if they had just been invented." In a follow-up article Taubman said, "Since Mr. Williams is one of the finest writers in the theatre today, he could not touch any subject without bringing to it grace of style and a sure feeling for the stage. His latest play is shot through with felicitous moments. There are lines that sparkle with freshness of insight. There are scenes that erupt into laughter. There are affecting passages of barely articulated tenderness." Williams' most impressive ability, the critic continued, is his "gift for capturing the way his people talk." However, he pointed to "barren stretches."

A number of critics thought it "not one of Mr. Williams' best," and one felt that it was "perhaps his weakest." John McCarten, in the *New Yorker,* damns the seriocomedy in these unequivocal words: "Unfortunately, his attempts at comedy are all too often aimless or vulgar, and when he tries to be earnest, he advances ideas that are hopelessly banal. While he is plainly mad about sentimentality, he is determined to show us that he is well up on Freud and thinkers like that, and he goes on interminably about impotence, incest, homosexual tendencies in the very young, castration complexes, and frigidity in women. In short, before *Period of Adjustment* has run its ragged course he has transformed what might have been a simple domestic comedy into a turbid stew of immiscible ingredients." The principal complaints were the shallowness of the characterization, the "insistent gabble about sex" for sheer shock effect, and the strictly un-comical nature of Williams' view of the world as a gigantic sick room.

Williams himself is always surprised that the public is willing to buy his stuff at all. *Period of Adjustment* is certainly not his first experiment in "turbid stews" and yet he continues to rate high in box-office appeal. Businessmen have come to consider investment in Tennessee Williams' dramas as safe as blue-chip stocks. Theatre parties continue to buy huge blocks of tickets long before a Williams play opens on Broadway and the critics sagely speculate on its worth. So, it would seem that, even if he should never again equal the poignancy of *Menagerie* or the power of *Streetcar,* Tennessee Williams is secured of a comfortable and productive old age.

Although still certain that each of his plays is his last, that he might die at any moment, the sun-tanned author considers his "black period" over. He feels that his sessions with Dr. Lawrence Kubie, "a great and sympathetic analyst," might account for this "up-beat" mood. "He made a vast difference in my feelings, and from now on my plays will be different. I'll still deal with life and reality, of course—and sometimes caustically, perhaps. But I won't be pointing out the bestiality in life." To those worried about his future and his sanity after a taste of *Sweet Bird,* this statement comes as a relief. "Bestiality still exists," he says, lest we think he has entirely changed, "but I don't want to write about it any more. I want to pass the rest of my life believing in other things. For years I was too preoccupied with the destructive impulses. From now on I want to be concerned with the kinder aspects of life."

Of these non-black plays coming up, he has briefly outlined several. He has already completed the first draft of *Night of the Iguana,* planned for Katherine Hepburn. Based partially on the short story of that same name, and making use of his world tour experiences, its chief character is a world-tour guide who runs into difficulties with his group. Another is *The Milk Train Does Not Stop Here Any More,* a play about a seventy-year-old former musical-comedy star. In his own description it is "Rabelaisian in spots—but it ends up on a note which I would describe as tender or compassionate." He has started a third play, as yet untitled, for Maureen Stapleton. Another, called *Kingdom of Earth,* was begun while he was still working on *Sweet Bird of Youth;* and still another is called *The Poem of Two.* These are all on his "workbench" in different stages of completion. As commentator Lewis Funke has said of him, Tennessee Williams "is just full of plays."

By now, it should be clear to even the most cursory reader what to expect of a Williams play. It will be set either in the American South or in a tropical country. On stage there will be a bed or a fountain; the atmosphere will suggest decayed past glories. Significant props will include lamps with rose shades or naked light bulbs, wine bottles, pictures, shrines, clocks, etc. From the distance will come delicate background music while fantastic lighting streaks dimly across the stylized stage.

If the play is a comedy, it will be grotesque, funny only in parts, and mainly because it lacks a tragic ending. On the whole, the viewer is likely to find himself more worried than the author appears to be about what is transpiring on stage. The comedy theme is generally some aspect of the sexual relationship. A lusty, probably Mediterranean-type woman, who appears to the audience to be in a tragic situation, occupies the stage. Her life is doomed, we soon discover, for some deficiency in the relationship—no marriage, no love, or no sex. Suddenly a lover stumbles into her life to the accompaniment of music, wine, flowing fountains, and rustling trees. He can be identified by his magnificent torso and accompanying phallic symbols—bananas or whips or shoes. After a brief resistance in observance of conventional decorum, she will hurl herself into his arms. The two will rush up some stairs, through a door, and into a dark room. If the play should picture her afterwards, she will look narcoticized, wear a rose-colored slip or wrapper, and hug a pillar of the decrepit old mansion, a neighboring tree, or a purse, while mumbling disjointedly about roses and babies.

If the new offering is a tragedy, although there may be as many laughs in it as in the comedy, the ending will be frustration. We may also recognize that it is tragedy by the fact that the heroine is more intelligent and sensitive—though not less erotic. She will probably have outlived her stage of physical beauty.

Like the heroine of the comedy she will avoid discussing sex, since her background will not allow her to acknowledge her drives. As a consequence of this repression she will sound faintly hysterical, talk too much, too fast, too shrilly, in an outdated vocabulary, about unattainable and very vague ideals. Since her life is virtually over, she spends her time in a dream world, looking at scrapbooks, narcoticizing herself with drink or dope. Her physical needs having overmastered her, she precipitates disaster by her desperate search for sex, becoming a prostitute if she has no independent means, keeping a gigolo if she has. The Adonis of her sexual salvation is young and athletic. Because he looks his best without a shirt, the blond hair glistening on his sun-tanned chest, he rips off his shirt at the first opportunity. (But if she is blonde he will be swarthy and keep his shirt on.) His life also has its flaws and frustrations. He is growing old, too (turning thirty). He, too, has ideals. The vestigial traces of his innocence emerge from the general corruption in a moment's contact with this other lost spirit. Their liaison is, however, in opposition to the code of the community. Anyway, the two never marry. Then society, or heaven strikes, and they die or incur mutilation. (Sometimes the heroine is a little younger; if so, consummation is denied her. Our author is determined to thwart her. Sex, it would seem, is the answer to the world's problems, but is not usually tied to marriage.)

In its movement the drama will be practically static. The real action is already over; what we see is the conclusion of that story, almost always anti-climactic, recalling the excitement of remembered youth.

The amazing thing about all this is not that it is formularized, but that Williams can construct such varied stories around the formulas. His talent for thematic variation can be seen in the very different yet essentially identical stories of *Summer and Smoke, A Streetcar Named Desire*, "The Lady of the Larkspur Lotion," and "Portrait of a Madonna." Some whole plays have been given dozens of different forms, yet each work has its own freshness and truth.

Involved theories have been propounded to explain the typical youth-age relationship in the tragedies (and the comedic *Baby Doll*). One is that the plays are all really about incest. The little boy of the story, either, like Oedipus, lusts after his own mother and wants to kill his father, frequently turning to perversion and waiting for the punishment he secretly desires from Big Daddy. Whether he chooses other boys or older women, he attributes his drives to ideals, loathes corruption, and is horrified that Big Daddy and society think *him* corrupt and believes that he is simply rejecting normal sex relations. Williams has said that most women castrate their husbands and their sons, in the latter case by the incestuous attachment which replaces the umbilical cord. The older women in Williams' plays entangle their lovers in similar bonds.

Sometimes we wonder if Williams men aren't really women and vice versa. Or the debate is over whether a character is or is not homosexual, whether nymphomania can result from psychic traumas, whether dipsomania can be cured by therapeutic conversation, etc. The characters are often Freudian case-studies; their actions arise from hysterias and obsessions.

Are his characters, as some theories propound, Williams' alter egos, reflecting or distorting his own life? Tennessee Williams himself has averred that his plays are a direct outgrowth of his life. "Of course, it is a pity that so much of all creative work is so closely related to the personality of the one who does it.

"It is sad and embarrassing and unattractive that those emotions that stir him deeply enough to demand expression with some measure of light and power, are nearly all rooted, however changed in their surface, in the particular and sometimes peculiar concerns of the artist himself, that special world, the passions and images of it that each of us weaves about him from birth to death, a web of monstrous complexity, spun forth at a speed that is incalculable to a length beyond measure, from the spider-mouth of his own singular perceptions."

Williams makes constant use of the people he knows, the places he loves, the conflicts he feels. This he calls "organic" writing. He is incapable of creating any plays outside the orbit of immediate experience.

This organic work he distinguishes from non-organic according to its potentiality of alteration: "It is possible to reform . . . the nature of a non-organic (synthetic) work of the arts, meaning that work which is produced through something other than a necessity as built into a worker as his heartbeat and respiration. But you could flay the skin off a writer whose work is organic and you would still not get out of him a sincere or workable recantation of his faith in what he is doing, however abominable that work may be, or strike you as being."

In his continued self-analysis Williams makes use of standard dream symbols—largely sexual. Added to these are personal symbols. The playwright is at his best when he is creating symbols out of situations rather than superimposing them or hauling in irrelevant or traditional ones. One of Tennessee Williams' outstanding talents is his ability to see his life and his world metaphorically. The most exciting Williams symbols are those fashioned from his own experience.

The author's enthusiasm for metaphor and symbolism comes partially from modern psychology and partially from an enduring regard for the French symbolist poets. John Gassner believes that, had Tennessee Williams restricted his creative efforts to poetry, he would have been a symbolist. "Fortunately," the critic adds, "he did not, for he would have been a distinctly minor, perhaps only barely tolerable, lyric poet." The use of symbolist atmosphere and musical accompaniment provides stimulating contrasts to the realism of his characterization and dialogue. Because his sense of theatre restricts him to a basic realism, he seldom allows the atmosphere of his plays to thin out into a symbolist fog. It has been hard for Williams to use other influences effectively, but in his use of symbolism his talent and his literary tastes are happily united.

Among his influences are D. H. Lawrence, Strindberg, Lorca, Chekhov, E. E. Cummings, Hart Crane, Dylan Thomas, Irwin Shaw, Erskine Caldwell, William Faulkner, Lillian Hellman, and dozens of others, but he has adopted effectively very little of their styles and ideas. As George Jean Nathan had said, Tennessee Williams, for some reason known only to himself, chooses to lose his own considerable gifts "in the marshes of either juvenile or borrowed and ill-assimilated philosophies on life, sex and whatnot." His literary tastes are seldom "organically" incorporated into his plays, and consequently they most often sound like ventriloquists' tricks. He is not an effective preacher of the *mystique de la merde* (filth for its own sake) or an outstanding member of the Pound-Eliot allusive school of poetry.

Lawrence's influence has been the strongest, longest, and most unfortunate. Williams is not at home in the glorification of sex. He is really much closer to Strindberg's love-hate than to the cerebral sexuality of D. H. Lawrence (who also seems to express a perverse Puritanism). Williams' love of "life's delicate children" hardly lends itself to animal sexuality.

A truer affinity is Strindberg, who saw the mixture of compulsion and revulsion in the human sex drive as it had evolved in social organization. Both Williams and Strindberg see man as a victim of conflicting desires. Although he is driven to the act of sex by nature, he hates himself and his partner for the compulsion. Williams appears to have arrived at Strindbergian views of life even before reading Strindberg. Both place the same emphasis on the Dionysian element in man. To quote Joseph Wood Krutch. "To seek difficulty, pain and madness is irrational and therefore to the Dionysian peculiarly human. If happiness is unobtainable, some sort of fulfillment in the Dionysian orgy is. The pain of life becomes the key to its values and the proof of the being's humanity."

Another influence discerned by some readers of Williams' novel, *The Roman Spring of Mrs. Stone,* is Marcel Proust, whom Williams considers the outstanding genius of our century. For Williams, as for Proust, the fountainhead of his work "can only be his life." Of this writer, Williams has recently said, "No one ever used the material of his life so well as Marcel Proust, who made out of his life, recollected and continuing, what is possibly the greatest novel of our time, *The Remembrance of Things Past,* in which he made the passage of time (from past to present and to the future shadow) a controlled torrent of personal experience and sensibilities to it. . . . It contains all the elements of a man's psychic history—his love, fear, loneliness, disgust, humor and, most important of all, his forgiving perception of the reasons for the tragicomedy of human confusion. . . . The midnight dark of the final picture was irradiated and purified by a genius that no other writer of our century has in his command, not even Chekhov or Joyce." Proust confirmed for Williams a lesson he had already learned, that art is the process of transposing the contents of life into a "creative synthesis of it."

Pirandello is another understandable influence. For both playwrights truth has many faces, and reality can be found only in fragments. Williams has said, commenting on William Faulkner's Stockholm speech asserting faith in man's dignity, that he believes, not in the essential dignity of man, but in the essential ambiguity of man. Of Faulkner's statement, he says, "It's a damned good platform. The only trouble with it, from my POV [point of view], is that we are not agreed about exactly what the high-sounding slogan really means in the way of truth about dignity and mankind. . . . People are humble and frightened and guilty at heart, all of us, no matter how desperately we may try to appear otherwise. We have very little conviction of our essential dignity nor even of our essential decency, and consequently we are more interested in characters on the stage who share our hidden shames and fears, and we want the plays about us to say, 'I understand you. You and I are brothers, the deal is rugged but let's face and fight it together.'" Such ambiguities between appearances and reality, between what we are and what we admit are the very things that Pirandello explored in his philosophical drama *Naked*, a play closely parallel in its basic themes to *Streetcar*.

Chekhov, whose characters pursue their own thoughts, even when with others, has been another influence on Tennessee Williams. Both dramatists imbue isolated and outwardly trivial events with a sense of spiritual significance; both can develop warm but unsentimental moods; both deal with the isolation of human beings and their tragic inability to understand one another; both writers' plays are, in part, elegies to a decaying aristocracy. Unable, like Arthur Miller, to take the more forceful social tone of Ibsen, Tennessee Williams finds Chekhov's approach to drama more compatible. Yet he likes the way Ibsen builds his symbols, and therefore adopts that technique from the more socially conscious playwright.

He likes Wilder's fantasy, O'Neill's black tragedy, Lorca's blood-drenched stories of passionate people. Decadent poets appeal to him for their anarchy and their denial of Puritan standards, a perverse sort of romanticism. He enjoys Hart Crane for the same reasons, and for the mad, frightened, ecstatic, frenzied, Bohemian life he led. Williams likes to feel that his taste is "catholic," but examination discloses a preference for the romantic, the decadent, and the *avant-garde*.

An out-and-out romantic, he builds his stories on conflicts between delicate ideals and disgusting tabus. He has told Marya Mannes, in *The New York Times,* that "no significant area of human experience and behavior reaction to it, should be held inaccessible" to the modern artist. Although his ladies aren't so fair as Miss Mannes would desire, they are not so sick, he believes, as she contends. "I think that there has not been a very sick but a very healthy extension of the frontiers of theme and subject matter acceptable to our dramatic art, to the stage, the screen and even television. . . ." Having spent the last two decades exploiting violence and shock about as far as the human mind and stomach can bear, Tennessee Williams certainly can say that the frontiers of acceptance have become practically limitless. His plays describe rape, prostitution, murder, perversion, castration, and cannibalism—an imposing set of extensions.

In his role of extending frontiers, Williams has been credited with opening the way to such authors as Robert Anderson, Paddy Chayefsky, Jean Anouilh, Jean Giraudoux, and others. According to Robert Rice, such plays as *The Chalk Garden, A Hatful of Rain, The Potting Shed,* and *Waiting for Godot* would not have reached or thriven on Broadway or off-Broadway if Tennessee Williams had not prepared the way. More recently, *The Visit, Krapp's Last Tape, Zoo Story, Toys in the Attic, The Balcony,* and *Caligula* reflect the same world out of which Williams writes. His influence has been a partial cause of the O'Neill revival, and the angry young Britons were probably better able to vent their rage after *Streetcar* had come to London. Prostitution, dope addiction, homosexuality are now permissible dramatic subjects. The first nighter now perhaps expects them at a "serious" play.

Both good drama and sensationalism have come to the fore in this enlarged territory of dramaturgy. For the time being, it is difficult to separate the valuable from the tawdry; they are often mixed within a single play. Much of this has resulted from the continuing popularity of Tennessee Williams. Although he is the leader of no movement, his influence is powerful. As William Inge said of this man to whom he owes much for personal encouragement and literary help, "One writer helps another writer, I think just by being. Tennessee's being has helped me a lot."

The boundary expansion has been almost entirely in the sexual area, but that was the area most infested with tabus. Perhaps Williams and his associates have also been cashing in on the modern "Philistinism," feeding, as Alfred Kazin says, "a secret hunger for wickedness found in rich, middle-class society." With a writer as eager as is Williams for fame and fortune, the critic has a difficult time estimating how far he is exploiting his own talents in catering to that hunger. Underneath, there is undoubtedly the sincere desire to help other people rid themselves of the Puritan repressions that, in his view, accounted for so much in his own tormented history. But this seems to be adulterated with deliberate infusions of the violence and filth that can help a play to commercial success.

As for the rest of the human being—the virtually ignored areas above the belt—Tennessee Williams has had little to offer. He is a visceral rather than a cerebral writer. Bragging that he is no intellectual, he intends his appeal to be consistently and consciously low-brow—again probably because of his obsession with popularity. This is not to say that he is a stupid man or an ignorant one. Indeed, he is widely read in many fields; and his work reflects a good education. Before he reached Broadway, he was considered the awards man of the younger generation, having won so many of the prizes offered to encourage young talent. Nevertheless, he is no intellectual; his decisions are usually emotional rather than rational, and he has not developed any clear or consistent philosophy. His most positive tenet is that the world needs romanticism. Tennessee Williams will not go down in history as one of the twentieth century's outstanding philosophical minds.

Nor is he social-minded. His "cause" enthusiasms as mentioned earlier, are limited to direct experiences or emotional involvement. He has no program for reform, is no polemic writer. He sees the basic problem of the world as personal; "The crying, almost screaming, need of a great worldwide human effort to know ourselves and each other a great deal better, well enough to concede that no man has a monopoly on right or virtue any more than any man has a corner on duplicity and evil and so forth. If people, and races and nations, would start with that self-manifest truth, then I think that the world could side-step the sort of corruption which I have involuntarily chosen as the basic, allegorical theme of my plays as a whole."

Nor is he any clearer on religion. He believes in God, but makes fun of organized religion and of the Puritan ethic, although he knows how ingrained both are in him. Actually, Christianity is a source of his symbolism, and often the key to his story. His outcast women may sometimes be the Virgin Mary, sometimes Mary Magdalene; the male of salvation is invariably Christ. But Christianity, in his treatment, acquires Williamsian features. As the Old Testament was for his grandfather, the Bible, as a whole, is to him an allegory; but unlike the old clergyman, he has no world view. There are no absolutes for him, no system of values outside of man, no morality outside of personal anguish. His ultimate ethic is *sympathize*. In a universe that rolls on its inevitable way, living in a society that we cannot change, we are powerless to influence or even understand our fate. The best we can do is face our doom with fortitude and reach out our hands in sympathy to our doomed fellow-beings.

The Williams world lacks the stability of philosophy, government, or religion. It contains two forces in constant conflict: flesh and spirit, reality and dreams, brutality and ideals. This dualism once again stresses his Puritanism. The idealistic dreamer in this surrealistic universe vainly seeks an innocent way through the jungle world. He retreats more and more into himself, seems more and more pathological to the people around him, suffers beatings and rapes, mutilation, and castration, until, tainted at last with foul and fatal corruption, he dies. Williams says of the writer's life and safety, "especially in his middle years" if he began writing in his adolescence, that they lie "in one of two things, whichever one is more personally suitable to him—living in a remote place, particularly on an island in the tropics, or in a fugitive way of life, running like a fox from place to place. I have tried both and am still trying both."

The real world is not only destructive to the delicate and the idealistic, it is also corrupt. The diseases of mendacity, cupidity, and stupidity spread like cancer through the body social, making man hate and torture and kill. In this jungle world the romantic can only destroy himself in attempts to compete with the other beasts. Yet his destruction, for all of its seeming horror, is the only possible salvation. Damnation, says the romantic Williams, comes not through destruction, but through apathy. Action, the author insists, is salvation. The brute eats the dreamer, but this strange and repeated ritual brings a solution. Revolt, that will lead to this inevitable sacrificial offering of the revolutionary, seems to be the only possible positive action.

This is the vision Williams has acquired in his painful struggle to live in a world he never made. His job as a playwright is, he feels, to make X ray photos of "the ravages of tissues turning malignant." Speaking of man's mortality, he says, "This is God's or the devil's way of removing us to make room for our descendants. Do they work together, God and the devil? I sometimes suspect there's a sort of understanding between them, which we won't understand until Doomsday."

Tennessee Williams considers himself a member of a school, which he terms the Gothic, uniting in a specific American combination, expressionist, impressionist, surrealist, symbolist, and naturalist elements. He, Carson McCullers, Truman Capote, Lil-

lian Hellman, William Faulkner, and other Gothics use the South
as the proper setting for insanity and horror. "There is something
in the region," he says, "something in the blood and culture, of the
Southern state" that fostered this group.

It has been suggested that the South is the regional embodiment
of non-conformity. Henry Popkin, a critic who has analyzed Williams' drama in the *Tulane Drama Review,* says the disappointment, repression, and poverty of the South have fostered eccentricity, making it the natural ground for the "American Gothic."
Tennessee Williams considers this movement akin to French
Existentialism, except that the "motor impulse of the French
school is intellectual and philosophic while that of the American
is more of an emotional and romantic nature." The common link
between the two movements, he says, is a "sense, an intuition, of
any underlying dreadfulness in modern experience." This "dreadfulness" he finds impossible to explain. It transcends the horrors
recorded in the daily papers, and is rather a "kind of spiritual
intuition of something almost too incredible and shocking to
talk about, which underlies the whole so-called things. It is the
incommunicable something that we shall have to call *mystery*
which is so inspiring of dreams among these modern artists. . . ."
With this characteristic evasion of explicit definition, he goes on
to defend his "crazy people doing terrible things" as being external symbols of this inward, brooding reality. Art must select
and compress. The terror that Williams has seen for years as the
key to his universe is mirrored in his dramas.

In a real sense, Tennessee Williams is right about his dread.
The choices open to the modern artist are terrifying for the sensitive man to contemplate. In a world coldly indifferent or harshly
antagonistic to his values, he finds himself constantly fighting the
stream of life. Insisting on inner realities, the timeless value of
beauty and truth, he is lured by the sirens of fame and wealth. He
has a choice of integrity at the risk of poverty and obscurity, or

"prostituting his art" for emotional or material security. The attempt to satisfy both the world and himself is the poet's agony.

In the early years, our author willingly dedicated himself to his romantic faith, and was inevitably led to Bohemia, the essence of which, according to John Gassner, "is preoccupation with the artist's singularity or specialness, which is often the same thing as a sense of alienation defensively exaggerated into exhibitionist defiance." Williams denies that the eccentricity of the artist is exhibitionism or specialization. Our age is one that is violent and disturbed; artists, functioning as the nervous system of society, are bound to be disturbed in a disturbed world. "I am giving away no trade secret," Williams comments in illustrating the artists' reaction to international horror, "when I point out how many artists, including writers, have sought refuge in psychiatry, alcohol, narcotics, way-in or way-out religious conversions, and so forth."

For a while, the pleasure of flouting the Philistines can assuage quite physical hungers. The carefree life of the hobo has a temporary appeal; but the degradation of cadging from poor grandparents, or stealing eggs, or waiting tables and fighting over tips begins to take its toll. When the artist sees himself growing older without security or hope of recognition, the charms of Bohemia can fade. The easier way is to adapt himself to the non-poetic world. By vulgarizing his work he can flatter that world into believing that it knows something of poetry and understands philosophy.

Since the function of art should be communication, the artist can easily justify reaching for popularity. However, when he has a vision of pure art, he is haunted by a fear of cheapening the object of his worship. He also finds that his vision of the world makes him look like a lunatic to the more prosaic and practical. As Williams expresses this relationship between insanity and art: "If artists are snobs, it is much in the humble way that lunatics are: not because they wish to be different, and hope and believe that they are, but because they are forever painfully struck in the face with the inescapable fact of their difference which makes them hurt and lonely enough to want to undertake the vocation of artists." Therefore he believes that men are sentenced to solitary confinement within their own skins. In his forays into a cold-eyed, rational world, he feels like Jack in the Beanstalk Country.

The genius of Tennessee Williams is his ability to transform this fearful world into living and universal art. He says that he has spent his entire life trying to master the trick of "rising above the singular to the plural concern." He can't always do it; when out-of-character lyricism and disembodied fantasy take over, he fails; and he also trips frequently over his symbolic regalia. But at his best, he shows a genius for realism, an ear perfectly attuned to conversational speech and an eye keenly perceptive to human idiosyncrasies. He is then unsurpassed in achieving living characters and expressing deep emotional realities.

It is Tennessee Williams' good fortune to have lived in the renaissance of American drama, when he could find appreciative audiences for his work. He is lucky that Europe had spent a century developing techniques and attitudes for him to choose from. The twenties gave him the nihilism and iconoclasm of any age without answers. The thirties gave him love of humanity and sympathy with human pain. Freud gave him his concept of man's inner deeps, Darwin his concept of the evolving animal, and Marx his concept of evolving society.

Although typical of his age, Tennessee Williams is no typical artist. Perhaps, as he himself has said, he is only a minor artist who has written some major plays. Whatever time and the critical consensus may decide, Tennessee Williams is an author who has brought power and beauty to the American stage. Out of the stuff of his own tormented life, he has created dramas of rich humanity. Writing for him is an act of faith, and writing such as his gives us a new respect for the human mind and heart.

Bibliography

Bibliography

ARTICLES AND ESSAYS BY TENNESSEE WILLIAMS

Tennessee Williams has made a habit of publishing an essay prior to the Broadway opening of his plays. These illuminating descriptions of the plays and of the author's ideas and attitudes have served as prefaces to the dramas when the plays have later appeared in published form. Especially interesting are: "The Catastrophe of Success" (published with *The Glass Menagerie*), "The Timeless World of a Play" (with *The Rose Tattoo*), "Forword" and "Afterword" (*Camino Real*), "Well of Violence" (*Sweet Bird of Youth*), "Person-to-Person" (*Cat on a Hot Tin Roof*), "Something Wild . . . " (*27 Wagons Full of Cotton*), and "The Past, the Present and the Perhaps" (*Orpheus Descending*).

Other essays, which like those listed above, also appeared in *The New York Times,* include:

"Laurette Taylor 'An Appreciation,' " (December 15, 1946).

"Questions Without Answers," (October 3, 1948).

"Reflections on the Revival of a Controversial Fantasy" (May 15, 1960).

"Point of View," (June 12, 1960).

Other notable essays, serving as introductions, include those published in the following volumes:

Five Young American Poets, third series. Norfolk, Connecticut: New Directions, 1944.

INGE, WILLIAM. *Dark at the Top of the Stairs.* New York: Random House. 1958.

McCULLERS, CARSON. *Reflections in a Golden Eye.* New York: New Directions, 1941.

BOOKS BY TENNESSEE WILLIAMS

American Blues. New York: Dramatists Play Service, 1948.

Baby Doll. New York: New Directions, 1956.

Camino Real. Norfolk, Connecticut: New Directions, 1953.

Cat on a Hot Tin Roof. New York: New Directions, 1955.

The Glass Menagerie. New York: Random House, 1945.

Hard Candy. New York: New Directions, 1954.

I Rise in Flame, Cried the Phoenix. Norfolk, Connecticut: J. Laughlin, 1951.

In the Winter of Cities. Norfolk, Connecticut: New Directions, 1956.

One Arm, and Other Stories. New York: New Directions, 1948.

Orpheus Descending. New York: New Directions, 1955. (There are earlier editions of *Battle of Angels* available, and Signet has published the film script for *Fugitive Kind.*)

The Roman Spring of Mrs. Stone. New York: New Directions, 1948.

The Rose Tattoo. New York: New Directions, 1951.

A Streetcar Named Desire. New York: New Directions, 1947.

Suddenly Last Summer (also under *Garden District*). New York: New Directions, 1960.

Summer and Smoke. New York: New Directions, 1948.

Sweet Bird of Youth. New York: New Directions, 1959.

27 Wagons Full of Cotton and Other One-Act Pays. Norfolk, Connecticut: New Directions, 1946.

with Donald Windham. *You Touched Me!* New York: S. French,
1947.

Williams' latest play, *Period of Adjustment,* as well as many of his
one-act plays and short stories may be found in *Esquire* magazine.
Period of Adjustment is in the December, 1960 issue.

BIOGRAPHY

Williams' agent, Liebling-Wood (MCA), has published several
press releases by and about the author, including two brief, but
helpful ones:

"Facts About Me"

"Tennessee Williams"

The best source I discovered for material about Tennessee
Williams' life was a series of articles by Robert Rice, appearing in
the *New York Post* (April 24–May 4, 1958), entitled "A Man
Named Tennessee." Other good sources were:

BARNETT, LINCOLN. "Tennessee Williams," *Life* (February 16,
1948).

MOOR, PAUL. "A Mississippian Named Tennessee" *Harper's* (July,
1948).

TYNAN, KENNETH. "Valentine to Tennessee Williams," *Mademoiselle* (February, 1956).

Much of the material included in this book was drawn from
articles and interviews appearing in *The New York Times, Time,
The New Yorker, Newsweek,* and *Theatre Arts.*

CRITICISM

Most of the major newspapers and magazines have carried cri-
tiques on each of the Williams' plays from *The Glass Menagerie*
through *Period of Adjustment.* Among those I found especially
helpful were the many by Brooks Atkinson, the *Times'* loyal
Williams defender. Lewis Nichols, John Rosenfield, Howard

Taubman, and Myra Mannes have also produced interesting and perceptive criticism. Other critics whose ideas I have drawn upon include: Harold Clurman, George Jean Nathan, David L. Stevenson, Robert E. Fitch, Anthony Hartley, Howard Hewes, Stanley Hyman, Dudley Fitts, John Woods, John Mason Brown, William Hawkins, Wolcott Gibbs, John McCarten, and many others. The most useful analyses of the body of Williams' drama were:

BENTLEY, ERIC. *The Dramatic Event*. New York: Horizon Press, 1954.

———. *In Search of Theatre*. New York: Alfred A. Knopf, 1953.

———. *What Is Theatre?* Boston: Beacon Press, 1956.

BRUSTEIN, ROBERT. "Sweet Bird of Success," *Encounter* (June, 1959).

GASSNER, JOHN. *Best Plays of the Modern American Theatre*, second series. New York: Crown Publishers, 1947.

———. "Tennessee Williams: Dramatist of Frustration," *College English* (October, 1948).

———. *Theatre in Our Times*. New York: Crown Publishers, 1955.

KRUTCH, JOSEPH WOOD. *Modernism in Modern Drama*. Ithaca, New York: Cornell University Press, 1953.

POPKIN, HENRY. "The Plays of Tennessee Williams," *Tulane Drama Review* (March, 1960).

BIBLIOGRAPHY

CARPENTER, CHARLES A., JR. and ELIZABETH COOK. "Addenda to 'Tennessee Williams: A Selected Bibliography,'" *Modern Drama* (December, 1959).

DONY, NADINE. "Tennessee Williams: A Selected Bibliography," *Modern Drama* (December, 1958).

OTHER SOURCES

COURTNEY, MARGUERITE. Laurette. New York: Rinehart and Co., Inc., 1955.

JONES, MARGO. *Theatre-in-the-Round*. New York: Rinehart and Co., Inc., 1951.

Index

Index

315

DATE DUE

PRINTED IN U.S.A.